THE
SHEPHEARDES
CALENDER
An Introduction

THE SHEPHEARDES CALENDER

An
Introduction

Lynn Staley Johnson

The Pennsylvania State University Press
University Park and London

Library of Congress Cataloging-in-Publication Data

Johnson, Lynn Staley, 1947–
    The shepheardes calender : an introduction / Lynn Staley Johnson.
        p.   cm.
    Includes bibliographical references.
    ISBN 0-271-00699-4
    1. Spenser, Edmund, 1552?–1599.   Shepheardes calender.
2. Pastoral poetry, English—History and criticism.
I. Title.   II. Title: Shepherd's calendar.
PR2359.J65   1990
821'.3—dc20   89-26611

It is the policy of The Pennsylvania State University Press to use acid-free paper
for the first printing of all clothbound books. Publications on uncoated stock
satisfy the minimum requirements of American National Standard for Information
Sciences—Permanence of Paper for Printed Library Materials, ANSI Z39.48–
1984.

To my parents

Contents

Acknowledgments

O ne of the final and most agreeable tasks in preparing a manuscript for press is that of acknowledging the help and support of others in the academic community.

I am grateful to the Huntington Library for permission to publish the plates for the 1579 edition of *The Shepheardes Calender*. I would also like to thank the Beinecke Rare Book and Manuscript Library of Yale University for permission to publish the plate of Sloth from Stephen Bateman's *Christall Glasse*. AMS Press has granted me permission to use portions of my essay, "Elizabeth, Bride and Queen: A Study of Spenser's April Eclogue and the Metaphors of English Protestantism," formerly published in *Spenser Studies*. *The Spenser Newsletter* has permitted me to use my note, "And Taken up His Ynne in Fishes Haske."

The staffs of both the Rare Book Room of Princeton University's Firestone Library and of Harvard University's Houghton Library have been generous with their time and knowledge.

Colgate University has offered invaluable support. The Research Council has funded both research and typing expenses. The heads of Acquisitions, Inter Library Loan, and Reference of Colgate's Everett Case Library have helped me to acquire or borrow the materials I have needed for my research.

Patricia Ryan has typed and retyped portions of this book with her usual care and speed.

Though I have acknowledged his help in chapter 5, I would like to thank Anthony Aveni of Colgate University's Department of Physics and Astronomy for answering my questions about astronomy and for reading that final chapter. Needless to say, any "cosmic" errors are my own.

Anne Lake Prescott of Barnard College has read portions of this manuscript and offered some important suggestions. I am pleased to be able to thank her for her help and encouragement.

I would also like to thank Elaine V. Beilin of Framingham State College for many fine conversations about sixteenth-century literature and for reading portions of this manuscript. Her own work on sixteenth-century women writers has enriched my own.

I am especially grateful to Roland Greene of Harvard University and Thomas P. Roche of Princeton University for their comments upon my manuscript. In revising the manuscript, I have had the opportunity to use what I think are two extraordinarily intelligent and graceful readers' reports.

A special word of thanks is in order for Philip Winsor, Senior Editor, of The Pennsylvania State University Press. His frankness and courtesy have created an easy and productive climate for preparing a manuscript for publication. It has been a pleasure to work with him and the staff of the Penn State Press.

Finally, and, as always, I thank Linck C. Johnson of Colgate University, who encouraged me to move forward from the age of Chaucer in order to explore what many have thought of as the last medieval poem, Spenser's *Shepheardes Calender*. He has generously read and reread the manuscript, listened to what must have seemed endless cogitations on topics only marginally related to those of nineteenth-century American literature, and offered comments and suggestions that have allowed me to bring my work into focus. Gratitude seems a poor word to use in response.

Working on a poet such as Spenser is always a privilege, but working with such aid and comfort transforms scholarship into conversation.

Introduction: The English Poet

he *Shepheardes Calender* is a poem about the English poet, his debts to the past and his duties to the present. It is a poem about the poet's ability—or responsibility—to remake that present, to offer his age a picture of a new and potentially more glorious reality. Consequently, *The Shepheardes Calender* describes conflict—literary, social, historical, philosophical, and psychological—presenting what can seem an unfocused picture or an irresolute dialogue. However, the *Calender*'s discord is strategic, meant at once to reflect the conflicts and anxieties of the age out of which it emerges and to offer a refiguration of the social formation and a rewriting of literary tradition, a reformation at once broadly national and intensely personal.

Though he had contributed translations of poems to Jan van der Noot's English edition of *A Theatre for Worldlings* ten years previously, *The Shepheardes Calender*, published in 1579, marked Spenser's true debut as a poet. Even to its first readers, the poem must have appeared a curious hybrid: It seems to join Virgil to Chaucer, the classical pastoral to the homely almanac, the aesthetic of the French Pléiade to the ideals of the English reformers, the scholarly traditions of the humanists to the moralizations of didactic poets, and the formal niceties of accomplished pastoral poetry to the rough metrics and archaic language of native English verse. Most obviously, the poem is a shepherd's calendar, composed of twelve eclogues, one for each month, that not only describe the rotation of a year, but address what were the conventional

issues of the renaissance pastoral—the purpose of poetry, the role of
the poet, the pains of unrequited love, clerical purity, and the meaning
of death. In addition, a gloss is attached to each eclogue—supposedly
the work of a figure simply identified as E.K. The fact that a gloss
follows each poem is in itself less surprising than the fact that the glosses
are sometimes unreliable and frequently confusing. Each poem is also
accompanied by a woodcut, providing us with a sort of pictorial gloss
upon the eclogue. Like the prose glosses, however, the woodcuts are
not always reliable guides to the poems. Each poem concludes with yet
another form of commentary, an emblem in English, Italian, Latin, or
Greek, which, like the glosses and the woodcuts, can seem either out
of place, bathetic, or puzzling. Finally, the *Calender,* like most sixteenth-
century editions, begins with essays explaining the themes and justifying
the method of the poem. Unlike most sixteenth-century prefaces, how-
ever, E.K.'s essays on the *Calender* tease rather than enlighten, forming
one more apparently opaque commentary about a poem that is difficult
enough on its own.

   Even the briefest of descriptions suggests that Spenser intended the
Calender to mediate political, social, and religious, as well as literary,
texts. To do so, he created a poetic language that allowed him to analyze
what are usually conceived of as distinct levels of reality and to create
a poem whose fundamental contradictions serve as keys to its very
structure and purpose.[1] Annabel Patterson's suggestion that Spenser
saw himself as following Marot in adapting the pastoral to a corrective
or didactic social end can be taken even further.[2] For in the *Calender,*
Spenser exploited the pastoral and all its centuries of complex coding
in order to articulate the actual realm he saw and the ideal realm he
envisioned. The very pastoral language that Spenser used gave him a
scope far broader than that available to the preacher, teacher, or politi-
cian; for he chose neither to rant nor to blame, but to present dialogues,
tell stories, offer pictures, and sketch characters. That his language was
designed both to mirror the present and to praise its unrealized symbolic
worth suggests his sense of the role that the poet and his poetry might
play in reconstructing England's history and, inevitably, its literature.

   The immediate context for the *Calender* is what we know of Spenser's
early years, and we know more about the intellectual companions of
those years than we do about Spenser himself.[3] We can locate Spenser

   1. See Jameson, 39–43.
   2. Patterson, *Pastoral and Ideology,* 130. For another view of Spenser, see Shepherd.
   3. See Judson.

in a particular circle as a student, first at the Merchant Taylors' School in London and later at Cambridge. During the last years of the 1570s, he was associated with John Young, Bishop of Rochester, and with Robert Dudley, the Earl of Leicester.[4] As the work of A. C. Hamilton, William Ringler, Eleanor Rosenberg, and J. A. van Dorsten has demonstrated, the climate of Leicester House was a beneficent one for the growth of aspiring minds. Indeed, from 1569 to 1579, Spenser's world served as one of the most demanding of universities. His teachers were the finest. From Richard Mulcaster, the master of the Merchant Taylors' School, supposed author of the Londoners' coronation pageant for Elizabeth and friend of Jan van der Noot, to the Puritan-dominated atmosphere of Cambridge, through John Young, and those frequenting Leicester House, Spenser received an inestimable education both formally and informally. During that decade Spenser would have been made especially sensitive to political shifts, rhetorical nuances, and social tensions in ways not possible when he was later situated in Ireland, far from the economic, religious, cultural, and political heart of England. It is therefore crucial to see the *Calender* as a "London poem," as a poem deeply rooted in its time and its city. Nor could it have been produced by any save Edmund Spenser who, even as he launched his poetic career, gave evidence of having mastered the tastes of the literary marketplace, the syncretic cast of contemporary thought, and the terms of a poetic discourse that Annabel Patterson has described as "*functional ambiguity.*"[5]

Spenser's actual associates and probable associations during this period also need to be considered in relation to the social and religious concerns of the decade. In 1579 the Elizabethan political and religious compromise was twenty years old. Those who had hailed Elizabeth as a new Solomon, as a prince of reform, envisioning a role for England as the head of European Protestantism, had become restless. The economic prosperity, peace, and relative religious calm that Elizabeth had brought to England seemed to presage a new age that had not yet dawned. It would be inaccurate to describe the English as disenchanted

4. In "Sidney and Spenser at Leicester House," a paper delivered at the 1985 meeting of the Modern Language Association, S. K. Heninger, Jr., examined the evidence linking Spenser to Leicester, challenging the view that Spenser served as Leicester's secretary. However, the intellectual life of Leicester House during the 1570s provides important clues to the tastes and habits of England's best and brightest.

5. Patterson, *Censorship and Interpretation,* 18. For a discussion of the renaissance reader, see Quilligan, *Milton's Spenser,* Preface and chapter 1.

during the 1570s, but the decade was characterized by a certain dissatis-
faction. Spokesmen for the crown and representatives of ecclesiastical
or social factions, all of whom noted England's growing materialism
and warned of the dangers that envy and ambition posed to the social
fabric, voiced similar sorts of concerns. Both officially and unofficially,
England chastised itself for its fondness for old ways, for tastes and
modes of behavior that tied it to its past rather than fitting it for a future
society as unencumbered as the ecclesiastical structure the Puritans
envisioned for the English church. Many have attempted to link Spenser
to a particular faction in the ongoing debate during the 1570s about
clerical and ecclesiastical purity.[6] However, religious issues must be
placed within a larger social context since the religious debate was
matched by a more secular debate, prompted, in part, by shifting
social categories.[7] The most important political debate of the decade
concerned the Queen's marriage negotiations with the Duc d'Alençon,
the younger brother to the King of France. The question of Elizabeth's
marriage was essentially a matter of national security, so the topic of
marriage underlies much of the occasional verse and the pageantry of
the last years of the decade.[8] Each of these subjects—England's religious
atmosphere, its social fabric, and its political conflicts—can only be
understood as parts of a complex and composite picture. Though the
Calender is sometimes seen as an explicit social commentary or a reli-
gious or political allegory, it is best described as informed—rather than
defined—by current social and political issues. Rather than a passive
reflection of the events or the rhetoric of the early Elizabethan period,
the *Calender* should be seen as an attempt to present the past and the
present in ways that might affect the future.

The literary background of *The Shepheardes Calender* is as important
as its immediate social and historical context. Spenser's relation to the
literary sources for his inspiration is an issue that undergoes a continual
reevaluation as our understanding of the nature of literary influence
becomes increasingly attuned to the renaissance attitudes toward imita-
tion.[9] The *Calender*'s diffuse, sometimes disorienting surface has to
some extent dictated the sorts of questions modern critics have asked
of the text. In an early essay, A.C. Hamilton argued for the essential

6. See Hume; McLane; Norbrook, chapter 3. For another view, see King (1985).
7. Helgerson, chapter 2; Montrose (1979), (1980), (1983).
8. Both McLane and Norbrook devote attention to the subject of the Queen's marriage.
See also Iser.
9. See particularly Greene.

unity of purpose and design of Spenser's first poem, exploring the relation between Spenser and Colin Clout, the most important of the poem's many voices. Hamilton saw the poem as a rejection of the pastoral mode and therefore as an affirmation of a life of duty and service. Hamilton established two broad categories of concern for later readings; the *Calender*'s relation to the pastoral mode and Spenser's attitude toward his own art figured in his handling of Colin Clout. More recent critical studies of the poem—such as those of Paul Alpers, Harry Berger, Jr., Patrick Cullen, and Jonathan Goldberg—have discussed the *Calender* as dialogic, underlining its intertextuality, its allusiveness, and its relation to conventional modes of discourse. Where these studies have examined the nature of the poem's *literary* discourse, Richard Helgerson, Louis Adrian Montrose, and Annabel Patterson have focused upon the relation between the *Calender*, its pastoral mode and apparatus, and the social tensions of the Elizabethan period, prompting an inquiry into what the poem reveals about Spenser's attitude toward his own poetic ambitions in an age of social change. The issue of Spenser's feelings about his own talent has likewise guided the work of Nancy Jo Hoffman and David R. Shore, whose studies of Colin Clout span Spenser's entire career and touch on some of the social and personal changes that inevitably influenced Spenser's appraisal of the poet's role. On the other hand, John N. King has argued that we should reconsider our approach to literary contextuality, insisting that the literature of the early Protestant period in England exerted a strong influence on the Elizabethan imagination and thus upon Elizabethan writers. King's focus upon the Protestant sources for Spenser's inspiration locates conflict and tension in society rather than in the poet or the text, pointing up the relation between the *Calender* and its cultural context. King argues that in the *Calender* Spenser translates the pastoral from one language and cultural tradition to the homely English of Chaucer and the cultural traditions embodied by writers like John Skelton and John Bale, both associated with the English Protestant cause, insisting that we see Spenser's first poem as emerging from an indigenous literary tradition as well as from a contemporary set of concerns.[10]

As recent theorists have reminded us, the relation between a complex text and its various contexts—biographical, social, cultural, or histori-

10. See also the remarks by Judith Anderson in the Introduction to *The Growth of a Personal Voice: Piers Plowman and the Faerie Queene.*

cal—is problematic.[11] In my own effort to relate the *Calender* to its background and times, I have defined context as encompassing both literary and cultural traditions and the immediate historical, political, and social atmosphere of England during the first twenty years of Elizabeth's reign. Rather than viewing Spenser as a Protestant poet, a transmitter of the classical tradition, or a mouthpiece for the Elizabethan state, we should understand him as a reformer in the broadest sense of the term, a stance that links the religious, literary, social, and political concerns manifested in the *Calender* and throughout the later works. These Spenser shared with his age. But his *Calender* does more than reflect the inherent and emerging tensions of his own world; he also used it to suggest a program for social, ecclesiastical, and literary reform that would usher in that new or golden age whose nascence preoccupied many during the decade. Though the *Calender* looks and sounds conventional enough, an exploration of its relation to conventional themes and forms suggests how radical a departure it actually is. Whether we juxtapose its poetry to Virgil's eclogues, Aesop's fables, or the conventions of the pastoral elegy, or compare the entire poem to conventional calendars, the *Calender* is only superficially faithful to its models. It is not simply filled with metric experiments, but with formal experiments—parodies, truncated forms, false closures—which frequently suggest meanings submerged beneath the ongoing dialogue of the shepherds on Spenser's pastoral stage.[12] The poem, in fact, is a rewriting, a refiguration of the literary tradition Spenser inherited.

The most elaborate of Spenser's formal experiments is his division of the eclogues into three *ranckes,* Moral, Plaintive, and Recreative. The division itself suggests an older literary and philosophical tradition, for the ranckes seem intended to recall the division of philosophy into moral, speculative or natural, and divine. Spenser uses this division as a means of suggesting not only the underlying theme of each type of eclogue, but also the dominant literary heritage and the style appropriate for each rancke. For example, each rancke has its particular resident literary genius: Chaucer's presence is most felt in the five Moral eclogues, which concern the fabric of the body politic; Virgil, the genius

---

11. See DeNeef (1987); Jameson, chapter 1; Iser; La Capra, chapter 1; Martines.

12. On the *Calender's* metrical innovations, see Woods. The *Calender's* metrical complexities have also occupied Seth Weiner, whose paper, "The Impress of Renaissance Musical Theory on Spenser's Prosodic Thinking," delivered at the Spenser at Kalamazoo conference in 1982, linked the poetry of the *Calender* with a broader interest in re-creating the primordial harmony between words and music.

of Roman poetry, hovers over the Plaintive eclogues in which Spenser explores more speculative problems like love, the role of the poet, and mutability through his handling of Colin Clout; the spirit of Theocritus informs two of the three Recreative eclogues, which depict the traumas of love. In the other Recreative eclogue, "Aprill," Spenser draws from the traditions of the biblical epithalamium to create a new form that celebrates a new queen and a new land. Spenser thus fuses the conventions of indigenous and classical verse with the traditions of philosophic inquiry and the concerns of what Andrew Weiner, Barbara Keifer Lewalski, and John N. King have referred to as a Protestant poetic. By bringing together these various themes and forms in a single poem, Spenser gives evidence of seeking to create a new literature, a new aesthetic for a new age. It is therefore no coincidence that the heart of this reformed calendar is a vision of a different cosmos whose component parts are ranged around a truly stable center.

Such a general application of the principles of reform also informs Spenser's manipulation of his poetic personae. In the three dominant voices of the *Calender*—E.K., Colin Clout, and Immerito—Spenser establishes a dialogue concerning the relationship between the poet and the reader and between the poet and his own talent and inspiration. In some measure, E.K. both intercedes between the poem and the reader and moderates between Colin Clout and Immerito. E.K.'s identity has long been a subject of speculation. Whether we believe the initials are a cover for Spenser himself, as I do, or for Spenser's close friend, Gabriel Harvey, or for someone else, E.K.'s contributions clearly met with Spenser's approval since they figure prominently in a volume over which Spenser exerted much control. E.K. functions primarily as a link between the poem's present and its significant literary past: He defines words, points out sources and analogues, translates phrases, and identifies figures of speech. In his prefaces to the *Calender*, E.K. furnishes important clues to the poem's architectonics, hinting at its purpose and meaning. He at once links the poem to significant classical and European literary traditions and implies that in the *Calender* we may find evidence of an English aesthetic that joins past to present, Greece and Rome to England in a poem that is a sort of literary monument to English traditions, religion, statehood, and literature. E.K. is most helpful as a kind of literary memory who provides insights into Spenser's transmission of his literary and cultural heritage. In relation to Colin Clout, E.K. is somewhat more sympathetic to Colin's problems than Spenser is. Whereas Spenser allows Colin to entangle himself in inconsistencies, to misapply certain terms, figures, and forms, and generally to subvert his own arguments, E.K. is relatively uncritical of Colin.

Through Colin, Spenser explores the literary present and the tensions and temptations inherent in the poetic vocation.[13] Here we need to see Colin in relation to works like Sidney's *Apology*. As D. H. Craig has argued, Sidney's defense draws upon several schools of thought, finally urging the integral relation between the poet and the moralist and thus linking the poet, not to the contemplative, but the active life.[14] Throughout his career Spenser used Colin as a figure for his poetic talent, but the Colin of *The Faerie Queene* and *Colin Clouts Come Home Again* belongs to the world of the 1590s, to a more mature Spenser and certainly to a different England. The Colin of the 1570s must be seen in relation to the *Calender*'s other great poet and Colin's maker, Immerito. Spenser employs Colin to dramatize the effects of allowing personal appetites and desires to master the self, particularly the poetic self. To this end, he allows Colin to condemn himself, since his own argument, metaphoric language, and poetry combine to suggest just how far he has fallen from his early promise. As Colin's own words make all too clear, he is responsible for his decay and for a poetic talent that ends in silence. The best poems in the *Calender* provide us with the strongest evidence against Colin, for those poems belong to the past. What we are left with is the echo of Colin's despair. Using the legend of Narcissus as the analogue for the myth of Colin Clout, Spenser dramatizes the effects of a misdirected will, ultimately of poetic isolation. As Spenser powerfully suggests through Colin, the most deadly trap is the self.

I therefore think we do the young Spenser a disservice if we continue to view Colin Clout as simply a pseudonym for the poet. Instead, Spenser chose the name Immerito, using Colin as a foil to the true poet. Immerito later disappeared, as in the Prologue to *The Faerie Queene*, where Spenser adopted the role of the shepherd-poet, implicitly Colin, who, like Virgil, moves from pastoral to epic. Having necessarily cast aside the fiction of Immerito, Spenser began to adapt those elements of Colin Clout's legend that were appropriate to his later poetry and his sense of himself as a poet. In the *Calender*, however, he experimented with a number of voices: E.K., Colin, and Immerito. Thus the obvious surface dialogue of the poem is but the manifestation of a more sub-

13. For other views about Colin and the poetic vocation, see Mallette (1979); Miller (*ELH* 1979), (*MLQ* 1979); and Moore (1975).
14. Craig (1980). See also DeNeef, *Spenser and the Motives of Metaphor*.

merged and intense dialogue about the nature of the poetic vocation. Spenser projects his concern upon three figures: Colin, the talented poet who represents the extremes of the contemplative life, E.K., the pedantic moralist, and Immerito, the maker. It is finally the issue of control, of command, that distinguishes the maker of the *Shepheardes Calender* from any of his creations. He rises above E.K.'s moral vision and Colin's personal one, creating a poem whose total effect is greater than its parts. Spenser, in fact, offers a poem that does more than either criticize or celebrate; he offers a poem that rewrites England's history by offering it a new vision of itself. By its active engagement with its various contexts, the *Calender* suggests Spenser's conception of poetry as informed dialogue designed for social work or intended to prompt "virtuous action." He also offers a reinterpretation of the relationship between the poet and his community. Choosing not to be circumscribed by the voices of his significant historical and literary past, Spenser proclaims the poet an active and shaping force, historically, culturally, linguistically, and socially. Spenser, as he well knew, was the English Poet.

1

The Prefaces to *The Shepheardes Calender*

he *Shepheardes Calender* is designed to articulate the issues and concerns of its age by capturing the contradictions between the actual and the ideal, a purpose ultimately linked to the theme of reform. Although specific figures or issues can be used as points of reference, this is a theme that, for Spenser, transcends the specific issues of a particular decade since it is broadly relevant to the underlying power structures of all social institutions. Spenser introduces these concerns through E.K., who functions as one of Spenser's voices in the poem. E.K.'s two prose prefaces, in particular, hint at Spenser's plan for his poem, thus suggesting the poetic tactics or method he adopted. Both its external ornament and its structural underpinnings, as E.K. implies, point up the theme of national and personal renewal and hint at Spenser's own sense of his role as an Englishman, a Protestant, and a poet. As the prefatory material suggests, *The Shepheardes Calender* is at once a personal or poetic manifesto and a piece of political commentary that addresses both the mythic England Spenser envisioned and the actual England Spenser saw around him. As a personal manifesto, the poem served as Spenser's first genuine bid for poetic fame, an attempt to establish himself as the poet of his age.[1] As a mythic statement, the *Calender* addressed itself to certain immutable principles that operate

1. For a discussion of Spenser's activities during this period, see Judson, 24–72; Hamilton, *Sir Philip Sidney,* chapter 2; McLane; Ringler, ed., *The Poems of Sir Philip Sidney,* Introduction. See also Heninger, Introduction, *The Shepheardes Calender.*

in specific men and nations. As a poem directed to the England of 1579, it reflects the concerns, enthusiasms, frustrations, and expectations of its own time.

What we might call a principle of continuity is particularly evident if we consider *The Shepheardes Calender* within the context of the poetry of the 1560s and 1570s, a period of enormous literary vitality. The work of Sackville, Tusser, Googe, Turberville, Churchyard, and Gascoigne provided Spenser with a rich environment for his growing understanding of the role the English poet might play.[2] These poets, like Spenser, suggest a conscious effort to preserve, or reforge, the links with the English medieval literary past while maintaining the connection with Greece and Rome so important to sixteenth-century English humanists. Poems like *The Mirror for Magistrates* and *The Steel Glass,* in holding the mirror up to human folly throughout history, drew upon older medieval forms and modes of expression inherent in the still-popular traditions of the visionary poem *Piers Plowman* and Lydgate's *Fall of Princes.*[3] Similarly, poets like Googe, Tusser, and Turberville sought to translate into English the traditions of the pastoral, a form for the sixteenth century stamped with Virgil's name.[4] In relation to the works of these poets, there is nothing particularly startling about any of the forms and traditions Spenser wove into his *Calender*. The poem, whose title and general design evoke the older and still-popular *Kalendrier des Bergers,* is, despite its relation to the more homely world of the almanac, a poem whose divisions, speakers, and devices seem a sixteenth-century version of Virgil's ten equally artful eclogues.[5] *The Shepheardes Calender* also belongs within the traditions of sixteenth-century social criticism. Most obviously, Spenser linked his poem to these traditions by naming his most memorable speaker Colin Clout, originally the offspring of John Skelton, whose voice was raised against priestly excess earlier in

2. Here Sidney's interests seem to run parallel to Spenser's. Both men composed a prose piece dealing with English poetry, Sidney the *Apology,* and Spenser that tantalizing lost work, *The English Poet.* Furthermore, the *Old Arcadia,* like *The Shepheardes Calender,* explores the nature and uses of poetry and hence the role of the poet, the sources of poetic inspiration, and the outlines of the poetic personality. See also Golding's translation of Beza's *A Tragedie of Abrahams Sacrifice.* Golding's translation was finished in 1575 and published in 1577. In the preface, Beza directly addressed the problems of the Christian poetic vocation.

3. The significance of *Piers Plowman* was greater than that of any one poem. See King, *English Reformation Literature* 319–39; H. White, chapter 1.

4. On sixteenth-century pastoral traditions, see Cooper, Introduction and chapter 5; Cullen, Introduction; Grant; I. MacCaffrey; Montrose (1983); Patterson, *Pastoral and Ideology,* chapter 2; Poggioli, chapter 1.

5. On the popularity of both calendars and almanacs, see Bosanquet.

the century. Spenser's treatment of the problems and varieties of love drew upon images, points of view, and tags fully and frequently exploited by both medieval and renaissance poets in their efforts to describe the woes caused by Cupid's dart.

One of the overriding concerns Spenser shared with his age centered on the problem of tradition and the ways in which the traditions of the past might be transmitted to the more recent traditions of "modern" vernacular literature. Thus in France, writers like DuBellay and Ronsard affirmed the possibilities of French as the language of poetry, a concern central both to the poets of the Pléiade and the poets who clustered around the Protestant Henri of Navarre.[6] In England, the subject of translation was particularly interesting to intellectuals with Puritan sympathies. Leicester's name, or that of his brother-in-law, the Earl of Huntingdon, both men of decided Puritan leanings, was frequently invoked by translators looking for patrons to shelter them from the roughhouse of the literary marketplace.[7] Moreover, for Englishmen the issue of translation became allied with that same mood of nationalism that came to characterize England's approach to religion, a religion celebrated in the language of the people. Throughout the last half of the century, we may find a growing belief in the value and the flexibility of the English language. Just as, during the reign of Henry VIII, the early reformers had encouraged biblical translation, so we find writers like Foxe and Sir Thomas North in the 1570s affirming both the value of English and the need to make English works available to as many people as possible. Foxe thus explained in his Dedication to the Queen that he translated the *Acts and Monuments* from its original Latin so that the "ignorant flock of Christ" in its simplicity might be instructed. Similarly, North, in dedicating his translation of the cycle of fables *The Morall Philosophie of Doni* (1570) to Leicester, justified his labors and paid tribute to his patron by saying that, though Leicester himself needed no translation from the Italian, Leicester's patronage of North constituted a benefit to the common reader, who could now read the work in his own tongue and reap the wisdom of the ages.[8] The interest in English as the language of serious poets manifested itself in a devotion to Chaucer, the father of English poetry. From the beginning of the

---

6. For discussions of the French literary atmosphere of the same period, see Prescott, *French Poets and the English Renaissance,* and Richmond. For a contemporary discussion of the state of French poetry, see Joachim DuBellay, *La Deffence et Illustration de La Langue Francoyse.*

7. See Rosenberg, 37ff.; Dickens, chapter 12.

8. See also Rosenberg, 161.

century, poets had looked back to him as both a master poet and a critic of the Catholic church in his own day. Poets like Spenser consciously invoked Chaucer by drawing upon what they felt were rhythms, words, and literary forms that could be classed as Chaucerian.[9]

What emerges from this at once simple and complex effort to come to terms with the English language is a situation in which the seemingly distinct issues of poetry, translation, religion, and learning were subsumed into what, for lack of a better term, we may call nationalism.[10] England was not the only country where such a conglomerate was fused; for in sixteenth-century France, particularly in the circle around Baif, and notably in Ronsard, we can observe the same devotion to the ideals of poetry, the possibilities of the vernacular, the Catholic religion, and classical learning, all put to the service of *patria*.[11] The attempt to find a workable language for a national poetry is, in effect, an attempt to find a workable myth whose symbols, forms, epithets, and themes will combine in a poetic language capable of being understood. English writers were particularly lucky in this regard. Not only did England have a single figure of stable rule, but, in Elizabeth, a ready-made symbol. Unmarried, born with the Reformation, educated by the humanists, Elizabeth was a figure to delight the heart of an allegorist: as a virgin, a symbol for beauty and purity; as a Protestant, a symbol for righteousness and truth; as an educated princess, a symbol for learning and wisdom, and as a woman, the Zabeta, Eliza, and Elissa of poets and playwrights. As a Tudor, Elizabeth was also more than capable of understanding the value of symbols.[12]

The work of both Thomas Churchyard and George Gascoigne during the decade preceding the publication of *The Shepheardes Calender* shows

9. See the remarks about Spenser and Sidney and their experiments in English verse in Woods, chapter 5. See also Kerling, chapter 2. The experiments in English quantitative verse by Gascoigne, Sidney, Dyer, and Harvey—the latter three connected to the Areopagus group—were similarly efforts to broaden the scope of English poetry by testing English as a medium for another sort of verse. For discussions of and speculations about the Areopagus group, see van Dorsten (1981); Judson, 61; Phillips (1965); Upham, chapter 2.

10. See Yates, *Astraea,* 29–87.

11. See M. Adams; Castor; Lee; McFarlane, Phillips (1965); Prescott, *French Poets and the English Renaissance;* Richmond; Upham; Yates, *The French Academies.* For a discussion of the problems sixteenth-century writers faced in defining their own individual creativity in relation to the classical tradition, see Quint.

12. See particularly Strong and Wilson. See also Kipling. Though Kipling's study concerns the entire sweep of Tudor pageantry, it offers a unique perspective upon the contextual background for Elizabethan pageantry. See also the medals issued during Elizabeth's reign in Grueber I: Plates VI, VII, VIII.

clear evidence of an attempt to realize the Queen's potential as a symbol. In the courtly pageantry of Kenelworth and Woodstock in July and August 1575 and in the civic festivities of Bristol in August 1574 and Norwich in August 1578, Elizabeth herself functioned as the focal point for the action. Elizabethan civic pageantry seems to have followed the original pattern of the London festivities for Elizabeth in 1559.[13] Thus Elizabeth moved over a route, encountering at various stations *tableaux vivants,* where she halted and was entertained by speeches, songs, debates, or, perhaps, as was the case at Bristol, battles. Each of these diversions was focused—or placed in perspective—by the presence of the Queen, who at once provided the scene with its dominant symbol and its most important observer while herself, usually near the end, participating in the action at some crucial point.[14] At Bristol Elizabeth thus was present at a ceremony celebrating her role as Peace, as the figure whose virtue and might prevented dissension and brought about a national concord that emanated from her person. Four years later, Churchyard's handling of the festivities at Norwich was similar; but this time he underlined Elizabeth's role as a symbol for chastity.

In the more courtly entertainments at Kenelworth and Woodstock, both written by Gascoigne, whom Leicester had taken under his wing, Elizabeth was again the audience for and a dominant symbol in the pageants.[15] In both events Gascoigne explored the possibilities implicit in Arthurian legend, attempting to link Elizabeth to England's most persistent national myth. Furthermore, the mythic worlds that form the backdrop to both pageants were presented as frozen or static, their inhabitants fixed in problems that could only be solved by the presence of the Queen. Elizabeth was thus cast as a principle of vitality whose beauty, virtue, and grace could restore a world to harmony. Sidney seems to have followed Gascoigne's lead in the entertainment he prepared for the Queen as she walked in Wanstead Gardens in May of 1578. There Sidney implied that Elizabeth, in a sense a living symbol, was capable of resolving contraries, of bringing debate and its delay to

13. Bergeron, chapter 1. For other suggestions about Elizabeth's relation to the pageants, see Montrose (1980) and Norbrook, 83–84. For the pageants, see Nichols; Pollard; *The Quene's Maiesties Passage.*

14. The Queen seems also to have functioned as audience, spectacle, and actor in such courtly entertainments as Peele's *Arraynment of Paris* and, perhaps, if Roy Strong's hunch about it is correct, Thomas Blenerhassett's *A Revelation of the True Minerva.* On the latter, see Johnson (1984).

15. For a discussion of the relationship between Leicester and Gascoigne, see Rosenberg, 166–72.

an end. Like the Dame Nature of Chaucer's *Parliament of Fowles*, Sidney's Elizabeth ended the stalemate of a lovers' debate, freeing a world to marriage and thus to motion and life. Both the civic and the more courtly pageants are profoundly playful, designed to unite what Chaucer would have called "game and earnest." This sort of event depends, first, upon an audience prepared to accept a world that may well manifest the absolute through the actual, and, second, upon symbols that have validity for the audience. Symbols, like paper currency, are acceptable legal tender only if backed up by what is truly valuable. Elizabeth, who functioned as such a symbol, not only understood the principles of such an exchange but those with whom she traded. Thus she could play in the world of the pageants while affirming the underlying seriousness of the festivities and what they revealed about the ideals upon which the nation's image of itself was based.[16]

It is important to recognize that these early Elizabethan writers and statesmen participated in a world whose language was designed to function on various and sometimes contradictory levels. Much of their work appears to praise Elizabeth lavishly. However, the very language of praise was also intended to fix or to fashion a particular image of regal virtue. Thus in 1563, four years after Elizabeth acceded to the throne of England, John Foxe published the first English edition of the *Acts and Monuments* (originally *Actes and Monuments of these Latter and Perillous Dayes*). Like the first printing of the Geneva Bible in 1560, Foxe's accomplishment can be seen as a kind of landmark designed to celebrate the providential course of English history and to hail a new era of truth, righteousness, peace, and prosperity for England. Both the Geneva translators and Foxe dedicated their labors to Elizabeth, who, as actual and symbolic head of the English protestant cause, came to be inseparably linked with the ideals of nationhood and religion. From its inception, the *Acts and Monuments* was intended as a history of the English true church, a guiding principle nowhere so evident as in the prefaces Foxe attached to each of the editions (1563, 1570, 1576) published during his lifetime.[17] Throughout the prefaces, Foxe

16. Jameson's remarks about Burke are apposite here: "Kenneth Burke's play of emphases, in which a symbolic act is on the one hand affirmed as a genuine *act*, albeit on the symbolic level, while on the other it is registered as an act which is *merely* symbolic, its resolutions imaginary ones that leave the real untouched, suitably dramatizes the ambiguous status of art and culture" (80).

17. For an account of these editions, see Foxe, *The Acts and Monuments* 1:88, 103–12, 140. For a discussion of the importance of Foxe's work, see Haller.

elaborated upon the interrelated issues of history and truth. In so doing, he suggested the nature and hence the value of the work he offered to his English reading public: The *Acts and Monuments* is at once a genealogy of the apostolic church as it existed in England from the earliest times; a mirror in which England could gauge itself in relation to the past; a Protestant manifesto made possible by that technological marvel, the printing press, whose potential the reformers had so quickly seen; and a calendar intended to replace the calendars of holy days affixed to Catholic breviaries and missals. In each of its appeals, the *Acts and Monuments* was directed at a specific nation with a specific language, religion, queen, and, hence, destiny.[18] Foxe used England's view of itself as an elect nation and of Elizabeth as its divinely appointed princess as a lens through which he saw history. Thus Foxe introduced his work by preparing us for history seen from a particular point of view. Not only did he make order of the potential chaos of the events and persons of the past, he created of these a splendidly ornate setting for the gem of his collection, the story of Elizabeth herself. Rather than a panorama of random images, history, in Foxe's hands, is a well-focused glass, the *speculum* it was intended to be.[19] In it, Englishmen could detect the outlines of a myth that told them something fundamental about themselves and allowed them to perceive the providential working out of the absolute principle of truth in the particular and the actual.

Similarly, the courtly entertainments, like the pageant Londoners had prepared for Elizabeth's coronation in 1559, mingled advice with their *encomia*. In her progress through the city of London, Elizabeth, while enjoying the tributes of a truly joyful city, was also reminded that her country's prosperity was inextricably linked to her awareness of her duties as a Protestant and English princess. It is only logical to expect that the entertainments of the seventies might reflect some of the concerns and issues of a decade whose tone was set in 1568 with Mary Stuart's arrival in England. Norfolk's connivance at the Northern Rebellion in 1569, the Papal Bull releasing English Catholics from their allegiance to the Queen in 1570, and the Saint Bartholomew's Day massacre in 1572 inevitably influenced English appraisals of their queen. At Bristol in 1574, Churchyard praised Elizabeth for her symbolic value as a figure for might and peace; in 1578, when her courtship

18. See Foxe 3:719–22; Foxe, "The Epistle to the Reader," in *The Whole Works of W. Tyndall, John Frith, and Doct. Barnes.* On the importance of the printing press to the English Reformers, see Eisenstein, 305–6. On the book trade of the period, see Thompson.

19. See Campbell (1937–38); Hanning; Partner.

with the Duc d'Alençon was beginning to cause national concern, he praised her for her chastity. Similarly, references to her value as a symbol of chastity link Sidney's two productions for the queen, *The Lady of May* in 1578 and *The Foster Children of Desire* in 1581. The entertainments at Kenelworth and Woodstock also touched on the subject of matrimony, a subject with a good deal of interest for Leicester, who had a hand in both entertainments.[20]

What we know about Spenser at this point in his career suggests that he was ideally situated to look at the world around him and find in it evidence of another, more absolute world.[21] First, Spenser was the right age to view national events with a certain amount of idealism, perhaps absolutism. Born probably in 1552, he matriculated at Cambridge in 1569. The school would have offered an exciting intellectual atmosphere during the early seventies to a young man of vision and intelligence, especially if that young man already sympathized with the Puritan faction of England's national religion. Spenser received his B.A. in 1573, his M.A. in 1576. Aside from those stark facts we know little of importance about him at this point; in fact, there is some question as to whether he remained in residence at Cambridge from 1574 to 1576. Whatever Spenser himself did during the middle years of the seventies, they were also years of growing Puritan agitation in Parliament and years that witnessed the beginning of the Accession Day festivities for Elizabeth, so important to the Elizabethan myth during the eighties and nineties.[22] Spenser thus grew to maturity in a country committed to its idea of itself as a Protestant nation—and for many "Protestant" meant presbyterian, particularly at a place like Cambridge—whose prosperity was guaranteed by the righteousness, might, and wisdom of its queen.

From 1578, when Spenser was employed by John Young, Bishop of Rochester, to the summer of 1580, when he sailed for Ireland with Lord Grey, we can make more accurate guesses about the atmosphere

20. For suggestions about Leicester's involvement in both Kenelworth and Woodstock, see Rosenberg, 168. I differ with Montrose (1980), who has offered the most sweeping discussion of Elizabethan entertainments, in my reading of the pageants. Despite their official function, the pageants offer compelling examples of what was a frequently stressed dialogue between Elizabethan and her subjects.

21. For studies regarding the activities, friends, and interests of the young Spenser, see the introduction in Hume, *Edmund Spenser: Protestant Poet;* Jardine; Judson; Phillips (1969); Stern; van Dorsten, *Poets, Patrons, and Professors.*

22. See Strong, chapters 4, 5; Yates, *Astraea,* 88–111.

in which he moved. Although Spenser would not have encountered quite the extent of involvement in the Protestant cause in Young's household that he no doubt later encountered at Leicester House, Young was by no means dissociated from the issues of Puritan politics. Moreover, in Young's household at Bromley, Kent, Spenser would have been only a two-hour ride from London, the center of the nation's political and intellectual life. From the literal and metaphorical periphery, Spenser moved directly into the center of things when he became Leicester's secretary, at least by the summer of 1579. Not only was he likely to absorb the obvious lessons of Leicester and his circle, but, as a poet, he would have been the ideal listener for the sort of talk that probably emanated from a group of men as acute and rhetorically gifted as those attached to Leicester House. Spenser was thus probably involved in most of the major issues of the day: in addition to absorbing ideas and information from his job as Leicester's secretary, he was in the presence of men conversant in the political affairs of England, men, in fact, bred for responsibility, bred to serve the state. Though it would be inaccurate to describe Spenser as "friends with" men like Sidney, Dyer, and Greville, we can say that he was known by them and that he knew, more intimately than most, of the concerns of that group. Even leaving aside the tantalizing presence of Sidney and his circle of intimates, the atmosphere still seems a heady and auspicious one for a young man with a flair for philosophical poetry. Indeed, at Leicester House Spenser would have encountered in almost pure form that rare blend of learning, political acumen, and religious involvement that could characterize the Puritan party of the sixteenth century at its best.

In many ways Spenser's life from about 1562 to 1580 seems of a piece. Educated under the impressive Richard Mulcaster at The Merchant Taylors' School, he was bred in that same rare blend of classical learning, English chauvinism, and Protestant piety. His work translating the sonnets of DuBellay for Jan van der Noot's *Theatre for Voluptuous Worldlings* was likewise a Protestant labor. Like his own first work ten years later, the *Theatre for Worldlings* is a curious hybrid composed of translations from Petrarch and DuBellay, emblems, and a long prose gloss clarifying both the poems and the pictures which, in forecasting the apocalypse, urged repentance on sinners and conversion on Catholics. Van der Noot was an important figure in the international world of Protestantism, who, in exile in England during the sixties, oversaw the English edition of his work, perhaps aided by advice from friends like Mulcaster.[23] From his early days as Mulcaster's student, Spenser went on to Cambridge, bastion of Protestantism, where Thomas Cartwright, staunch advocate of presbyterianism, was given the Lady Margaret Chair of Theology in 1570. Then in the late seventies Spenser was back in London, or at least in its precincts at the Bishop's Palace in Kent. When in residence at Leicester House, he had returned—not only to the city but to the atmosphere, only now more charged—from whence he came.

The importance of his Protestant orbit for his own intellectual development is underlined if we recall how important these same years were for the country. In addition to the feelings aroused by the Saint Bartholomew's Day Massacre early in the decade, by the almost continuous revolt in the Netherlands, and by Mary Stuart's vexing presence in England, in 1578 Elizabeth reopened marriage negotiations with the Duc d'Alençon, who in January of 1579 sent his agent Simier to woo Elizabeth for him. In August of that year, Alençon himself came to England. Elizabeth's apparently serious negotiations with a Catholic prince, the younger brother of Henry III, the King of France, did little to still the fervor of committed Protestants. Particularly in the circle around Leicester, the queen's intentions aroused anxiety and, sometimes, frenzy. Through a decade characterized by an ongoing and frequently heated debate between those devoted to Protestantism and those who, like Cecil, were less eager to see England commit itself either to religious or political extremes, Spenser, when he appeared, appeared in circles associated with the side of devotion. The very title page of *The Shepheardes Calender* proclaimed his connection with those of Puritan leanings, since only three months before the appearance of Spenser's poem, the printer Hugh Singleton had narrowly escaped losing his hand for printing John Stubbs's panegyric against the Queen's marrying a French Catholic. Spenser's choice of Singleton was a curious one: there were better printers in London, certainly printers more accustomed to printing volumes of poetry. Spenser's choice of Singleton for his first poem seems to indicate political sympathies even if it was not an overt political statement on Spenser's part.[24]

I do not, however, mean to give the impression that the England of the seventies was solely a forum for a Protestant debate, or that Spenser

23. For contextual discussions of *A Theatre for Voluptuous Worldlings,* see Rasmussen; van Dorsten, *The Radical Arts.*

24. See Byrom (1933); Dickens, 272. For another view of Spenser's choice of Singleton, see King (1985), 20–21.

could only have been concerned with this particular issue. On the contrary, even from this distance, it seems as idiosyncratic, as lively, and as enjoyable a decade as any might wish, a variety that is underscored if we glance at the publishing trade during the same period. It is of course impossible to posit a single reader for all the books and pamphlets published from about 1569 to 1579, or to determine what Spenser and his circle of acquaintances read. But from the evidence provided by booksellers' lists, library catalogues, and other scraps of information, it is possible to look at the records in the Stationers' Register with an eye to what might have appealed to men like Spenser and to what they might have noticed about the book trade.[25] The reader of the 1570s had a particularly rich diet laid out for him by the printers.[26] Choosing from among "scientific" literature, translations, games, history, literature, devotional tracts, philosophy, and jeremiads, a reader could indulge his or her appetite for light or heavy fare or, as is more likely, balance the one with the other. Speaking only in terms of the market for books, we can generalize about the varied taste of the reader of the seventies. Volumes like Tusser's *Five Hundred Points of Good Husbandrie* maintained a steady popularity.[27] The chronicles of Grafton (1569), Stow (1573), and Holinshed (1578) were all published within ten years of one another. In numerous apocalyptic treatises, Stephen Bateman warned England of the results of unrighteousness. In addition, books about chess and other games, literature by Gascoigne and Spenser, translations of the eclogues of Virgil and of Mantuan, of Ovid's *Metamorphoses,* of Plutarch's *Lives,* of the tales of Doni, of the works of Calvin and Beza, and of *Lazarillo de Tormes,* along with William Baldwin's still popular *A Treatise of Morall Philosophy* offered readers a considerable choice.

In addition to attesting to the variety of works that were available, the evidence also suggests a country whose eyes were turned in on itself.

25. The following have been particularly useful as guides to the publishing world of the 1570s: Thompson, ed., *The Frankfurt Book Fair;* Jahn (1923); Jayne, *Library Catalogues of the English Renaissance;* MacDonald, ed., *The Library of Drummond of Hawthornden;* Stern (1972); Arber, ed., *A Transcript of the Registers of the Company of Stationers of London: 1554–1640;* White. See also Dickens; Harvey, *Marginalia;* Holliwell; Yates, *Theatre of the World.* In addition, I have relied upon the records provided by Pollard and Redgrove.

26. For a sense of this variety, see, for example, Rosenberg's appendix, which lists chronologically those books dedicated to Leicester. These were books no doubt on the shelves of Leicester's library and probably available to Spenser.

27. *A hundreth good pointes of husbandrie* was issued in 1557, 1570, and 1571. *Five hundreth points of good husbandry* was issued in 1573, 1574, 1577, 1580, 1583, 1586, 1590, 1593, 1597, 1599.

The many translations, histories, and jeremiads all bear witness to a country intensely interested in discovering or in defining its national identity. In looking to the heritage of its past, its language and its history, England sought to ascertain the link between past and present and thereby to reinforce its belief that the new age under Elizabeth was a fulfillment of history, of the mistakes and triumphs of the past. The Elizabethan rose trees declared just such a point: these were secular adaptations of the medieval trees of Jesse that appear throughout Europe in the windows of churches and in manuscript illuminations, and their iconography exploited the Tudor hybridization of the red rose of York and the white of Lancaster. Whereas Christ is the final and perfect blossom on the tree that springs from Jesse's loins, Elizabeth, the Tudor rose, occupies that position on a tree springing from Edward III.[28] More explicitly, John Foxe in his dedication to the Queen of his edition of the Anglo-Saxon Gospels (1571) stressed the continuity between past and present, the kinship between the Anglo-Saxon church and the modern, and the importance of acknowledging the relics of the past. Explaining his reasons for publishing the volume, Foxe bemoaned England's lack of national awareness by pointing to its historic ignorance, "whereby hath happened, that for want of true history, truth hath lacked witnesse, tyme wanted light, new thynges were reputed for olde, and olde for new." He went on to justify his translation as a sort of monument, or memorial to the past, "that the said boke imprinted thus in the *Saxon* letters, may remaine in the Church as a profitable example & president of olde antiquitie, to the more confirmation of your gratious procedings now in the Church agreable to the same."[29] Grafton and Stow made similar points about the need for accurate histories, since by history's mirror we can see ourselves. The reasons given for translations, like those for chronicles or volumes of antiquarian interest, likewise turn on England's need to assert or understand itself as a separate and special nation.[30]

Almost without exception, writers stressed the utility of their volumes. The banality of his subject matter notwithstanding, Thomas

28. See the title page for John Stow's *Chronicles of England.* On Trees of Jesse, see Male, 165–70. See also King (rev., 1984).

29. *The Gospels of the fower Euangelistes:* sig. Aijv.

30. See, for example, Colvin. The frontispiece (a reproduction of the frontispiece to Saxton's *Maps of England* [1579], engraved by Augustine Ryther?) depicts the Queen as Patronness of Geography and Astronomy. The engraving suggests the need to link the symbolic figure of the Queen with the issue of national identity.

Twyne in the preface to *The Schoolmaster* (1576) underlined the moral and philosophical values of his book on table manners. In the blurb to *The Philosopher's Game* (1563), a complicated arithmetical game whose inventor was still disputed in the early seventies, William Fulke puffed the value of such games in a way that foreshadows present-day pitches for video games.[31] Different in kind if not in degree are the prefaces to books dealing with moral or theological subjects. In his prefaces to his translations of the popular series of fables, *The Moral Philosophy of Doni,* and Plutarch's *Lives,* North carefully outlined the lessons each work had to offer, in both cases stressing their applications to an understanding of good government of men as of nations. Gascoigne, drawing upon his own "ill-spent youth" in the epistle "To al yong Gentlemen" that introduces his *Poesies* (1575), affirmed the ability of such examples—and, by extension, of poetry—to alter the direction of men's lives. Thus E.K.'s statement in the Dedicatory Epistle that one purpose of *The Shepheardes Calender* was "to warne . . . the young shepheardes .s. his equalls and companions of his vnfortunate folly" would hardly have surprised a reading public used to hearing writers affirm the use of the works they offered the reader.

Writers also frequently explained or sought to clarify the rhetorical structure underpinning the work. Just as Foxe was careful to explain the *Acts and Monuments* to as many sorts of readers as he could imagine for it—Queen Elizabeth, the learned Protestant reader (in a Latin preface), the less erudite English Protestant reader, the Catholic reader—so authors of less exalted works explained their methods of organization, usually in a letter to the reader. Partly to excuse the slightness or the unpleasantness of some of his entries in *The Poesies,* Gascoigne explained that the volume contains "three sundrie sortes of Posies: *Floures, Hearbes,* and *Weedes.*" The first includes light but elegantly turned verse, the second "morall discourses," and the third exemplary narratives meant to make the reader wary of tasting "Hemlocke" for himself.[32] Even Twynne explained that he organized *The Schoolmaster* according to the principles of natural and moral philosophy. Thus, in the first book he discussed the "nature & quality of all manner of meates, drinkes, and sauces," whereas he considered behavior at meals under the heading of moral philosophy.

In *The Shepheardes Calender* Spenser revealed how keenly he appraised

31. See Rosenberg, 39–42, for a discussion of the contemporary taste for such games.
32. Gascoigne, 1:12–13.

his audience and how well he understood the literary codes of his day. Even the sketchiest of composites of the publishing world of the 1570s suggests a reading public with certain tastes and predispositions. First, readers were prepared to appreciate a work designed as an English translation—in that word's most fundamental sense—of a classical and continental form. In its emphasis upon the English language, including the persistent use of archaic words; in its handling of older, in some cases rustic or indigenous, metrical patterns; and in its Colins, Hobbinolls and Cuddies, *The Shepheardes Calender* insists upon a native language, rhythm, and landscape for dialogues more often declaimed in Latin by shepherds named Mopsas, Amyntas, or Coridon. Second, the reader of the seventies was eager that the present not be dissociated from the past. In this regard, Spenser's first volume is a tribute to his understanding of the art of *trompe l'oeil*. The design of the volume not only appears deliberately archaic—the woodcuts themselves are out of date in method and technique—but the layout appears designed to evoke two distinct literary traditions: the humanist tradition of editions of Virgil and Marot and the more humble tradition of the calendar or almanac.[33] Thus to its original readers Spenser's first volume must have seemed both familiar and strange, a hybrid revealing its links to the various traditions mingled between its covers. Though its format suggested an age by then several generations in the past, the volume might also have prepared a reader for a poem that was intended to herald a new age for England and for English poetry. In evoking such traditions, Spenser evoked authority, thereby giving the poem he described as his bastard child a pedigree as impeccable as any in Western culture.

Furthermore, in aligning himself with poets such as Marot and Virgil and calendrical poems like the *Kalandrier des Bergers,* Spenser signaled that its author intended *The Shepheardes Calender* as a vehicle for allegorical meaning. Both sorts of pastoral traditions—the artful and the artless—were intended to instruct, and both were frequently used as forums for social commentary.[34] Thus E.K.'s remarks in the "Generall Argument" that several of the eclogues in the *Calender* contain hidden meanings, some relating to matters of state, would not have surprised

---

33. Luborsky (1980, 1981).

34. See Cullen, chapter 1; Grant; I. MacCaffrey; Montrose (1983); Patterson, *Pastoral and Ideology,* 106–32. For the habit of using agricultural language to express dissatisfaction with contemporary social conditions, see Dickens, 224 ff.; Lamond. See also Otis, *Virgil: A Study in Civilized Poetry,* chapter 4, for remarks about the relationship between the actual, the literary, and the mythic worlds in Virgil's pastorals.

a reader in 1579 or 1580 accustomed to pastoral conventions and aware of issues and events of his own time that might demand veiled writing. The fact that the title page of the volume contained no author's name and that Spenser only signed himself Immerito in "To his Booke," the poem that succeeds the title page, probably heightened the suspicion that the volume touched on political issues. However, despite the poem's usefulness as a calendar for 1579, it is also, as Spenser claimed in the last poem in the volume, "A Calender for euery yeare." The lines suggest how highly the young Spenser estimated his own still-unproven talent; for like Foxe, who meant to displace a leaden legendary with a golden history and thus restore England's memory or its sense of identity, Spenser claimed for his poem a place in a literary tradition going all the way back to classical times and extending to the beginning of time itself.

E.K. and Immerito: Between Game and Earnest

Spenser used the front matter to *The Shepheardes Calender*—title page, the dedicatory poem "To his Booke," the letter to Harvey, and the "Generall Argument"—to ground his work in the authority of the past, relate it to the exigencies of the present, and suggest for it a place among the great and timeless works of literature. In that sense, the front matter was a truly intelligent bit of self-advertising on Spenser's part, designed to lure, mystify, and instruct. The first two components of the front matter seem especially effective snares for the curious. If the absence of an author's name on the title page were not enough to tantalize a reader, the name of the printer, Hugh Singleton, in letters larger than those used for the title, might well net a prospective and politically astute reader. The dedicatory poem, wherein the author signed himself Immerito, only compounds the mystery, as does the presence of a second unknown, an E.K. whose two prose pieces suggest the *Calender*'s generic and formal antecedents. E.K.'s first piece, the "Epistle to Harvey," can be read as an *apologia* for the *Calender*'s style, diction, syntax, poetics, and mode, while his second, "The Generall Argument," focuses upon the poem's rhetorical structure, hence upon its underlying thematic unity. Thus, in addition to tempting a reader into imagining all sorts of things about the volume and its author's possible political beliefs and associations, the four components of the *Calender*'s front matter also combine to form a coherent introduction to the art and design of Spenser's first work. From the homely title page to the Chaucerian "To His Booke" through the two prose pieces by the wordy and officious E.K., the front matter appears at once serious and droll, an elaborate bit of foolery, every bit as carefully contrived as the least of a great pantomimist's gestures.

Particularly effective is E.K., our master of ceremonies and Spenser's frequently ridiculous go-between for the backward Immerito and the poetic fame to which he aspires. Although any number of suggestions have been made about E.K.'s identity, there are very good reasons for supposing E.K. to be the creation of Edmund Spenser.[35] Both Gabriel Harvey and Edward Kirke have been advanced as likely authors of E.K.'s contributions to the *Calender*. But we have nothing of Kirke's to compare with E.K.'s passages, while Harvey's prose from about the same period, even his so-called comic prose, is more ponderous and a good deal less effective than any of E.K.'s arguments or notes. Moreover, the fact that Harvey and Spenser attempted to imitate Chaucerian English, exchanged letters whose mock solemnity and hyperbole were clearly jokes between them, and even adopted private pen names for some of this correspondence suggests the likelihood that Spenser might have created in E.K. an alter ego, half scholar and half buffoon.[36] Spenser would have found a literary model for such a creation in the works of the two figures whom he describes as his literary guides, Chaucer and Virgil. Most of Chaucer's poems contain a figure—a persona or a literary alter ego—who is at once helpful and misleading, halfway between "game and earnest." Thus the comically uncomprehending narrators of the *House of Fame* and the *Boke of the Duchesse*, the elusive narrative voice of *Troilus and Criseyde*, and, most important of all, the sly pilgrim Geoffrey, who recounts the tales told by the Canterbury pilgrims, provide Chaucer's poems with yet another layer of narrative complexity or perspective.[37] Virgil was also commonly thought to have embodied various aspects of himself in many of the shepherds who

35. For arguments supporting the view that E.K. is Spenser's creation, see Jenkins; Starnes (1944); Stephenson. For remarks about E.K.'s role, see Goldberg, *Voice Terminal Echo*, 62–63; McCanles (1982).

36. For a sense of Harvey's style, see Scott. For the correspondence between Spenser and Harvey, see *Works*, 10. See also Harvey, *Ciceronianus*.

37. See Donaldson. For Chaucerian influence, see Spearing.

occupy the *Eclogues*.[38] Considering the space he occupies and the brilliance of his effect on the *Calender,* as well as the precedent of both Chaucer and Virgil, it is difficult to avoid the suspicion that E.K. was created by Spenser. Indeed, E.K., Immerito, and Colin Clout, the *Calender*'s protagonist, are all perhaps best understood as embodiments of the various attitudes, stances, and points of view assumed by the author of *The Shepheardes Calender*.

Of the three characters in the poem, E.K. affords Spenser the most opaque cover. From his opening words, E.K. dares us to take him too seriously:

> Vncovthe vnkiste, Sayde the olde famous Poete Chaucer: whom for his excellencie and wonderfull skil in making, his scoller Lidgate, a worthy scholler of so excellent a maister, calleth the Loadestarre of our Language: and whom our Colin clout in his Æglogue calleth Tityrus the God of shepheards, comparing hym to the worthines of the Roman Tityrus Virgile.

Using what he called Pandarus's "Baudy brocage," the worldly advice Pandarus offers Criseyde on the benefits of seizing the day, to describe a poet, unknown and hence unkissed by the public, E.K. launches into a stretch of rhetoric whose arch tone and metaphoric logic can only be described as absurd. E.K. takes his general conceit from the second component of the front matter, the poem "To His Booke," in which Immerito describes *The Shepheardes Calender* as a child whose parent is "vnkent" (unknown), a child "begot with blame." Picking up the suggestion that the *Calender* is Immerito's illegitimate offspring, E.K. carries the metaphor to ridiculous lengths. Thus he notes that as soon as the new poet's worth is "sounded in the tromp of fame . . . he shall be not onely kiste, but also beloued of all, embraced of the most, and wondred at of the best." He knits up the implied comparison between the new poet and an unkissed maiden by ending the "Epistle" even more absurdly with the suggestion that *The Shepheardes Calender*—or the "maydenhead of this our commen frend's Poetrie"—was long ago dedicated to Sir Philip Sidney. The sexual innuendo of the "Epistle to Harvey" leads into the bombast of "The Generall Argument" and E.K.'s lengthy dilation upon the different ways of ordering the year adopted

38. Harvey's *Marginalia* reveals his awareness of the literary and psychological uses afforded by a *persona*. See Stern (1972) 6.

by the Romans, the Israelites, and the Egyptians. Aside from the fact
that Egyptian lore was associated with arcane knowledge, there appears
to be as little reason for the pedantry here as for the comparison between
The Shepheardes Calender and a maidenhead in the "Epistle to Harvey."

While I think E.K.'s two prefaces provide a reader with important
clues to the poem, we nonetheless do Spenser a grave injustice if we
ignore their comic effect. The droller aspects of E.K.'s two prefaces in
some measure reflect similarly bombastic discourses with which Spenser
was probably familiar, notably Langham's well-known account of the
festivities at Kenelworth, published in 1575, and Sidney's tongue-in-
cheek characterization of a scholar in the Rombus of *The Lady of May*.
Rombus's solemn pomposity, his inflated and hence ineffectual use of
language convey just how little his learning has to do with life, how ill-
suited he is to discuss a simple matter like love. With his first words he
establishes himself, like the later and better-known Peter Quince, as a
fool of a particular sort:

> Now the thunderthumping *Jove* transfund his dotes into your
> excellent formositie, which have with your resplendent beames
> thus segregated the emnitie of these rurall animals: I am *Potentis-*
> *sima Domina,* a schoole-maister, that is to say, a Pedagogue, one
> not a litle versed in the disciplinating of the juventall frie,
> wherein (to my laud I say it) I use such geometricall proportion,
> as neither wanted mansuetude nor correction, for so it is de-
> scribed.[39]

Bowing and scraping before Elizabeth as she walked in Wanstead
Gardens, Rombus must have provoked a good deal of genuine laughter
from the Queen and her urbane and superbly competent courtiers, the
sort of laughter that Gabriel Harvey's own earnest self-absorption and
ambitious attempts to curry favor elicited on several occasions.[40] Some
of Spenser's letters to Harvey suggest that he was well aware of the
potential uses of rhetorical pomposity, since he adopted a teasing or
ironic tone when touching on subjects of a particularly lofty nature
such as friendship or poetry.[41] If, as seems likely, E.K. is Spenser's

---

39. Sidney, 2:331.

40. On Harvey's difficulties in attaining preferment at court, see Rosenberg, 323–36.

41. Compare Spenser's side of the correspondence with Harvey's. Harvey strains for a
rhetorical effect that mingles hyperbole with sense. Though Harvey's efforts are clearly
directed at displaying his own wit, Spenser's letters—shorter and more modest—are wittier,
achieving with a sentence or two what Harvey never achieves in paragraphs of turgid prose.

creation, in his voice we have evidence of a comic talent that, like Sidney's, is too often overlooked.

E.K., and perhaps Rombus, may also owe something to the letter Robert Langham published in 1575, providing an account of the festivities he attended at Kenelworth of that same year. Leicester had taken Langham into his household as Clerk and Keeper of the Council Chamber Door, giving him clothes and granting him favors. In return, Langham kept peace at the door of the Council chamber, also barring the curious from the keyhole.[42] Langham himself, as he reveals himself in his letter, is worthy of Jane Austen; in his self-complacent and solemn account of how he rubbed shoulders with his betters and in his lengthy descriptions of what he himself ate and wore, we see the world of *Pride and Prejudice,* where Lydia or Mrs. Bennett also indiscriminately mingle the inconsequential with the important. The opening sentence of Langham's letter to his friend, Humfrey Martin, Mercer, gives a good indication of the matter, tone, and style of the subsequent account:

> After my harty commendacionz, I commend me hartely too yoo. Understand ye, that syns throogh God and good freends, I am placed at Coourt heer (as yee wot) in a woorshipfull room: Whearby, I am not only acquainted with the most, and well knoen too the best, and every officer glad of my company: but also have poour, a dayz (while the Councell sits not) to go and too see things sight woorthy, and too be prezent at any sheaw or spectacl, ony whear this Progress reprezented untoo her highnes: And of part of which sportez, having taken sum notez and observationz (for I cannot bee idl at ony hand in the world) az well too put fro me suspicion of sluggardy, az too pluk from yoo doout of ony my forgetfulnes of freendship: I have thought it meet to impart them untoo yoo, as frankly, az freendly, and az fully az I can.[43]

Langham's apparent lack of self-irony makes his letter all the funnier, its tone even more absurd. Since genuinely learned men like Gabriel Harvey came in for their share of ridicule, it is hard to imagine someone like Langham faring any better at the hands of the younger men connected to Leicester House.

42. See Langham, 13–16; Nichols, 1:421. Despite remarks about Langham's probable identity (see Langham, 12 n. 27), it is nonetheless tempting to see the *Letter* as a spoof.
43. Langham, 36.

If E.K's unwieldy style and arch tone owe something to the house humor and comic conventions of the circle around Leicester, his prefaces are nonetheless significant. Spenser places them where we would expect to find an author's own dedicatory epistle and epistle to the reader, giving E.K. a prominent position in his first publication and, in the glosses that accompany each eclogue, almost as much space as Immerito, the poet. Spenser's possible reasons for prefacing a serious poem with a comic prologue must remain as mysterious as E.K.'s actual identity, but we can guess at several reasons for the decision. First, E.K.'s jocular tone, pedantry, and carefree handling of Immerito's own metaphors are disarming. It may well be that Spenser felt certain that the eclogues glanced too sharply at the persons and issues of the late 1570s; if so, E.K.—half clown, half capable exegete—served to screen the author from political reprisals. The suspicion that Spenser might well have felt himself in danger of damaging a career he certainly cared about is borne out not only by the disfavor endured by Leicester and Sidney, men far more highly placed than Spenser, when they made their views too well known, but by the two references to Envy, the first in "To His Booke," the second in the "Epistle to Harvey."[44] While the references to Envy signal Spenser's recognition of a link between the poet and the social critic, especially a poet in the tradition of Chaucer, by his use of E.K. he seems to disavow any responsibility for the poem as a radical statement. Here Spenser may be following Chaucer's lead, for Chaucer uses the pilgrim Chaucer to equally good effect in *The Canterbury Tales,* warning us that, if he offends, he is merely reporting

44. "Envy" strikes a curious note. First, it links Spenser's poem with a Chaucerian antecedent, *Troilus and Criseyde* (V, 1789), the source for most of the Chaucerian allusions in the front matter. Second, the word seems to have had both metaphysical and political associations since it was frequently singled out as the vice most seriously threatening the social fabric. Envy was seen as reflecting the effects of the Fall; the printer's epistle to William Patten's *Calender of Scripture* (1575) described Cain as bearing envy to his brother, Abel. John Baret in his *Alvearie or Triple Dictionarie* (1573), originally a text compiled by and for students at Cambridge, defined *Envie* as "hatred, malice, ill will, spite." In royal proclamations of the decade November 1569/70–November 1579/80, traitors were frequently accused of envy. That the word *envy* may also have had even more pointed associations is suggested by the "Epistle Dedicatory to Lord Robert Duddely" of Robert Fills's translation of *The Laws and Statutes of Geneva* (1562). The "Epistle" contains several injunctions against the envy and malice of those who dislike both Dudley and the Genevans. This book was in Harvey's library (Stern [1972], 29); the Quaritch catalogue listed it with Harvey's autograph and manuscript notes. Spenser ends Book V of *The Faerie Queene,* the most political of the books in that poem, with a long description of Envy, one of the final trio of Arthegall's antagonists. See Hume (1969) for a discussion of certain words that had political associations and for remarks about the need to investigate the contextual background of the language Spenser used.

the actions and words of others. The poet Chaucer is thus free to use the pilgrim Chaucer as a mouthpiece for some direct hits on the institutions of state and church. Similarly, though several of the eclogues in *The Shepheardes Calender* contain only a thinly veiled political allegory, E.K.—with his tendency to point out the obvious and to wonder at what is not puzzling—interposes himself between Immerito and wrath in high places.

E.K. throws dust in the air about another, equally serious matter, Spenser's own ambitions for his poetry. The front matter alone suggests how well Spenser had gauged his own talent and how high his hopes were for recognition and preferment. In fact, in choosing to publish his first poem anonymously, Spenser implicitly made a bid for fortune's sweepstakes. He follows the at once humble and audacious "Immerito" with an Epistle that places the "newe Poete" in a direct line from Virgil and Chaucer, the first seen as the greatest of all western poets, the second as the father of English poetry. Not only does E.K. interlard his Epistle with classical references and explanations, he compares *The Shepheardes Calender* to other first poems by poets who chose to take their first flights in the pastoral mode: Theocritus, Virgil, Mantuan, Petrarch, Boccaccio, Marot, and Sannazaro. The list generically places *The Shepheardes Calender*, but it also places Immerito within the most authoritative of Western literary traditions. Although it is probable that Spenser saw himself in terms of that poetic tradition, E.K.'s *encomia* allow Spenser to claim and disclaim in the same breath. For example, the opening paragraph of the Epistle suggests that this new poet is an heir to Chaucer, but the bawdy Chaucerian allusions undercut the high seriousness of Spenser's claims, saving him from charges that his pretensions are no different from those of men like Langham. "Uncouth, unkiste" follows "Go little booke," and between the maiden Immerito and the "Pandar" E.K., it is hard to find exactly where Spenser himself stands.

As a comic prologue whose voice continues to influence our apprehension of the poem in the glosses following each eclogue, E.K. is splendid; as a veil between the poet and his public, he is more than serviceable; however, as a learned reader, he offers some genuine clues to the purpose and design of *The Shepheardes Calender*. In both the "Epistle to Harvey" and "The Generall Argument to *The Shepheardes Calender*," he stresses the decorum and fundamental orderliness of the poem, implying that its structure is a vehicle for its meaning. For his sixteenth-century readers, a poem's meaning was finally relevant to the issue of its utility; thus E.K. joins his voice to those as revered as Horace and Saint Augustine and affirms the union the true poet effects between form and function, or eloquence and wisdom. The need for such a union provided the Renaissance world, as it had the classical and medieval worlds, with the underlying logic for its division of education into disciplines pertaining to eloquence (the *trivium*) and wisdom (the *quadrivium*) and for the many critical treatises on the art of poetry, including Sidney's *Apology for Poetry*.[45] Fittingly, and like the schoolmaster he at times resembles, E.K. begins with eloquence, or the literal aspects of *The Shepheardes Calender*, enabling us to understand the language of the poem.

In an argument designed to establish Immerito's claim to the mantle of Chaucer, E.K. organizes the "Epistle to Harvey" around the idea of the English language. Rhetorically, he moves from simple to complex, from a consideration of words to a discussion of poetry, and, finally, of form. After the comic Chaucerian opening with its nod to Pandarus, he follows up Lydgate's more sober description of Chaucer as "the Loadestarre of our Language" by focusing on the smallest unit of poetry, the word. Even in his own time, Spenser's language in *The Shepheardes Calender* would have been seen as deliberately, and perhaps needlessly, archaic, so E.K. begins by defending the words in the *Calender* as forgotten elements of the native tongue: "And firste of the wordes to speake, I graunt they be something hard, and of most men vnused, yet both English, and also vsed of most excellent Authors and most famous Poetes." He goes on to stress the authority these "obsolete wordes" lend *The Shepheardes Calender* and the wisdom of joining "rusticall" speech to the humbler pastoral mode. But the most striking of E.K.'s comments about Immerito's use of language by far concerns his description of the new poet as a champion of the English language:

> for in my opinion it is one special prayse, of many whych are dew to this Poete, that he hath laboured to restore, as to theyr rightfull heritage such good and naturall English words, as haue ben long time out of vse and almost cleane disherited. Which is the onely cause, that our Mother tonge, which truely of it self is both ful enough for prose and stately enough for verse, hath long time ben counted most bare and barrein of both. which default when as some endeuoured to salue and recure, they

---

45. For a discussion of medieval education, see Stahl and Johnson, 1:90ff; Robertson, 297.

patched vp the holes with peces and rags of other languages,
borrowing here of the french, there of the Italian, euery where
of the Latine, not weighing how il those tongues accorde with
themselues, but much worse with ours: So now they haue made
our English tongue, a gallimaufray or hodgepodge of al other
speches.

E.K. here defends Immerito's use of obsolete words by emphasizing
the importance of a linguistic heritage threatened by the influx of loan
words. Notwithstanding the fact that Chaucer's language contained a
number of loan words, particularly from French, Chaucer's English was
the implicit standard by which the Sixteenth Century measured its own
speech. Moreover, sixteenth-century Englishmen were not sure how to
scan Chaucer because certain words were no longer pronounced the
same way, an uncertainty that seemed to underline just how far English-
men had distanced themselves from their linguistic roots. It is for this
reason that, a few sentences later, E.K. cries out against those who,
though they may be conversant in other languages, are "not ashamed,
in their own mother tonge straungers to be counted and alienes."[46]
Implicitly E.K. urges us to see *The Shepheardes Calender* as a manifesta-
tion of the nation's new awareness of its own unalloyed identity, as a
poem whose building blocks are hewn from native rock.

Proceeding from the building materials to the edifice itself, E.K. turns
his attention to poetic form, specifically to the pastoral. In discussing
Immerito's handling of the pastoral, E.K. suggests two broad categories
for pastoral verse, one humanist, one reformist. E.K. considers the first
variety of pastoral under the heading of the Æglogue, calling the role
of poets from Theocritus and Virgil to Marot. In so doing he describes
the pastoral as appropriate for a "first flight," thereby seconding the
closing lines of "To His Booke," "Come tell me, what was sayd of
mee: / And I will send more after thee." Both the poet and the critic
give fair warning: The *Calender* should be seen as the opening salvo
from a poet who intends to join the ranks of the great. E.K. therefore
emphasizes Immerito's serious poetic ambitions by pointing to the
ultimate seriousness of the pastoral mode. E.K.'s references to the
tradition of pastoral eclogues suggest links between Immerito and one
type of tradition; his discussion of the title Immerito chooses for his

---

46. These words, of course, echo or anticipate Sidney's lament in the *Apology* that a man
should have to relearn, or go to school in, his native tongue.

first poem intimates his eagerness to place the new poet within another
sort of pastoral tradition. As E.K. observes, Immerito "complied these
xij. Æglogues, which for that they be proportioned to the state of the
xij. monethes, he termeth the SHEPHEARDS CALENDAR, applying
an olde name to a new worke." In choosing that particular old name
for a new work, Spenser had implicitly chosen to ally himself with the
spirit of the Reformation. Despite the fact that neither the author of
the *Kalendrier des Bergers* nor John Skelton, from whom Spenser got
the name of Colin Clout, would have considered themselves Protestant
nor their works as belonging within a Protestant pastoral tradition,
both works were seen as manifestations of the desire for reform. The
Kalendrier des Bergers, or its English edition, *The Kalender of Shepherdes*
(1506), had from the beginning been associated with Lollardy, with
those fourteenth-century followers of John Wycliffe who raised their
voices against clerical abuses and corruption in high places.[47] Similarly,
Skelton, whose popular *Merie Tales* Spenser gave to Harvey in 1580,
was inextricably linked to causes dear to the hearts of the Reformers.[48]
E.K. thus places Immerito squarely within an indigenous tradition of
pastoral verse. This native pastoral tradition formed a common bond
among works as seemingly unlike as *The Kalender of Shepherdes;* the
numerous almanacs published throughout the century; Thomas Tus-
ser's *Fiue Hundred Pointes of Good Husbandrie;* and the early sixteenth-
century addition to *The Canterbury Tales, The Plowman's Tale.* Further-
more, this particular lineage was frequently traced back to Chaucer,
whose *Canterbury Tales* stood as the standard by which lesser poets
measured their efforts to amend the times.

    E.K. ends his beautifully balanced argument by closing on a Chaucer-
ian note. He supports Immerito's poetic dexterity by alluding to some
of his unpublished and still lost works, "his Dreames, his Legendes, his
Court of Cupide." Both Spenser and Harvey refer to these poems in
their correspondence, so there is no reason to doubt the existence of the
works; however, the list nonetheless sounds suspiciously Chaucerian. A
sixteenth-century reader might well have been reminded of the most
recent edition of Chaucer's works compiled by Stow in 1561, the title
of which read, *The Woorkes of Geffrey Chaucer, newly printed with divers
Addicions which were neuer in printe before.*"[49] In addition to genuine

    47. See Dickens, 30; King, *English Reformation Literature,* 446; White, 24ff.
    48. Stern (1972), 49. On Skelton, see King, *English Reformation Literature,* 43; Kinney.
    49. The sixteenth-century editions of Chaucer were Thynne's edition of 1532, which was revised in
1542; Thynne's "booksellers" edition of ca. 1550; and Stow's edition of 1561. See *Chaucerian and
Other Pieces,* xv. See King, *English Reformation Literature,* 50–52; Miskimin, chapter 8; Yeager (1984).

"dreames" like *The Boke of the Duchesse* and *The Parliament of Fowles* and "legendes" like *The Legend of Good Women,* the volume contained such spurious works as *The Court of Love, The Judgment of Paris,* and *Chaucer's Dream.* If Spenser wrote his own dreams, legends, and a *Court of Cupide,* he appears to have apprenticed himself to Chaucer from an early date, modeling his career on that of the poet whom E.K. describes as a master workman. If, however, Spenser never wrote such poems, he apparently wished his readers to think he had, no doubt intending that they see this "newe" poet as firmly rooted in the excellencies of the past.

Only when we consider the "Epistle to Harvey" as an argument do we apprehend its rhetorical strategy and therefore understand that E.K., in establishing this "newe" poet's links to the past, seeks to establish Immerito as a reformer or as a restorer. In fact, E.K. claims for Immerito what had been claimed for the English Protestant church, in particular for its head, Queen Elizabeth. E.K.'s statement that Immerito had "laboured to restore . . . such good and naturall English words, as haue ben long time out of vse" resonates with the language of the Reformation. Not only had Foxe in 1570 praised Elizabeth for "restoring the country in a manner to itself,"[50] but the Dedicatory Epistle to the Queen that prefaced the 1560 edition of the Geneva Bible described her as rebuilding the temple, as restoring a practice of religion that had been forgotten. Just as the Reformers stressed the vitality of the primitive English church—in other words, the church established by Joseph of Arimathea, thus predating the Roman foundation by Augustine of Canterbury[51]—so E.K. describes Immerito as returning to the purer and still vital language of Chaucer. From those older words, he builds a form at once old and new, a form that, like the Elizabethan compromise itself, is cast as a restoration of the past and thus a reformation for the present.[52]

In describing Immerito's achievement as an act of poetic reformation,

---

50. In a letter to the Queen after her visit to Cambridge, Foxe wrote that "you restored their own country to them, and not only to them, but the country in a manner to itself." Quoted in Strype I, 2:110.

51. England's interest in its own ecclesiastical lineage underlay the antiquarian interest in very early English writers like Gildas. For example, an edition of Gildas's *De excidio* in 1525 contained a prefatory epistle ascribed to Polydore Virgil and another in 1541 in which Gildas's treatise is the tenth article in *Opus Historicorium nostro seculo convensenli.* In 1558, John Josseline edited another edition of the *De excidio,* dedicating the volume to Matthew Parker.

52. Not only were all sorts of writers sensitive to the nuances of words like reformation (re-formation), but, in particular, John Foxe exploited English in ways that suggest his interest in a revolutionary rhetoric. On this subject, see Billington.

E.K. suggests that *The Shepheardes Calender* presages a future as brilliant for English as that forecast for England with the accession of Elizabeth to the throne. This is because *The Shepheardes Calender* is not only a labor of semantic restoration, but a work of translation in the truest sense of the word. In presenting us with twelve English eclogues, Spenser unites English with its own linguistic roots as well as allying the native tradition with the literary traditions of the past. He accomplishes this in two ways. First, Spenser does more than translate Virgil or Theocritus, as a comparison between Barnabe Googe's *Bucolics* (1563) and *The Shepheardes Calender* illustrates. In translating the spirit of Virgil's eclogues into English, Spenser provided the classical pastoral with a renewed vitality, precisely because he made it relevant to the present.[53] In addition to translating words or dialogues in *The Shepheardes Calender*, Spenser translates forms, joining the classical eclogue, with its humanist breeding, to the rustic native almanac. As England's own hybrid, a bizarre mingling of Rome, Geneva, Basel, Strasbourg, and Salisbury, was the marvel of its age, so E.K. seems to suggest that the *Calender* is a new and wonderful creation. Both linguistically and formally, Spenser shows the way to his contemporary English poets; for in returning to the language of Chaucer, he helps to create a new language for English poetry. Similarly, his pastorals, though cast in the form of eclogues, speak in the language of England to readers whose ideals, frustrations, tastes, and predispositions are those of the Elizabethan and not the Augustan age.

E.K. implicitly claims even more for his Immerito. The union he effects between present and past is, like Foxe's in *The Acts and Monuments*, an effort to awaken a nation to itself. In his prefaces to *The Acts and Monuments*, Foxe justified the study of history in general—and his history in particular—by linking history to memory, hence to a nation's sense of its identity. E.K. hints at just such a connection when he bewails England's ignorance of its own forgotten language: Lacking a memory, it lacks a language and, consequently, a poetic identity. E.K.

---

53. On Spenser's transformation of pastoral language, see Fowler, *Kinds of Literature*, 77. The subject of translation was a charged one. Translations made elitist knowledge available to the masses and thus were seen as acts that could have political consequences. See R. F. Jones, 32–67; Rosenberg, chapter 5. That sixteenth-century translators were alive to the methods and thus the aims of translation is clear from Fills's remarks in the "Epistle Dedicatory" to *The Laws and Statutes of Geneva*. After stressing the moral value of these laws, Fills remarks that he will sacrifice style for matter and translate word for word rather than sense for sense.

thus describes Immerito's use of the language of Chaucer as strategic, as a decisive rejection of the foreign in favor of the indigenous. The motive justifies the apparent oddness—the difficulties it may pose for the reader—of Spenser's decision. By giving them an opportunity to refamiliarize themselves with their mother tongue, Spenser makes it possible for his readers to begin to know themselves. The reader will then begin to regain his or her memory, and the amnesia that had clouded the present should no longer threaten the future.

Whereas the "Epistle to Harvey" is designed to illuminate the underlying logic of the stylistic and formal characteristics of *The Shepheardes Calender*, the "Generall Argument" illuminates the poem's rhetorical structure, hence its unity of design. After stressing the origins of the Æglogue in goatherds' songs and thus the pastoral antecedents of the mode, E.K. goes on to offer two important clues to the poem's meaning. Both adumbrate a series of conventions, or codes, that serve as coordinate organizing principles for *The Shepheardes Calender*. First, E.K. divides the eclogues into three *ranckes,* Moral, Plaintive, and Recreative, intimating the sorts of lessons appropriate to each type of eclogue. Second, he elaborates upon the calendrical structure of *The Shepheardes Calender*, suggesting that we consider the twelve eclogues as units in one work whose proportions reflect those of the natural year. By relating each of the eclogues to a grander pattern, E.K. prevents us from taking them separately and directs us to all twelve, to a work Spenser clearly conceived as a single poem. In addition, E.K.'s discussion of the internal organization of *The Shepheardes Calender* implies that an inquiry into the poem's design is inevitably an inquiry into its meaning: The patterns he finds in *The Shepheardes Calender* have fairly widespread associations for a sixteenth-century reader. By describing the eclogues as either Moral, Plaintive, or Recreative, E.K. points his reader toward the idea of wisdom; for the three *ranckes* would have recalled the three types of philosophy, likewise reflected in other conventional triads associated with that of the *triplex vita*. E.K.'s justification of Spenser's reasons for beginning his year in January, rather than March, for example, alerts us to Spenser's insistence upon a Christian frame for the poem and the wisdom that informs it. E.K. ends by offering his reader what Saint Augustine, Chaucer, or Spenser himself might tag "Egyptian gold"— wisdom focused by Christian truth, like the pastoral mode of *The Shepheardes Calender*, a genuine transformation of traditional views, ideas, and patterns.

E.K.'s discussion of the first of these patterns, like the design of the volume Spenser himself seems to have overseen, is at once familiar and foreign:

> These xij. Æclogues euery where answering to the seasons of the twelue monthes may be well deuided into three formes or ranckes. For eyther they be Plaintiue, as the first, the sixt, the eleuenth, and the twelfth, or recreatiue, such as al those be, which conceiue matter of loue, or commendation of special personages, or Moral: which for the most part be mixed with some Satyrical bitternesse, namely the second of reuerence dewe to old age, the fift of coloured deceipt, the seuenth and ninth of dissolute shepheards and pastours, the tenth of contempt of Poetrie and pleasaunt wits.

He seems to speak a conventional enough language here. Any of Spenser's readers would have expected a prefatory Epistle or Argument explaining the plan of the work itself. It is only when we begin to scrutinize the passage that we realize that we only think we understand him.

The problem with the passage, like many of E.K.'s utterances, is one of semantics. His tone implies that he speaks of what everyone knows, that the terms he uses are standard critical usage, as familiar as terms like "elegy," "eclogue," or "encomium." But "moral," "plaintive," and "recreative" are in no dictionary of rhetorical terms, no handbook of poetic forms. The *OED* only returns us to E.K. and *The Shepheardes Calender*. The terms are particularly tantalizing since we know Spenser was in the habit of coining words.[54] Used as terms of literary criticism, Moral, Plaintive, and Recreative sound logical, but they exist only within the closed world and language of *The Shepheardes Calender*. E.K.'s definitions are as opaque as the terms themselves: He defines each by saying what months it designates. When we turn to his gloss on an individual month, he then tells us whether the eclogue is Moral, Plaintive, or Recreative. We appear to have stumbled into a particularly zany world where unknown but familiar-sounding words are defined in terms of what they define.

However, E.K. offers a cipher for this code in his statement that the three terms correspond to three *formes* or *ranckes*. His use of *rancke* as a synonym for *forme* is particularly significant, since together the two

54. For a discussion of Spenser and wordplay, see Hamilton (1973).

words imply gradation, or orderly progression. Where *division,* which he uses a few lines later in reference to the entire triadic pattern, implies only category, *forme* or *rancke* suggests that the eclogues are not necessarily of equal significance, but that they can and should be seen proportionally in relation to one another.

E.K.'s subsequent identification of these *ranckes* might well have then alerted a careful reader to another triadic pattern, a pattern conventionally associated with the pursuit of wisdom. Traditionally, philosophy was divided into three types: practical, theoretical, and theological, or divine. This division, which was frequently ascribed to Plato, was not simply a convenient way of categorizing the studies of ethics, metaphysics, and theology, but was thought to adumbrate a process of increasing complexity that had its ideal end in the soul's union with God. Each unit of the triad was appraised in terms of its utility. As Pierre de la Primaudaye put it in his popular *French Academy,* moral philosophy taught ethics and concerned "the correction of life and manners." Natural or theoretical philosophy was the study of natural causes, ultimately an inquiry into the origins of the universe, the master plan and the "masterbuilder." Divine philosophy was the queen of the triad since it culminated in the love of and union with God.[55] In his series of prose dialogues published between 1552 and 1575, Pontus de Tyard also remarked on the hierarchical structure of philosophy. Noting that moral philosophy is the study by which "we are freed from barbarism and made fit for society" and natural "the study of nature and natural causes," he assigned theology to the highest rank since it is the study "by which the soul rises to God."[56]

In the Middle Ages and the Renaissance, the three types of philosophy were also linked to the three goddesses of the Judgment of Paris, who were of course the three figures for the *triplex vita,* Juno, Athena, and Venus. Here, too, each unit in the triad was defined according to its end. Therefore, an understanding of practical philosophy, or ethics, was thought to lead to the pursuit of the active life, symbolized by Juno; an involvement with purely speculative philosophy to the contemplative life, figured by Athena; and a devotion to divine philosophy to the mystic or spiritually voluptuous life, symbolized by Venus.[57] Whereas

55. Pierre de la Primaudaye, 38–42. See also Reynolds, *Mythomystes,* 163.

56. In Yates, *The French Academies of the Sixteenth Century,* 83. See also Valerius, "The Epistle," Baldwin, chapters 3, 4.

57. See *Scriptores Rerum Mythicarum, Latini tres,* 144, 241. For Bruno, see Memmo, 105; for Ficino, see Jayne, *John Colet and Marsilio Ficino,* 59.

we might expect Athena to occupy the highest rank in a triad of goddesses, as she does in conventional treatments of the Judgment of Paris, the celestial Venus, as a symbol of spiritual, rather than carnal, *voluptas,* displaced Athena. The shift is less surprising in relation to Renaissance Neoplatonic thought and its accompanying iconography, whereby Venus was elevated from Paris's bane to man's salvation. Metaphorically, Venus has more to offer us than either Juno or Athena.[58]

This same triad was thought to be reflected in the three books of Solomon. Solomon's reputation for great wisdom (see I Kings 3) made him a special figure during the Middle Ages and the Renaissance. Like Moses, Solomon was credited with secret knowledge of God, and he was frequently mentioned in works dealing with arcane wisdom. Moreover, in the three books of Solomon—Proverbs, Ecclesiastes, and the Song of Solomon—commentators had a clearly defined canon of works that were not only grouped together but discussed as divinely inspired poetry whose outer veil concealed wisdom. The three books thus received the type of scrutiny devoted to other allegorical poetry. Saint Ambrose, the first and most succinct of a venerable line of commentators upon Solomonic literature, stated that Solomon treated Moral philosophy in Proverbs, Natural in Ecclesiastes, and Mystical in the Song of Solomon.[59] As a celebration of mystic union, the Song of Solomon was thought the climax of a movement that began in ethics, moved to metaphysics, and culminated in delight. For example, in his *Mythomystes,* Henry Reynolds initiated his consideration of Solomon by stating that "the powerfullest of al the affects of the minde is Loue,"

---

58. On the importance of Venus to Neoplatonic thought, see Gombrich, *Symbolic Images,* 31–81; Panofsky, *Problems in Titian,* 109–38; *Renaissance and Renascences,* 182–200; Sturtz, 10. Reynolds, *Mythomystes,* 176, noted that the Hebrew word *Eden* meant *voluptas,* or delight, and that only through love does man regain Eden.

59. Saint Ambrose, *De Isaac et Anima,* 512. See also his sermon on Ps. CXVIII, 1200; *Expos. Evang. Secundam Lucam,* 1529; *Comm. in Cantica Canticorum,* 1853. In *PL* 15:1529, the editor notes that the philosophic division was attributed to Plato, citing further references for Saint Augustine, *Civitas Dei,* VIII:4; Cicero, *Acad. quaest.,* I; Laert., *Vita Platonii;* Eusebius, *de Praepar. Evang.,* XI, 2; and Plutarch. In *De Bono Mortis,* Ambrose associated the Song of Solomon and Plato's *Symposium,* linking Plato's garden of the mind with Solomon's garden of the soul. *De Bono Mortis* was translated into French by Philippe de Mornay and in 1607 *Six Excellent Treatises on Life and Death* appeared, collected (and published in French) by P. Mornay, and now (first) translated into English. For a discussion of Ambrose and Neoplatonism, see Courcelle, 120–22. For a discussion of medieval Platonism as it influenced Renaissance thought, see Constable (1971), 24, 29. See also Walker (1953). For a discussion of the continuity of the medieval exegetical tradition, see A. Williams. For a discussion of biblical genre theory in relation to the works of Solomon and the seventeenth-century lyric impulse, see Lewalski, 53–59.

of which there are two kinds, Celestial or Intellectual, and Carnal or Vulgar:

> Of both these kinds Salomon hath spoken exellently; of the Vulgar, in his Prouerbes as a Morall, and in his Ecclesiastes as a Naturall Philosopher; and diuine-like of the diuine and Intellectual Loue in his Canticle; for which it is called among all the rest of the holy Scripture *Canticum canticorum* as the most sacred and diuine. The obiect of this Celestiall or Intellectuall Loue . . . is the excellency of the Beauty of Supernall & Intellectual thinges. . . .[60]

For Reynolds only the Song of Solomon taught celestial love and, more than other scriptures, enticed the soul to an ecstatic love of Beauty.

In prefaces and glosses to sixteenth-century English editions of scripture or translations of Solomon's poetry, we may find ample proof that the tendency to see the three books of Solomon as reflecting the three types of philosophy was not confined to recondite treatises accessible only to philosophers, divines, and university students. References to the triadic structure of wisdom, to the *triplex vita,* to the Judgment of Paris, or to the tripartite canon of Solomon's poetry are so common that it is hard to believe any literate sixteenth-century person with even passing interest in either philosophy or scripture would not have been familiar with several of these homologous triads. Spenser was no ordinary reader, and even during his lifetime he was thought to have tried his hand at biblical translation. As early as 1591, in his preface to *The Complaints,* Ponsonbie stated that Spenser had translated Ecclesiastes and the Song of Solomon. These two translations, along with seventeen other works, were supposed to have burned with Spenser's home in Ireland and continued to haunt Spenserians well into the eighteenth century.[61]

60. Reynolds, *Mythomystes,* 150.
61. In 1660–61 John Worthington wrote to Samuel Hartlib, enclosing a catalogue "of those pieces of the renowned Spenser, which are only mentioned, but were never printed." The first two entries were "A Translation of Ecclesiastes" and "A Translation of Canticorum Cantorum." Worthington continued, "Next to his Faery Queen, I should most desire to see the English Poet, & the Diuine Poems: for that in his latter years he most relish'd the more diuine strain of poesie, appears by seueral passages in his printed poems." Samuel Woodford in the preface to *A Paraphrase Upon the Canticles* (1679), remarked that he regretted nothing so much as the loss of Spenser's "Version of the Canticles." Quoted in Heffner, et al., 251–52, 272. For a discussion of these lost works, see Judson, 46. For discussions of the ways in which these works relate to Spenser's extant poetry, see Baroway (1934); Buck (1908); Sandison (1910).

Although there is no way of proving that Spenser actually translated these works, there is just cause for linking him to the traditions of biblical poetry. First, Solomon held a particular fascination for Elizabethans. As the ruler who completed the temple his father David envisaged for the true worship of God, Solomon was frequently invoked in addresses to the Queen, who was praised for continuing the work of her father and brother by establishing the true church in England, or, to adopt the metaphors of the times, by building a more lasting temple for a chosen people in a land thought to be a new Israel. Second, given the interest the reformers had in Old Testament poetry, which exerted a particularly strong pull on the circle surrounding Sir Philip Sidney, it seems reasonable to suppose that a young poet still searching for his direction as an English and Protestant poet might have investigated the design, intent, and ultimate meaning of biblical poetry. The poetry of Solomon would probably have seemed especially rich and suggestive to a poet who would go on to make the celestial Venus central to the theme and design of his mature works. From his accounts of Amoret and Britomart in *The Faerie Queene* to his *Epithalamion* and *Four Hymns,* Spenser played variations upon that chord whose harmony emanates from Venus herself. If Spenser translated Ecclesiastes and the Song of Solomon, he no doubt checked other English translations of these works, where he would have encountered prefaces and glosses linking the three books of Solomon to moral, natural, and divine philosophy. These Protestant glosses upon the Solomonic canon of poetry would also have seconded the feelings of the Neoplatonists that, in its capacity for love, the will could apprehend truths inaccessible to the intellect.

A similar triadic model underlies Richard Willes's discussion of the three types of poets in his *De Re Poetica* (1573). Willes was, of course, influenced by French literary critics, notably Scaliger; he had spent time on the continent as a Jesuit but in the early 1570s recanted and returned to England, where he added his voice to those of other English poets and critics concerned with formulating an identity for the English poet. In the *De Re Poetica,* he identified three types of poets, linking each to one of the three types of philosophy. He remarked that the first type of poet is theological and therefore capable, like such classical poets as Orpheus and Amphion, of making inanimate things live. He next described a second type of poet, the philosophical poet, who, like Lucretius, writes about nature or natural causes. Willes's third type of poet is the poet of manners, the political, economical, or general poet.[62] His remarks seem to anticipate those of E.K.; he arranged the three types of poets in a descending hierarchy, placing in the highest position those with re-creative powers. Moreover, E.K. not only suggests a similar hierarchy of forms or concerns, but implies that in Immerito we have a poet who, like the biblical Solomon, fulfills all three poetic roles in a poem whose hierarchies manifest the fundamental order of sapience itself.

By describing the eclogues as belonging to three *ranckes,* E.K. suggests that the *ranckes* themselves can be seen as literary kinds that function as stylistic and thematic codes.[63] E.K. thus places the poem within a specific series of considerations that govern not only the more obvious differences among eclogues but the fundamental unity among the *Calender's* many, and apparently various, parts. First, the suggestion that the eclogues are ranked puts Spenser's emphasis upon proportion in a new light: not only are the eclogues not equal, they are intended to have a focal point, a center. Second, if the design reflects that of wisdom, then we can expect the eclogues to fall into three broad areas of concern: The Moral eclogues should treat the subject of man as he exists in society; the Plaintive should consider man from a more speculative or metaphysical perspective; and the Recreative should, as E.K. says they do, "conceive matter of loue." Third, we can, before we begin, guess at what lies at the heart of the maze—Venus, and a recreation that may finally be re-creative. The suggestion is radical since it has the effect of displacing Colin Clout from the position of prominence he has enjoyed among critics for the past fifty years. In taking the vantage E.K. offers us upon the *Calender,* however, we displace Colin only to place his song to Elisa, the earthly manifestation of celestial harmony, in the spot he formerly occupied. Moreover, by intimating that the eclogues fall into such triadic proportions, E.K. implies that the barrenness of December is in reality the fallow earth from which the growth of another year will spring. What we learn from

---

62. Willes uses the noun *classis,* which connotes hierarchical ranking. Of the first class he writes, "quorum opera tam diuina sunt habita, vt rebus etiam inanimis metem addidisse crederentur." Willes 59, 63. *De Re Poetica,* which forms a section of Willes's *Poematum liber* (London, 1573), seems especially interesting in relation to the *Calender* and to Sidney's *Apology.* In *French Poets and the English Renaissance* (96–98), Prescott discusses Willes. For a consideration of Sidney as a critic, see Craig (1980); Robinson.

63. See Colie, 114, 115, 128; Fowler, *Kinds of Literature.*

a scrutiny of either social inequities or private miseries and frustrations cannot be compared to the revelations of love, most perfectly captured by the lay in "Aprill."

Such an emphasis upon re-creation is also apparent in E.K.'s handling of the poem's second organizing principle, its calendrical structure. Like E.K.'s ranking of the eclogues, that structure forces us to consider the twelve eclogues as a single poem whose unifying patterns hint at a higher order that Spenser would ascribe only to the creator of the whole. E.K. begins his discussion of the poem's calendrical structure by defending Spenser's decision to begin his year with January rather than with March, the first month of the year of grace.[64] E.K. begins by discussing the various methods of organizing the months adopted by Roman, Hebrew, Egyptian, and Christian civilizations. In each case he juxtaposes a calendar to a particular civilization's religious beliefs, in effect using the calendar as a backdrop for the activities of human beings. Thus, E.K. tells us, the ancient Hebrews began their year in March to commemorate the Exodus; the Romans called their first month after the god of beginnings, Janus; and the Egyptians began with September since they believed God made the world in that month. In contrast to these other methods of organizing the year, the Christian calendar is a "memorial" or a "monument" to Christ and the resurrection he offers man. E.K. implies that whereas other civilizations have sought to organize the year around the idea of creation, only with the birth of Christ is it possible to make a calendar a monument to re-creation:

> But sauing the leaue of such learned heads, we mayntaine a custome of coumpting the seasons from the moneth Ianuary, vpon a more speciall cause, then the heathen Philosophers euer coulde conceiue, that is, for the incarnation of our mighty Sauiour and eternall redeemer the L. Christ, who as then renewing the state of the decayed world, and returning the compasse of expired yeres to theyr former date and first commencement, left to vs his heires a memoriall of his birth in the ende of the last yeere and beginning of the next. which reckoning, beside that eternall monument of our saluation, leaneth also vppon good proofe of special iudgement.

64. For a discussion of Renaissance ways of ordering the months of the year, see Hawkins (1967).

The Christian calendar is the sign of a unique perspective upon time, a "reckoning" that celebrates grace and not nature. March indeed marks the point where the earth awakens, but by beginning with January, E.K. suggests we affirm a more perfect nature.

In his handling of the calendrical underpinnings of *The Shepheardes Calender*, E.K. plays upon the subject of proportion, a subject he not only addresses in his remarks about the three *ranckes* or *formes* of the eclogues, but one of manifest importance to Spenser given the complete title of the poem as it appears on the title page: "The Shepheardes Calender, Conteyning twelue Æglogues *proportionable* to the twelue monethes." (Italics added.) E.K.'s explicit and implicit emphasis upon proportion encourages the reader to read the individual poems in relation to one another and the whole; for the word implies relation whether we apply it to buildings, monuments, geometric ratios, or musical harmonies.[65] Thus, in underlining the calendrical structure of *The Shepheardes Calender*, E.K. alludes to a fundamental principle of the *Calender*. We can no more isolate one poem than we can one month; in order to grasp the purpose behind the grand design, we must take all twelve, proportionable to one another, that comprise a year, or a poem. E.K.'s comments about this calendar's beginning in January make it clear that E.K. values the calendar's structural and thematic "decorem" as much as he values the linguistic decorum of Immerito's "Chaucerian" English. Spenser indeed manages to attune his eclogues to the labors or lessons of each month, allowing the poem to function as a calendar.[66] We need only look at its French model, *The Kalender of Shepherdes*, to realize how well Spenser adapted an old French, Catholic, and relatively unsophisticated form to a modern, English, Protestant, and certainly sophisticated purpose. The resemblance is there: if we place *The Shepheardes Calender* alongside *The Kalender of Shepherdes* and a series of Labors of the Months, we see the similarities. But even more noteworthy are the differences of purpose, design, and effect.

Neither of the two most obvious prototypes for the *Calender, The Zoadiake of Life* (translated by Barnabe Googe in 1576) or *The Kalender of Shepherdes* actually merges literary mode with thematic purpose; Spenser nonetheless took these literary offshoots of the almanac seri-

---

65. The word itself was a signifier for a series of concepts important to a number of disciplines. See Heninger, *Touches of Sweet Harmony;* Wittkower.

66. See Cheney (1989); Cullen, 120–50; Heninger; Parmenter; Tuve, *Seasons and Months*.

ously.[67] In *The Zodiake of Life,* which begins its rotation under the sign
of Aries in March, its author, Palingenius, attempted to link each of
the twelve long poems to the weather and tone of each astrological
sign. But it remains a collection of discursive poems, each chastising
man or his institutions for folly or corruption. *The Kalender of Shep-
herdes,* though far more harmoniously joined to its dominant idea, the
calendar, is characterized by a similarly overt didacticism. Its frequently
labored language and crude versification contribute to its air of rustic
charm. Both works, however, proclaim a message also found in Spen-
ser's *Calender.* All of these poems underline the necessity of trying to
achieve a harmony humanity may find manifested in nature, which, like
itself, is the work of that greater artist Jehovah. Thus the natural year,
though it appears but to teach the lesson of Ecclesiastes ("Vanity,
vanity, all is vanity"), urges us to look beyond transience and decay to
what is permanent. The prologue to *The Kalender of Shepherdes* stressed
the book's fundamental utility by saying that it inspires health and
good governance in recognition of the finitude of this life. Similarly,
Palingenius enumerated the many frustrations and disappointments of
human life in order to turn our eyes to the light evoked in the first
book, Aries, and the twelfth, Pisces, where he stressed the relationship
between God and the sun. Indeed, such works were more literary
reworkings of the calendars found in prayer books and devotionals; all
were efforts to graft man onto eternity by using finite time as a glass
for infinity.[68]

E.K.'s discussion of the calendar frame would therefore have sug-
gested to its readers a second series of stylistic strategies and thematic
concerns. Since the poem's consecutive fiction is organized around the
figura of the year, it is natural to expect it to explore the issue of time
and to do so using the metaphors of agriculture. Furthermore, E.K.'s
emphasis on reform suggests that the *Calender* is a document of new,
or reformed, time and will join social commentary to an abstract explo-
ration of man in time. Finally, since the poem is composed of eclogues
within a calendrical structure, it is implicitly linked to works like Pe-
trarch's *Trionphi* or *Canzoniere,* both of which juxtapose human and

67. For example, under the ABC of our Vulgar Astrologers, Harvey refers to the *Shepherdes
Kalender* as a primer. Harvey's marginal comments about Spenser's admiration for DuBartas's
astronomical poem make it clear just how seriously readers like Harvey and Spenser took such
works. See Harvey, *Marginalia,* 163, 51, 161, 162.

68. Nowhere are such lessons as pronounced as in the prayers and lessons for November
17, Accession Day. See, for example, Hake; Pit.

transitory events to a greater cycle of transcendant, or providential, time.[69] Calendrical patterning was frequently used by both medieval and renaissance authors to adumbrate the providential ordering of a universe whose motion was conceived of as but the manifestation of a great and stable love.

Both ways of organizing the poem that Spenser describes in the letter bespeak his overarching concern with order. E.K.'s discussion of the calendar frame implies that the poem will consider subjects like time, fruitfulness, and reform, employing a consecutive fiction whereby we move from the year's beginning to its end. Colin Clout's history, which points up the relationship between individual achievement and time, serves as the unifying thread for this scheme. The *ranckes* also serve to organize the eclogues. If the calendar frame suggests linear (or, more accurately, circular) progression, the category of the *ranckes* underlines an internal progression, culminating in the love that for renaissance as for medieval man bound contraries together in fruitful relationships. The pattern of hierarchical relationships traced by the *ranckes* serves to link Colin and his personal concerns with those of the greater social body. However, neither the fruitfulness we might expect Colin's year to embody nor the orderly love figured by the celestial Venus is manifested in the *Calender*. The very order that undergirds Spenser's design in the poem is, in a sense, frustrated by the poem itself, and the renewal promised by the prefatory material remains unrealized in and by the world that the *Calender* depicts.

Conclusion: A Monument of Reform

In seeking to explain E.K.'s prefaces to *The Shepheardes Calender*, I have drawn upon architectural language and metaphors, a language that at once reflects the rhetorical habits and strategies of Spenser's contemporaries and illuminates the grand design behind *The Shepheardes Calen-*

---

69. The comments of Bernardo Lapini, frequently referred to as Bernardo Illicino, were a standard feature of the many sixteenth-century editions of the *Trionfi*. In addition to seeing the poems as sketching a process of enlightenment, in his discussion of the first poem in the series, Illicino hinted at an astrological allegory that informs Petrarch's poem. On the *Trionfi*, see Carnicelli, Introduction; Bernardo Lapini, sig. CXIXv, XXIIv. On calendrical patterning in the *Canzoniere*, see Roche (1974).

der.[70] For example, two of the most important publications of the
Elizabethan age, Foxe's *Acts and Monuments* and the Geneva Bible,
were described in architectural terms. Foxe not only gave his work a
title that evoked an actual structure, but underlined the relationship
between monuments and memory throughout his prefaces, implying
that the book was an edifice designed to endure where those of brick
and mortar crumble—that, in fact, he had rebuilt the past in a way that
gave true permanence to the acts of history. Elsewhere, Foxe was equally
prone to using the analogy between a book and a monument in order
to stress the relationship between the present and the almost forgotten,
hence dead, past. The Geneva translators, like many others during the
early years of Elizabeth's reign, linked her achievement to the rebuilding
of the temple. Thus they embroidered an elaborate conceit whereby
Elizabeth "whome God hath made as our Zerubbabel for the erecting
of this most excellent Temple," will overcome all obstacles to the com-
pletion of a spiritual temple in the new Israel, Protestant England. They
sustained the conceit throughout the dedicatory epistle to the Queen,
concluding, "This Lord of lordes & King of kings who hath euer
defended his, strengthn, comfort and preserue your maiestie, that you
may be able to builde vp the ruines of Gods house to his glorie, the
discharge of your conscience, and to the comfort of all them that loue
the comming of Christ Iesus our Lorde." Their choice of metaphors
was natural, considering the emphasis throughout the Old Testament
upon the temple. From the Ark of the Covenant to Solomon's temple
to the rebuilt temple described in Ezra and Nehemiah to Ezekiel's vision
of the temple, the structure dominated the imaginations and hence the
language of the Old Testament writers. That such a vision struck a
sympathetic chord in the English Protestants is apparent from the
Geneva Bible—whose twenty-six woodcuts are dominated by various
structures, especially the ark or the temple. Since the temple was mod-
eled upon the ark, whose divinely inspired pattern was given to Moses
by God, the proportions of both edifices were thought to reflect the
pattern or order of the cosmos.[71] Furthermore, the fact that the English
Protestants saw themselves as a chosen people made them eager to
suggest ways in which the England of the late sixteenth century served
as a stage for working out God's plan in history. As Solomon or
Zerubbabel, Elizabeth ushered in a new age—an age frequently de-

70. For a study linking calendrical patterning and architectural metaphors, see Prescott
(1978).

71. See Wittkower 91, 105–6.

scribed in evocative pastoral language—by erecting the true spiritual temple in a land once a bond slave to Rome. The proportions of England's temple, like those of the Ark of the Covenant, should manifest God's own order, an order Elizabethans also thought inherent in the human frame.

At the risk of out-conceiting E.K. himself, we can describe *The Shepheardes Calender* as a Protestant monument, stripped of its Roman encrustations, now cleansed and restored to its true identity. It is the garrulous but helpful E.K. who, as if he were showing us where to stand in order to attain the best vantage upon this at once strange and familiar work of Immerito's, suggests that we see the poem as a unit whose individual components combine to point up a single ideal. As E.K. implies in his two prefaces to the poem, the union Immerito effects between *littera* and *sententia*, or between eloquence and wisdom, is an essential aspect of the function of the *Calender*, just as it is a crucial element in the formation of the English poet. E.K., in fact, hints at what *The Shepheardes Calender* itself bears out: It is impossible to separate such issues as politics, religion, literature, philosophy, theology, and poetry. For, as beliefs conceived of in relation to a man, all might happily serve the same queen, just as all knowledge, pursued wisely, should lead to the same place. E.K. acts as a valuable guide to the poem since in both of his essays he focuses upon the harmonies of the *Calender*—harmonies of design, structure, function, and ornament that are integral to Spenser's purpose in writing the poem.

Both the "Epistle to Harvey" and the "Generall Argument" stress the fundamental harmony of *The Shepheardes Calender* by praising first, decorum and second, proportion. Like a schoolman, E.K. begins with the obvious, with the exterior, pointing out and explaining Immerito's choice and use of language, praising his handling of rhyme, rhythm, and imagery, and the fitness of the genre he chooses for a first poem. All these considerations can be grouped under the umbrella of decorum, a topic E.K. introduces early in the "Epistle":

> No less I thinke, deserueth his wittinesse in deuising, his pithinesse in vttering, his complaints of loue so louely, his discourses of pleasure so pleasantly, his pastorall rudenesse, his morall wisenesse, his dewe obseruing of Decorum euerye where, in personages, in seasons, in matter, in speach, and generally in al seemely simplycitie of handeling his matter, and framing his words . . .

The word "Decorum" dominates this clause. Not only does E.K. capitalize it for visual effect, but the sentence itself concerns the decorousness of *The Shepheardes Calender*. E.K.'s choice of this word is at once significant and ironic; he chooses a term that an acute reader would have recognized as a fairly recent loan word, a word, moreover, that French critics were only beginning to employ as a critical term. Despite the paradox, E.K. has chosen justly since decorum implies relation. Nothing alone can be decorous; in order for something to observe decorum, it must relate harmoniously to something else. Throughout the "Epistle," the principle of decorum remains the implicit standard by which he measures Spenser's achievements of style and method. Gascoigne in *Certayne Notes of Instruction concerning the making of verse or ryme in English* (1575) had advised the poet to begin with an idea, then to suit style to invention. If we take as Spenser's purpose the creation of an English pastoral suited for his own age, then the issues of words, sentences, rhyme, meter, and metaphoric language fall smoothly into place.

E.K. does not stop with the more obvious features of *The Shepheardes Calender*, but in the "Generall Argument" goes on to intimate ways in which Immerito has created a work of genuine unity. The principle of decorum E.K. finds in the poem's style is the physical manifestation of a more fundamental principle we may call proportion that informs the entire poem. For this reason, both of the ordering principles adumbrated in the "Generall Argument" are based upon the idea, or ideal, of order. In his *Calender* Spenser does more than praise the actual Elizabeth, he celebrates her as an earthly vessel for an order that, should man perceive it, can realign him with himself, his fellows, and the realm of nature. The calendrical structure of *The Shepheardes Calender*, as carefully and strategically executed as any cycle of the Labors of the Months upon a Gothic cathedral, is informed by the same principle of order, in effect, a principle of re-creation. E.K. insists upon a calendar that is made in the image of something greater than itself. Rather than stress a natural or astrological cycle, E.K. emphasizes the fact that Immerito has chosen to make his poem proportionable to a calendar that is a "memoriall" or a "monument" to Jesus Christ. By linking Immerito's year to the theme of renewal, E.K. once more hints that the *Calender* is unified thematically by its emphasis on re-creation, love, and harmony.

In his handling of both classical and indigenous literary tradition and significant events and persons of his own age, Spenser is equally intent on elaborating upon this same principle of renewal. First, as a maker, he uses what he finds around him. However, he does not build in slavish imitation of Virgil or Chaucer, but erects—like John Foxe himself—a monument to and for his time. Thus, while we can see here and there a detail he surely borrowed from another, Spenser borrows but to make his own. He joins past to present in a work that, though cast in a language and genre and informed by a habit of mind no longer familiar or meaningful to us, nonetheless retains its second function as a calendar for every year. Though we cannot lift *The Shepheardes Calender* away from the world and the reading public of the 1570s, neither can we fix it solely in that world. The force the poem still exerts is a genuine measure of Spenser's success in finding and sustaining a workable myth: In the pastoral world of the *Calender*, he draws upon the actual and concrete only to figure the ideal and abstract. Spenser used the world around him as the material for a myth grander than any Leicester or Walsingham or even Elizabeth. The poem's proportions suggest this myth of renewal and order, a myth that reflects his appraisal of and hopes for human societies. That Spenser's is an Elizabethan, Protestant, and humanist vision goes without saying; he offers England—her citizens, her priests, her poets, and her statesmen—a way out of decay and decline. He offers the possibility of a world truly re-formed.

2

The Moral Eclogues: Pastoral Cares

n the five Moral eclogues, Spenser focuses on matters related to the well-being of the body politic. He explores the conflicts inherent in the institutions and relationships of his own day, drawing on a variety of poetry and poetic devices that his readers would have linked to figures such as Chaucer, Mantuan, and Skelton, as well as to the ethical concerns of moral philosophy. In Cuddie's scorn for Thenot, "Februarie" introduces the group by taking up the quarrel between youth and age, a conflict that not only points up the difficulties of harmonizing the two conditions, but the difficulties men face when they try to coexist. "Maye," "Julye," and "September" carry the debate into another realm of pastoral concerns by exploring ecclesiastical conflicts and inequities. Moving from the duties of priests to those of poets, "October" offers yet a third type of shepherd and depicts a debate about the duties the poet assumes in relation to his fellows and his society. The five Moral eclogues thus comprise an elaborate commentary on pastoral duties and cares, offering a sweeping vision of man's relation to his fellow citizens. To a large extent, in the pastoral world of *The Shepheardes Calender*, Spenser describes a realm whose conflict, misapprehension, self-interest, and folly evince a need for harmony that remains either unrealized, unwanted, or untenable for the shepherds, figures whose failures and longings bespeak not only those of human beings in general, but those of the second decade of Elizabeth's reign in particular. In fact, the Moral eclogues may be viewed as Spenser's sober appraisal of a commonwealth whose fundamental weaknesses demand radical reform.

The Moral Tradition

Because of their obvious topicality, the Moral eclogues have frequently been studied against the background of the 1570s. They must also be seen as emerging not only from a strain of pastoral poetry commonly associated with Mantuan,[1] but from a strong English tradition of moral tales, dialogues, and debates that continued to flourish throughout the seventies. Figures like Chaucer, Langland, and Skelton belong in this tradition, for Spenser and his contemporaries associated these poets with social commentary and hence with the poetry of national and individual morality. "Moral" is, in fact, the one term E.K. uses for which Spenser's first readers would have had an immediate equivalent; in addition to connoting a certain type of behavior, it was used as a critical term applied to works of literature. Frequently it was the only purpose or level of meaning an author would claim for his work, as Spenser himself does in the Epilogue to his *Calender,* wherein he insists that his purpose has been "To teach the ruder shepheard how to feede his sheepe, / And from the falsers fraud his folded flocke to keepe."[2] Spenser's words reflect the critical habits of his age. In keeping with a poetic that avowed poetry's higher and hidden meanings, sixteenth-century poets generally acknowledged only a moral level for their po-etry, leaving the possibility of further layers to the curious and diligent; higher meanings like pearls were not prizes for easy availability.[3] Thus, when E.K. ranks some of the eclogues as Moral, describing the five as employing satire and treating the problems of the age, the church, and the state of contemporary poetry, he signals the manner in which a reader should approach these eclogues. For his original readers, the term functioned as a code, linking the eclogues to a certain type of

1. For a discussion of the conventions of the Mantuanesque pastoral, see Cullen, Intro-duction.

2. Maren-Sofie Røstvig feels that the "Epilogue" is a "classical example of what Puttenham calls a square poem, the meaning of which is constancy or permanence" (72). Røstvig's reading intimates that what appears to be a simple poem asserting only moral purpose contains, in its structural design, a meaning beyond the literal.

3. See Murrin, 65, 75, 81, 114.

audience, to a characteristic poetic style or strategy, to a series of conventional themes and concerns, and therefore to a particular didactic purpose.

Moral literature, like the Proverbs of Solomon, was seen as the least complicated, one directed toward the beginner, the child, or the simpler sort of reader. For example, in the Prologue to the Book of Proverbs (1535), Coverdale stressed its usefulness for the uninitiated, observing "That the very babes might haue wyt, & that yonge men might haue knowledge & understonding." The Bishops Bible (1568) noted that the book was for "the nurture of those who begin to serve God." The Geneva translators were not as explicit, but they twice in the opening glosses described the Proverbs as parables, a mode frequently described as appropriate for the instruction of the young or unsophisticated reader. They went on to say that Proverbs instructed in both manners and doctrine, the reference to manners hinting at the book's association with moral or ethical philosophy.[4]

Similar remarks about teaching the young the rudiments of wisdom were offered in prefaces to less elevated forms of literature. Thomas North in the Prologue to *The Morall Philosophie of Doni* (1569/70), the cycle of fables he translated and dedicated to Leicester, stressed the benefits inherent in such tales by remarking on their value for the ignorant or young: "hee that understandeth these examples, knowing little, should by them knowe much. . . . if he were yong, and had small delight to reade much: yet he may with a short and pleasant waye be instructed with these delightful fayninges, and with those similitudes and examples taste the sweetnesse of the wordes, the pleasure of the sentences, accompanied with proper tales."[5] North, like moralists before and after him, intended to draw with honey rather than vinegar; moral philosophy in fable's clothing is far more likely to lure the ignorant than unadorned ethics.

In associating instruction of the young or untutored with a certain type of narrative, North reflected the conventional belief, frequently revealed in discussions of Proverbs, that similitude or example best served the concerns of moral philosophy. Works like *The Morall Philosophie of Doni*, the fables of Aesop and of Reynard the Fox, or the Spanish

<hr />

4. See also Cartwright, *A Dilucidation*, 13; *In Proverbis Salomonis*, sig. A. In his *Sermones in Cantica Canticorum* (785), Saint Bernard referred to the Proverbs as *parabolas*. See also the *Glossa Ordinaria*, 1079. According to Philip of Harvengt (*Cantici Canticorum Explicatio*, 186), Proverbs teaches the rude, unskilled, ignorant or young. See also Lewalski, 53–69.

5. North, *The Morall Philosophy of Doni*, Prologue.

picaresque tale *Lazarillo de Tormes,* all of which enjoyed a good deal of popularity during the late sixteenth century, were thought to teach virtuous behavior by demonstrating the consequences of folly, greed, wilfulness, or stupidity. From such stories the young might learn to recognize the dangers posed by certain situations and, knowing the face of evil, to avoid it in actual life. The emphasis was thus upon instruction through demonstration, as throughout sixteenth-century discussions of the value of such works, critical terms like *parable, example,* or *similitude* were used interchangeably. The success of any parable or similitude depends upon its creator's ability to suggest that the narrative elements of the story are analogous to certain abstract principles, principles usually associated with acceptable behavior.[6] Thus, rather than expand upon the inner harmonies of the "virtuous woman" (see Proverbs 31), Solomon described a woman whose activities—buying and selling land, spinning, weaving, and seeking out food—identified her as a figure of harmony by associating her with the common profit. Similarly, in *The History of Reynard the Fox,* the frequently ribald tales of animals tricked by Reynard are, in fact, pictures of animals undone by their own greedy desires for honey, fish, sex, or mice. In both cases, the narrator establishes his point by describing a figure, group of figures, or scene whose individual elements are inseparable from their moral function in the tale as a whole. The picture, then, of the virtuous woman or of Reynard becomes a means of understanding either female virtue or the sort of human craftiness that succeeds by capitalizing on the follies of others.

Though moral literature was relatively uncomplicated, it was nonetheless seen as important since its purpose was instruction in the art of living. As Cornelius Valerius in the "Epistle" to his *Casket of Iewels* (London, 1571) remarked, ". . . Morall philosophy [is] a matter comprehending the perfect trade of how to live amonge men soberly and honestly." In general, moral literature tended to underscore the ideals of individual and national concord and the necessity of working for the common good, inveighing against self-interested governors, priests,

---

6. Christ's parables were seen as perfectly embodying the form. In *The Arte of English Poesie,* II.xix, Puttenham linked the parable or proverb with "moralitee and good lesson." Fables were used to teach composition, and in the Middle Ages Aesop was a school text (Pearsall, 192, 193). Furthermore, in *A learned commendation of the politique lawes of England,* originally written in the reign of Henry VI, but translated by Robert Mulcaster and printed by R. Tottel in 1573, Sir John Fortescue referred to Aristotle's *Ethics* as "his book of Moral philosophie" (sig. 12r).

and citizens or self-indulgent behavior. Moreover, writers who saw themselves as mouthpieces for morality frequently focused on the moral laxity of the servants of Rome. Though Catholic, both Chaucer and Skelton were seen as moral guiding lights, as proto-Protestants, for castigating the wickedness they saw in the church of their days. At its least sophisticated, moral literature took the form of the wooden *Plowman's Tale,* which, though known to be spurious, was printed in editions of the works of Chaucer after 1542.[7] At its most complex, the strategies, themes, and purposes of moral literature could result in masterpieces like Shakespeare's dramatic recasting of the "legend" of Henry V in his portrait of Prince Hal's revolutions between court and tavern.

Considering some of the ideals, frustrations, and restrictions of the Elizabethan Age, moral literature offered modes of expression that answered the needs of the social critic. The euphoria that accompanied Elizabeth's accession in 1559 had, by the seventies, been replaced by more realistic appraisals of the English political and social scene. Although I do not mean to underestimate either the very real love and respect she aroused in her subjects or her genuine, sometimes brilliant, grasp of the exigencies of late-sixteenth-century political life, Elizabeth could and did prove frustrating to serve.[8] Directly relating to the queen's person were the worrisome subjects of her marriage and Mary Stuart's presence in England. Both were relevant to Elizabeth's safety, and the queen's unwillingness to discuss either for very long continually vexed her councillors. Second, though restoring stability to the English throne and economy, her conservatism could prove a stumbling block to the new and sometimes restless generation of seventies politicians. The tug between various interest groups, one of which, of course, orbited around Leicester, and the Queen resulted in a variety of national fears, frustrations, and attempts to change the mind of a sovereign whose very motives—*Semper eadem* and *Festina lente*—proclaimed her more than equal to the task she had set herself of preserving the *status quo.* Any society has its frustrations, particularly the closer one moves to the source of power, but Elizabethan England imposed an additional burden upon its writers. As William Ringler has observed, "the sixteenth century in England was a period when rigid censorship of speech

---

7. See Skeat, xxxi.
8. I am indebted to the following: W. T. MacCaffrey (1961); *Queen Elizabeth and the Making of Policy;* Neale, *Elizabeth I and Her Parliaments, 1559–1581;* Palliser; Pulman; Stone, *The Crisis of the Aristocracy, 1558–1680,* 68ff; Wrightson, chapter 1 and 125ff.

and writing, both public and private, was enforced by the government and the church. . . . To question the form of the government or the acts of the monarch was considered treasonable."[9] It is therefore little wonder that writers availed themselves of the conventions of moral literature, cloaking their assessments of contemporary issues and figures with garments handed down by Aesop, Skelton, and Chaucer.

It is clear from what we know of Spenser during the last years of the seventies that he was well aware of the possibilities that the various narrative modes of moral literature afforded the political commentator. During this period, when he was secretary, first to John Young and then to Robert Dudley, and therefore likely to be cognizant of some of the burning issues of the day, he was also trying his hand at writing poetry whose allegory glanced at affairs of state. He was of course writing *The Shepheardes Calender*, parts of which relate to political affairs. From his correspondence with Harvey, it is also clear that he was beginning to write something that he already entitled *The Faerie Queene*. While Spenser was engaged in these works, he read moral literature, sending Harvey in December of 1578 his copies of *Howleglass* and *Lazarillo de Tormes,* whose ribaldry, like that of Chaucer, was justified on moral grounds.[10] Spenser was probably familiar with other works of moral literature, particularly since he frequently alludes to Aesop and since North, another of Leicester's protegés, had published his translation of *The Fables of Bidpaie (The Morall Philosophie of Doni)* earlier in the decade. Indeed, it is possible that at this time Spenser wrote an early draft of *Mother Hubberds Tale,* a fable along the lines of some in the cycle North had translated.[11] *Mother Hubberds Tale* is thought by many Spenserians to be a political fable that occasioned some trouble for its author since its beasts were rather too like those two notable Frenchmen of the seventies, the Duc d'Alençon and his agent, Simier. Both the prince and his agent are also thought to figure in Spenser's account of Braggadocchio and Trompart in Book II of *The Faerie Queene,* another configuration that owes its comedy to the conventions of moral literature.

9. Ringler (1983). The subject of veiled writing has been treated by Annabel Patterson in *Censorship and Interpretation.*

10. See Judson, 52–53. Harvey appears to have been no more impressed with the risible comedy of *picaro* and rake than he was with that early draft of part of *The Faerie Queene.* See also King, *English Reformation Literature,* 229.

11. Rosenburg, 162.

The Moral eclogues suggest that Spenser intended his first readers to associate them with the forms and traditions of moral literature. Since Spenser and his contemporaries would have described some of the tales in *The Canterbury Tales,* the verse satires of Skelton, most of *Piers Plowman,* and the fables of Aesop and Reynard, both of which had been translated by Caxton, as moral, or as containing moral allegory, it is significant that the five Moral eclogues share certain characteristic verse forms, styles, techniques, and allusions that link them with native poetic traditions. Thus, with the exception of "October"—whose subject is poetry—the Moral eclogues employ native rhythms rather than the classical or continental forms we might expect from a new poet and which we do find in other eclogues, including "October." Moreover, the world of the Moral eclogues is composed of *tableaux,* of similitudes that consider not such abstractions as the nature of love, mutability, or the harmony of the universe, but subjects that directly concern humanity's efforts to form workable societies. Like other works seen as concerning matters of moral philosophy, Spenser's Moral eclogues explore subjects like ambition, desire, greed, luxury, folly, laziness, and duty. The eclogues fairly deserve to be called parables, for each teaches by providing us with speaking pictures whose voices debate, tell fables to one another, or recount experiences in ways that evoke other well-known parables or tales.

Because they are more didactic, the Moral eclogues are the most accessible, preparing us for more abstract considerations by developing our sense of moral distinctions. To this end, the moral eclogues and E.K.'s glosses upon them suggest links between these five poems and the moral didacticism found in works like Solomon's Proverbs and Mantuan's eclogues. In his discussion of the eclogues, for example, E.K. includes critical terms commonly used to describe moral literature. E.K. links the tale of the Oak and the Briar in "Februarie" to both Chaucer and Aesop, labeling it a "picture," an "Icon," and a "fable." In his comments on the Emblem for "Februarie," he goes on at great length, pointing out that Thenot's emblem serves him as "a moral of his former tale" and that Cuddie's reply is "a byting and bitter proverbe," juxtaposing it with one of Aesop's fables and one of the Adages of Erasmus. Elsewhere, he likens the tale of the Fox and the Kidde in "Maye" to one of Aesop's fables. Both the tale of the Oak and the Briar and the tale of the Fox and the Kidde function as moral emblems because they imprint themselves on our memories, leaving the impress of the morals they are designed to illustrate. Since the plot of each tale is its meaning, we cannot separate *littera* from *sensus* without destroying the whole.

The kinship between the Moral eclogues and the moral poetry thought to be found in Proverbs is also suggested by "Maye," where Palinode counters Piers's sagacity with language that echoes the language of Solomon:

> Three thinges to beare, bene very burdenous,
> But the fourth to forbeare, is outragious.
> Wemen that of Loues longing once lust,
> Hardly forbearen, but haue it they must:
> So when choler is inflamed with rage,
> Wanting reuenge, is hard to asswage:
> And who can counsell a thristie soule,
> With patience to forbeare the offred bowle?
> But of all burdens, that a man can beare,
> Moste is, a fooles talke to beare and to heare.
>   ("Maye," ll. 132–41)

Palinode achieves his effect here in two ways. First, the lines turn on the subtle distinction between bearing or enduring and forbearing or abstaining: Lusty women, an ill-used party, or a powerful thirst are all hard-pressed to forbear, but he, Palinode, must bear the heaviest burden, a fool's talk. Second, Palinode casts his reply in language that makes a hash of the cadences and epigrammatic style of such verses as "There be thre things that will not be satisfied: yea, foure that say not, It is ynough" (Proverbs 30:15; cf. Proverbs 30:18, 21, 24, 29). Palinode's formulaic rejoinder, like E.K.'s critical terminology, hints at the link between these eclogues and moral literature, a link strongly suggested by the more fundamental affinities between these five eclogues and the eclogues of Mantuan.

Mantuan's eclogues are generally acknowledged as important sources for *The Shepheardes Calender,* but the relatively straightforward Moral eclogues owe by far their greatest debt to what for the sixteenth-century reader was a schoolboy text.[12] Spenser signals his debt to Mantuan in several ways. First, E.K. refers to Mantuan in the glosses to three of

---

12. See *The Eclogues of Baptista Mantuanus*. For a sixteenth-century translation, see Spagnuoli, trans. Turberville.

the Moral eclogues, "Februarie," "September," and "October." More importantly, three of the Moral eclogues rely specifically upon the work of Mantuan. "Julye" mines Mantuan's seventh and eighth eclogues for its debate between Thomalin the shepherd and Morrell the goatherd, who scorns leaving his hill for Thomalin's valley. Diggon Davie's description of the evils of city life and his account of his experiences there draw upon the satires in Mantuan's sixth and ninth. "October"'s *apologia* for poetry is based, in part, on Mantuan's fifth eclogue and its complaint against stingy patrons. Like Alexander Barclay, whose influence is also felt in the Moral eclogues, Spenser drew upon what Patrick Cullen has referred to as the "characteristic stances and techniques of the Mantuanesque pastoral."[13] To some extent, the effect of Mantuanesque pastoral is didactic, frequently punitive: It seeks to restrain and to warn, describing human life in terms of combat and the world in terms of polarities. It thus pits country against town, youth against age, pleasure against duty, and the desire for worldly success against that for spiritual gain. The debate appears to be its natural mode, and, not surprisingly, in the eclogues that make the greatest use of the techniques and stances of the debate, Spenser relies most heavily on a variety of pastoral linked to morality, logical persuasion, and the values of the common good, all, in turn, associated with the methods and lessons of moral philosophy.

Although it is probably as hard today to work up an enthusiasm for Mantuan's lessons as for his style, his eclogues nonetheless captured the ideals—medieval, if you like—of Spenser's own world. With their satires upon civil and ecclesiastical corruption, their assumption that the individual exists for the good of the whole, that the state is only as strong as its weakest member, and that the common denominator of human behavior ought to be rational thought, they reiterate the ideals that underpinned the Elizabethan understanding of the individual, the family, and the state.[14] Though practically unknown now, the eclogues of Mantuan were then perhaps the best known forum for a message that Spenser's first readers could find repeated throughout discussions of literature classed as moral. We thus need to see the *Calender*'s five Moral eclogues as the point where a number of factors and traditions converge, as Spenser's effort to frame—and I use the word intentionally—his age and to present a remedy for its divisions by using the

13. Cullen, 25. See *The Eclogues of Alexander Barclay*.
14. As Pulman puts it, "Peace, quiet, order, wealth—these were the words that touched the hearts and minds of sixteenth-century Englishmen" (249).

techniques of the moralist and expecting his readers to sympathize with
the silent component of the five *tableaux:* the order, the harmony
among men that is never realized in the Moral eclogues themselves.
Like *The Canterbury Tales,* the Moral eclogues offer us voices whose
conflicts, dilemmas, and narratives force us to listen in order to discover
what they reveal about themselves. Spenser intends us to hear the age,
whose desires were frequently at variance with its ideals. Thus in the
five Moral eclogues he presents five aspects of the pastoral world of
The Shepheardes Calender. It is a world where debate reigns, a world
desperately in need of order, harmony, and resolution.[15]

Spenser's Moral Eclogues

The Moral eclogues comprise an elaborate dialogue upon the nature of
social bodies. Both formally and thematically, they function as a unit,
emerging from two contexts, one literary, the other historical. Like
many contemporary tracts, speeches, and sermons, the five eclogues
chide the age, suggesting that it is dominated by commerce, that a
corrupt notion of trade underpins human institutions and relation-
ships.[16] The eclogues therefore treat the traditional subjects of moral

15. See Berger (1969); Cullen 31, 32; Shore, chapter 1.
16. For official comments upon the tensions of the age, see *All Such Proclamations, as were
Published During the Reign of Elizabeth*. For sermons that convey the uneasiness that seemed
to characterize the seventies, see William James, "A Sermon Preached Before the Queenes
Maiestie at Hampton Court the 19. of February laste paste" (London: 1578). The text for
this sermon was Ezra 4, and James expanded upon the need to rebuild the Temple, an act
that he linked to the sovereign's will and to the obedience of the citizenry. See also John
Knewstubb, "A Sermon preached at Paules Crosse the Fryday before Easter . . . in the yeere
of our lorde, 1579" (London, 1579). Knewstubb urged contentment, exhorting his hearer
to find ease in the estate in which God had placed him. John Stockwood's "A Sermon Preached
at Paules Crosse on Bartholomew Day, being the 24. of August, 1578" (London, 1578) is
174 pages long and decidedly lugubrious. It is a warning to England, a call to repentance,
and a mild effort to nudge Elizabeth towards a more active Protestant stand. In "A Sermon
No lesse fruitfull then famous. Made in the yeare . . . 1388. And founde out hyd in a wall"
(London, 1579), R. Wimbleton bases his remarks on the Parable of the Vineyard and urges
his hearer to "see to what state God hath called hym." He then goes on to emphasize the
theme of judgment. John Young's "A Sermon preached before the Queenes Maiestie, the
second of March. 1575" (London, 1576?) is possibly a contemporary source for both *Mother
Hubberds Tale* and the fable of the Oak and the Briar. Young focused upon the evils of
ambition as detrimental to the commonweal. He ended by asking God for humility with no
immoderate desires for Englishmen. See also the appendix to Golding's *An Elizabethan
Puritan: Arthur Golding*.

literature—conflict between the generations; the need for clerical discretion, purity, and poverty; and the poetic vocation—by drawing upon the metaphors of a mercantilist society. As some of the speakers insist and the five eclogues imply, only when the citizens of this pastoral world transfer their allegiance from earthly to spiritual profits can they begin to realize the harmony of the Golden Age. Spenser's literary guides in these eclogues, which could be described as an extended and particularly graceful bow to his literary heritage, are the revered authorities of moral literature—Mantuan, Aesop, Barclay, and, most importantly, Chaucer.[17] As Chaucer borrowed from the authorities of his literary age, so Spenser recast Chaucerian debates, problems and situations, creating pieces that, in the truest sense, are Chaucerian. Like *The Canterbury Tales,* the Moral eclogues are meant to capture English voices, presenting us with figures who are both timely and timeless, figures whose very problems identify them as Elizabethans, but in whose voices echo the language and the rhetorical stances found in works like *Reynard the Fox,* Aesop's *Fables,* the eclogues of Barclay and Mantuan, and *The Canterbury Tales.*

"Februarie," the first of the Moral eclogues, provides us with important clues to Spenser's perspective upon the body politic and his attitude toward the conventions and possibilities of moral literature.[18] The eclogue is a deceptively simple altercation between two shepherds, Thenot and Cuddie, upon the traditional subject of youth and age. In response to Cuddie's complaint over the raw winter weather, Thenot counsels stability—or equanimity—in the face of Fortune, going on to warn the young and sexually active Cuddie that he, too, will find himself old someday. Under the guise of offering Cuddie some of his hard-won wisdom, Thenot recounts the fable of the Oak and the Briar, a fable that he mistakenly attributes to Chaucer. Thus, in the eclogue, Spenser not only presents a debate, but encloses a tale within the eclogue itself. Like Chaucer's pilgrims, who exist within one fiction and

17. Harvey's correspondence suggests his interest in Chaucerian imitation. Thus, in a series of letters to John Young that inform Young about Harvey's troubles at Pembroke, Harvey adopted a Chaucerian tone, employed a number of homely similes and tags, and evoked Chaucer by dropping the name Jynkin (a name immortalized by the Wife of Bath). He specifically alluded to the *Miller's Tale* in lines like "But by youre leave a litle her must first goe pisse" (*Letterbook,* 90) and "Tho arte so queynte felt" or tags like "piggesnye." Though Harvey's efforts are heavy-handed attempts to echo one of the most innocent bawdy tales in English literature, they nonetheless suggest his (possibly Spenser's) interest in Chaucer's verbal dexterity and Chaucerian turns of phrase.

18. For discussions of "Februarie," see Bond; Cullen 125–27; Montrose (1981).

go on to create secondary fictions, Thenot and Cuddie reveal their lack of sympathy for one another in their diverging perspectives upon the fable Thenot tells. They are the first in a series of paired shepherds who can have no sympathy for one another because they do not understand one another. Throughout the Moral eclogues Spenser suggests that the language that should be a common medium of exchange is not even legal tender in the *Calender*'s pastoral world: like those dwelling in the suburbs of Babel, Spenser's shepherds do not use and understand language in the same way. Within the frame of the *Calender,* words that should be symbols of higher values and that find their highest form in poetry are useless. Spenser prepares us for a world whose broken chain of commerce signals its disorder by his account in the first of the Moral eclogues of the conflict between Cuddie and Thenot, a conflict that is heightened, rather than resolved, by the tale Thenot tells.

Like Chaucer's Reeve and Miller, Thenot and Cuddie enjoy a relationship characterized by envy and scorn.[19] The Miller, a relatively uncomplex character though a brilliant storyteller, gives the Reeve, a carpenter by trade, occasion for malice by telling a tale about old carpenter John who, despite his care for his young wife, is nonetheless hoodwinked by a young student living in his home. While the *Miller's Tale* cuts many ways and, in fact, says more about Robin the Miller than John the Carpenter, Oswald the Reeve takes the tale personally as a slap at his declining sexual prowess. What therefore ensues is a good deal more complex than the Miller's tale of cuckoldry, for Oswald "requites" Robin, opening his own tale by stressing his continuing sexual vigor and by feigning a sagacity and a forebearance that he uses as a cover for malice. He goes on to recount a tale of a miller who loses both his wife and daughter to the lechery of students. More importantly, he paints a picture of the Miller that is a grotesque and judgmental version of Chaucer's own portrait of Robin in the General Prologue and, while purporting to offer wisdom to Robin, instead offers only the harsh justice of the law. Oswald's spitefulness is far more serious than Robin's annoying but relatively harmless dig. The one is merely instinctive and provocative, the other premeditated and well-aimed. Where Robin is hot, Oswald is cool; where Robin is drunk, Oswald is sober; where Robin is boisterous, Oswald is malicious.

A similar dynamic underpins Spenser's characterization of Cuddie

---

19. Berger (1982), also links the figure of Chaucer's Reeve to Spenser's images of age. On the relationship between the Miller and the Reeve, see Olsen (1962).

and Thenot. Cuddie opens the contest by complaining about winter: he feels himself too young and lusty to have to endure "rancke winters rage." Thenot replies to what is Cuddie's private quarrel with winter, using language that signals the outbreak of hostilities, "Lewdly complainest thou laesie ladde." The line's alliteration and pattern of stress force our attention to *lewdly, laesie,* and *ladde,* none of them terms designed to promote rational discourse. Thenot goes on to take cover behind sagacity, discussing the rotations of Fortune and the weather in more general terms, but what we in fact hear is Oswald the Reeve's equally hypocritical balm applied to the unquiet brow of Robin the Miller. Thus the Reeve's initial reaction to the Miller's tale and the Miller's sexual exuberance suggests his intention of using his age as a screen for his anger:

> "So theek," quod he, "ful wel koude I thee quite
> With bleryng of a proud milleres ye,
> If that me liste speke of ribaudye.
> But ik am oold, me list not pley for age;
> Gras tyme is doon, my fodder is now forage;[20]
>   (I, 3864–68)

Oswald here admits his age, linking age with sagacity and forebearance. But in the remainder of his speech, he dwells on the issue of sexual vigor, denying that age has had any effect on his abilities. He in fact offers us an emblem for old age in the leek, a vegetable with a "hoor head and a grene tayl" that suggests folly and weakness rather than wisdom and strength. Thenot's remarks to Cuddie follow much the same pattern, for, though he purports to offer counsel, his comments reveal his envy of Cuddie's youth and sexual prowess.

   In Thenot's two opening speeches, of about fifty lines total, Spenser demonstrates the deleterious effects of envy upon social relations, for Thenot very swiftly moves Cuddie from his initial, and desultory, dissatisfaction with the cold weather to wrath. Thenot begins by saying that when he was young he, unlike Cuddie, never complained about the weather. This opening speech is especially interesting, for it provides us with the outlines of Thenot's characteristic rhetorical habits in the eclogue. Thenot's speech falls into two parts, the first containing general

---

20. *The Riverside Chaucer.* All references to the works of Chaucer refer to this edition and will be designated in the text by line number.

remarks about fortune, the second focusing our attention on his own
prudence. Thus his first query, "Must not the world wend in his com-
mun course / From good to badd, and from badde to worse" ("Febru-
arie," ll. 11–12), serves as a preamble to

> Selfe haue I worne out thrise threttie yeares,
> Some in much ioy, many in many teares:
> Yet neuer complained of cold nor heate,
> Of Sommers flame, nor of Winters threat:
> Ne euer was to Fortune foeman,
> But gently tooke, that vngently came.
>   ("Februarie," ll. 17–22)

As laudable as this advice may be when taken out of context, it is
advice that nonetheless should be seen as coming from a spokesman
whose opening remarks to Cuddie suggest not charity but scorn. Fur-
thermore, the ensuing conversation reveals Thenot as less than objective
about his "thrise threttie yeares," making it hard for us to believe in his
portrait of his own youthful equilibrium. His remarks become more
pointed in his second speech to Cuddie, for he describes Cuddie and
his fellows as "little heardgroomes" and "fond flyes," filled with "careless
corage" and "surquedrie," who keep their beasts in the "budded
broomes" and spend time "crowing in pypes made of greene corne."
The language he uses to describe the youthful sexual vigor of Cuddie
and his friends has the effect, not of undercutting Cuddie, but of turning
our attention to the depths of his own envy for the younger shepherds.
Thenot reaps what he sows when Cuddie responds in kind, pointing
out that Phyllis, whom Cuddie "wonne" with a "gyrdle of gelt," is the
Abushag Thenot needs in his dry old age. From there on, the debate
disintegrates into name-calling until Thenot offers to tell one of Chau-
cer's tales. If Phyllis is Cuddie's remedy for Thenot's age, then the tale
should be seen as Thenot's remedy for Cuddie's youth. However, like
the *Reeve's Tale,* Thenot's is merely a tale of revenge masquerading as
one of wisdom and balance.

When we approach Thenot's tale of the Oak and the Briar, which is
usually viewed as embodying the moral lessons of the eclogue as a
whole, we need to recall the lessons in sleight-of-hand *The Canterbury
Tales* might have offered to the young Spenser. The *Tales* demand a
reader who is alive to the various perspectives Chaucer creates within
the frame of his Canterbury pilgrimage. We need to know which pilgrim

is telling a tale, and seek to understand why he tells it and what he thinks it means. We must then consider what the teller reveals about himself, judging whether or not he is in control of his own fiction and if he understands the implications of his own tale. Spenser seems to be aware of Chaucer's mastery of narrative perspective, for those same issues are central to the underlying purpose of the fable of the Oak and the Briar. Through the tale, Thenot purports to counsel Cuddie's heedlessness and scorn; however, he uses it to disguise his real purpose, which is revenge.

Although Thenot loudly proclaims his good intentions, his introductory description of youth suggests that he is less concerned with the idea of mercy than with the realities of justice:

> *Cuddie,* I wote thou kenst little good,
> So vainely taduaunce thy headlesse hood.
> For Youngth is a bubble blown vp with breath,
> Whose witt is weakenesse, whose wage is death,
> Whose way is wildernesse, whose ynne Penaunce,
> And stoopegallaunt Age the hoste of Greeuance.
> ("Februarie," ll. 85–90)

The fact that Cuddie will eventually get what he deserves—becoming old and withered himself someday—obviously charms Thenot. His desire for strict justice informs the fable, for Thenot tells a tale where age turns out to be right about the world and is even belatedly valued for its usefulness. Ironically, however, his wishful tale of the quarrel between an Oak and a Briar simply reveals the depth of his own frustration with change and fortune.[21]

Thenot characterizes the Oak and the Briar in terms of age, humility,

21. The motif of the tree and the briar or the tree and the vine was used in several ways: as an illustration of the interdependence of tree and vine, as a portrait of the decay (frequently "Romish") of the old tree, or as a depiction of the evils of ambition. Spenser's use of this motif is his own: it reveals his ability to recast and thereby transform those traditional elements that made up his literary heritage in ways that served the needs of a poetic designed both to transmit and transmute the past. For positive uses of this motif, see Peacham, 41; *Whitney's "Choice of Emblemes,"* 62. *The Dialoges of Creatures Moralized* depicts a number of pairs whose apparent conflict is used to demonstrate the necessity for concord. For negative or hortatory uses of the emblem, see *Whitney's "Choice of Emblemes,"* 34; "The Princely Pleasures at Kenelworth Castle, 1575," in Nichols 2:519; and John Young, "A sermon preached before the Queens Maiestie (1575). (On the relationship between Young's sermon and "Februarie," see Stirling.) On the other hand, Roger Ascham in *The Scholemaster* linked the Oak to Marian decay (see Rosenzweig).

and forebearance and youth, pride, and spite; as a storyteller, Thenot tells more than he knows. From the eclogue itself we know few facts about Cuddie: he is young, dislikes bad weather—or is unwilling to endure its adversities—glories in his sexual vigor, and, like Aesop's grasshopper, seems unaware that his green youth will decline to Thenot's withered age. As such, his high spirits and lack of foresight certainly contribute to one of the *Calender's* central lessons, which Colin's declension from potential to waste, from January to December, illustrates all too forcefully. Though Cuddie appears foolishly vulnerable to the threat of time, he hardly deserves the transformation he undergoes at the hands of Thenot. Thenot's briar is not only foolhardy, it is bragging (l. 115), proud (ll. 116, 160, 223, 228), foolish (l. 127), spiteful (l. 148), determined to stir up strife (l. 150), crafty (l. 162), ambitious, and slanderous. Only one of Thenot's observations seems to fit, for he links the Briar's boastfulness with what, in effect, is its sexuality:

> Yt was embellisht with blossomes fayre,
> And thereto aye wonned to repayre
> The shepheards daughters, to gather flowres,
> To peinct their girlonds with his colowres.
> And in his small bushes vsed to shrowde
> The sweete Nightingale singing so lowde
> ("Februarie," ll. 118–23)

The blossoms, the songs of the nightingale, the garlands—all suggest sexual exuberance. Foolish and boastful Cuddie may be, but we only have Thenot's word that he is spiteful, contentious, crafty, and ambitious. These are serious accusations, and would seem to demand more than the sort of nonevidence Thenot offers.[22]

Thenot's description of the Oak reveals even more about how he sees himself. He describes the Oak as goodly (l. 102), strongly built (l. 105), once fruitful, and rooted in the practices of the past. Thenot, however, seems not to realize that in describing the Oak he describes his own blindness and incapacity. First, he portrays the Oak as silent in the face of the Briar's spiteful verbosity, a silence that the fable itself exposes as a fanciful bit of self-fashioning. Although Thenot describes the Oak's forebearance as a means of pointing up the Briar's mean lineage ("Little him answered the Oake againe, / But yielded, with shame and greefe adawed, / That of a weede he was ouerawed" ["Februarie," ll. 140–

22. See Bond.

42]), he in fact reveals more about his own illusions about himself. Furthermore, despite his eagerness to expose Cuddie in his characterization of the Briar, Thenot inadvertently reveals his own insecurities by going on to praise the Oak's former service to the ungrateful Husbandman:

> For it had bene an auncient tree,
> Sacred with many a mysteree,
> And often crost with the priestes crewe,
> And often halowed with holy water dewe.
>   ("Februarie," ll. 207–10)

In this one detail, a detail, by the way, that does not appear in other contemporary versions of this fable, Thenot gives himself away, undercutting his entire argument. The suggestion that the Oak had once been sacred to the rites of England's old religion seems designed to evoke Lucan's description of Pompey in the *Pharsalia:* "The mere shadow of a mighty name he stood. Thus an oak-tree, laden with the ancient trophies of a nation and the consecrated gifts of conquerors, towers in a fruitful field; but the roots it clings by have lost their toughness, and it stands by its weight alone, throwing out bare boughs into the sky and making a shade not with leaves but with its trunk."[23] This passage is central to Lucan's characterization of Pompey as a figure from the past whose worth cannot be translated into the present; for Lucan contrasts Pompey's age and position to Caesar's energy and ambition. If Pompey is the ancient oak, Caesar is the bolt of lightning that will inevitably fell the old and unsound tree. DuBellay adapted Lucan's conceit, applying it to the idea of Rome in Sonnet 28 of his important *Antiquitez de Rome,* the sequence of sonnets that Spenser translated as *The Ruines of Rome* and published in *The Complaints* in 1591. Since Spenser probably made this translation fairly early in his career, perhaps as an undergraduate, it is likely that Lucan's description of the Oak served as the subtext for Thenot's description of himself as a wasted but venerable oak.[24]

23. Lucan I:135–43.
24. See Green, 225. On DuBellay's importance to English poets, see Prescott, *French Poets and the English Renaissance,* 37–75. On the *Antiquitez de Rome,* see Ferguson (1984); Russell (1972). For Spenser's translation of DuBellay's sonnet, see *The Works of Edmund Spenser* 8:152; *Commentary,* 389–90. It is possible that Spenser intended his description of the Oak in the fable as his contribution to an elaborate literary dialogue with DuBellay and Lucan, especially since DuBellay used the *topos* as a means of exploring the nature of the body politic and the future of France. Spenser's use of the *topos* in the first of the Moral eclogues suggests his awareness of the need to incorporate the past into the present.

Thenot, however, misses the point of Lucan's conceit or DuBellay's sonnet. By ignoring the underlying message of decay and illusory strength and honor that the emblem conveys, Thenot glories in the description of himself as an oak, heightening our sense of the glories of the past and thus of the pathos of the oak's present condition:

> But now the gray mosse marred his rine,
> His bared boughes were beaten with stormes,
> His toppe was bald, and wasted with wormes,
> His honor decayed, his braunches sere.
>   ("Februarie," ll. 111–14)

Thenot omits any hints of the Oak's responsibility for his advanced state of decay, hints that inform both Lucan's and DuBellay's handling of the Oak as a figure for diseased honor. Later, after describing the Oak as sacred to the old religion, Thenot admits that "sike fancies weren foolerie, / And brougthen this Oake to this miserye" ("Februarie," ll. 211–12). However, he shies away from any moral that might apply to his own condition, instead turning our attention to the Briar and its likely and deserved end. In his eagerness to malign Cuddie for his youth, energy, and impatience, Thenot inadvertently undermines his own position as a figure of wisdom and authority. Not only does Thenot's description of the Oak suggest the depths of his own self-delusion, but his fable reveals him as the spiteful, contentious, slanderous, and vengeful member of the debate.

He pretends to speak for Cuddie's own good, but in fact he tells a tale whose strict justice leaves little room for either amendment or appeasement. The moral he draws is singularly flat: "Such was thend of this Ambitious brere, / For scorning Eld." Cuddie interrupts, breaking Thenot's line after the second foot and leaving us with a tag whose didacticism resonates with all the self-righteous morality that young people generally associate with their peevish elders. Thenot's remedy for Cuddie's youth is suspect; like the Wife of Bath, who recommends old women for young men, Thenot self-servingly advises that the young should give place to the old. Since Thenot is hardly humble himself, the tale turns round on its teller, revealing him to be the divisive character he accuses Cuddie of being. For it is Thenot who speaks for most of the eclogue, and it is Thenot's wagging tongue that slanders Cuddie, praises his own virtues, and stirs up Cuddie to wrath. Moreover, since Thenot implies a vision of the world not unlike that found in the world of the *fabliaux,* where each man "gets his," the justice Thenot anticipates for Cuddie is just as likely to fall on himself, or the ax we see in the woodcut to "Februarie" is just as likely to hack at his own ancient roots. Both the tale he tells and the woodcut to "Februarie" evoke Saint John the Baptist's well-known forecast of doom for a corrupt Jerusalem ("Now also is the axe laid vnto the roots of the trees: therefore euerie tre which bringeth not forthe good frute, shalbe hewen downe and cast into the fyre." [Luke 3:9]). It is a lesson frequently applied to England's perceived weaknesses.[25] Thenot fails to understand the more serious, metaphoric lesson hidden in his own tale: Envy is a worse crime than lust, conscious malice far worse than simple anger. If the tree is known by its fruit, then Thenot should look to his own harvest, figured in the tale he tells, and let Cuddie tend to his own fragile spring bloom.

Spenser's handling of his various sources and analogues for his first Moral eclogue, however, offers us more than a series of narrative ironies. Like *The Canterbury Tales,* which cannot be fixed in topical or political allegory, the "Februarie" eclogue nonetheless offers a fundamental— and fundamentally Chaucerian—social commentary in its figuration of social tension. Rather than suggesting that we side with either member of the debate, the eclogue suggests that we affirm not one of the polarities of their verbal conflict, which reveals the utter lack of sympathy between Thenot and Cuddie, but a good outside the actual world the eclogue portrays. That good is implicit in the fable of the Oak and the Briar, for Spenser, like Chaucer before him, uses the device of the tale-within-a-tale to depict truths upon which all truly lasting social bodies are founded. It is Spenser the tale-maker and not Thenot the tale-teller who emerges as the genuinely moral center of the "Februarie" eclogue.[26]

The pattern of conflict Spenser establishes in "Februarie" dominates the other moral eclogues as well. Just as Thenot and Cuddie have no sympathy for each other, so Thomalin and Morrell in "Julye" have no hope for resolving two mutually exclusive points of view. Morrell

25. See, for example, Arthur Golding's "Discourse vpon the Earthquake that hapned throughe this Realme of England . . . the first of Aprill, 1580," in Golding, 195.

26. This is one of the problems in reading Thenot's tale as a strict political allegory (see McLane 61–76). First, such a reading inevitably ignores the frame that the conversation between Thenot and Cuddie provides for the fable. Second, it makes no sense to identify Leicester with an oak that Spenser links to the Roman rite. Given the fable's components and the relationship between the fable and the eclogue, it seems more potentially fruitful to investigate Spenser's attitude toward and exploitation of traditional materials.

shrugs off Thomalin's encomium to the humble shepherds of the past who lived contented in valleys with a bland "Here is a great deal of good matter, / lost for lacke of telling" ("Julye," ll. 205–6), going on to praise a state where there are fat folks of great wealth. Morrell and Thomalin speak at cross-purposes: there is no question of the two finding common ground, a point Spenser makes all too clear by having Morrell speak from his hill and Thomalin from his dale.[27] Thus the eclogue itself is predicated upon an impossibility; taken literally, the two could not hear one another. The truth of the eclogue is consequently both figurative and sobering; we are asked to agree to Spenser's fiction that the two can hear one another while having it borne in upon us that they cannot understand one another. The woodcut for "Julye" gives added force to the eclogue's atmosphere of babel. In it Morrell is tonsured, the likely spokesman for the ecclesiastical system of church government he espouses with his references to Saint Michel's Mont and Saint Briget's bower, comfortably established on his hill, while Thomalin, whose attitude suggests humility or supplication rather than comfort, stands below him. Thomalin's histories of good shepherds go unheeded by Morrell, and he ends the eclogue by digging at Thomalin, who will not climb his hill. Though Thomalin has the weight of history and the virtue of humility on his side, he has only "won" a debate, not a soul. His emblem, *In medio virtus,* professes moderation, but the eclogue itself, like "Februarie," describes polarities.

Like "Maye" and "Julye," "September" focuses upon the need for ecclesiastical reform. The eclogue depicts a conversation between Diggon Davie, who has just returned disillusioned from nine months in the greater world, and Hobbinoll, who has never ventured beyond the boundaries of his own pastoral world. In many ways, the eclogue is conventional enough. It owes its subject matter and its language to Mantuan and Barclay, both of whom castigate ecclesiastical corruption by decrying the mercantilist husbandry practiced by bad pastors, a theme that likewise underlies Chaucer's praise of the Parson in the General Prologue to *The Canterbury Tales.* This same subject, of course, provided Milton with a major strand of the rhetorical structure of *Lycidas,* where he distilled an entire school of pastoral poetry—compressed before him by Spenser—into the magnificent outcry against shepherds turned wolves. Spenser's handling of the subject of ecclesias-

---

27. Dialogue VII of *The Dialoges of Creatures Moralized* is a dialogue between "the hylle and the Dalez." For a discussion of this eclogue in terms of specific issues and figures from the contemporary church, see McLane, 188–215.

tical corruption in "September" brings to a climax the concerns voiced in "Maye" and "Julye" by shifting our perspective from the shepherds, figures near the apex of the ecclesiastical hierarchy, to the more humble citizens of the pastoral world. By depicting a world whose unsound economics can only lead to bankruptcy, the eclogue testifies to the likely plight of the sheep when shepherds are concerned with secular rather than spiritual values.

The monetary references and metaphors that dominate the eclogue underscore the disjunction between the different legal tenders of the kingdom of the flesh and the kingdom of the spirit. E.K. introduces the eclogue by identifying Diggon Davie as "a shepheard, that in hope of more gayne, droue his sheepe into a farre countrye." Diggon Davie goes on to describe that country as a place whose citizens "maken a Mart of theyr good name" (l. 37) and whose shepherds are robbers (ll. 39–41). He then draws a distinction between those who barter for personal gain (ll. 83–94) and Christ, or "great Pan":

> They boast they han the deuill at commaund:
> But aske hem therefore, what they han paund.
> Marrie that great *Pan* bought with deare borrow,
> To quite it from the blacke bowre of sorrowe.
> But they had sold thilk same long agoe:
> For they woulden drawe with hem many moe.
> ("September," ll. 94–99)

These lines outline two radically different approaches to spiritual economy, for the indefinite pronouns that focus each couplet can only designate the soul, that most precious commodity. Worldly shepherds engage in trade for gain, possibly in embezzlement, since they pawn what they did not purchase, selling what they do not own to obtain goods that cannot belong to them. In contrast, great Pan trades apparently at a loss, buying with his own pain souls otherwise lost. The fact that Diggon Davie is speaking suggests that his experience among these greedy and corrupt shepherds has alerted him to their unsound economies. Though impoverished, he is nonetheless able to draw moral distinctions, discerning the difference between a true shepherd and a false shepherd and recognizing a wolf when he sees one. In the truest sense, he has returned from his travels disillusioned.

"September," however, is informed by more than the spirit of satire; also present is a darker irony that owes more, perhaps, to the genius of Langland or Chaucer than it does to the jeremiads of Mantuan. The concerns we can associate with Mantuan and the conventional themes and modes of ecclesiastical satire provide Diggon Davie with the matter and much of the language for his remarks about the world. On the other hand, Spenser uses the dialogue between Diggon Davie and Hobbinoll to point up the more serious disunity between the two shepherds. For example, Diggon Davie laments his own folly in seeking his fortune in foreign lands: "Hobbin, ah Hobbin, I curse the stounde, / That euer I cast to haue lorne this grounde" (ll. 56–57); "I wote ne Hobbin how I was bewicht / With vayne desyre, and hope to be enricht" (ll. 74–75). Here he chastises his own greed, which impelled him into the world and thus into his present poverty. Hobbinoll responds by drawing a rather stodgy moral from Diggon Davie's cry of personal anguish:

> Ah fon, now by thy losse art taught,
> That seeldome chaunge the better brought.
> Content who liues with tryed state,
> Neede feare no chaunge of frowning fate:
> But who will seeke for vnknowne gayne,
> Oft liues by losse, and leaues with payne.
>   ("September, " ll. 68–73)

On first reading, Hobbinoll's words seem sound enough; however, what he is in fact counseling is less than wise, for he counsels stasis, contentment based on an unrealistic notion of human nature. While we do sixteenth-century writers an injustice if we apply our own ethics of personal advancement to an age that frequently saw the destructive consequences of ambition, there are equal dangers in ignoring the degree to which the sixteenth century offered opportunities for personal advancement, or change. Hobbinoll's words seem particularly disturbing if we compare them either to other contemporary descriptions of pastoral contentment or to Spenser's ambiguous and intelligent handling of the same subject in Book VI of *The Faerie Queene*. Both the hermit in the pageant of Woodstock and Meliboe in *The Faerie Queene* argue for pastoral retreat in terms of the opportunity it provides for an active pursuit of virtue.[28] In contrast, Hobbinoll sees the pastoral realm as offering the safety of retreat.

28. For remarks about the perceived evils of ambition, see Montrose (1981). See also Young's "Sermon preached before the Queenes Maiestie" (1575). For a discussion of Meliboe in Book VI of *The Faerie Queen,* see Berger (1961), esp. p. 61 and n. 25. Anthea Hume in *Edmund Spenser: Protestant Poet,* 38–39, likewise feels, though for different reasons, that Hobbinoll in "September" is inadequate.

The fundamental inadequacy of this view is highlighted near the end of the eclogue in a two-part exchange between Hobbinoll and Diggon Davie that points up Hobbinoll's inability to recognize a remedy for either general or personal misery. After describing the discernment and vigilance of an older shepherd, Roffyn, Diggon Davie rightly draws the only possible moral from the history of Roffyn's constant battle against wolves, "How, but with heede and watchfulnesse, / Forstallen hem of their wilinesse?" ("September," ll. 230–31). Hobbinoll responds by reminding Diggon Davie of the inevitable limits human nature places on human ideals,

> Ah Diggon, thilke same rule were too straight,
> All the cold season to wach and waite.
> We bene of fleshe, men as other bee,
> Why should we be bound to such miseree?
> ("September," ll. 236–39).

Hobbinoll is right about human nature, but wrong in assuming that struggles against evil are useless just because they are fought by men whose strength and forebearance can never be equal to the task. Hobbinoll is equally helpless in the face of Diggon Davie's personal misfortune; he counters Diggon Davie's anguished "What shall I doe? what way shall I wend, / My piteous plight and losse to amend?" ("September," ll. 245–46) with words that seem to mock the pastoral even as they echo the endings of countless eclogues:

> But if to my cotage thou wilt resort,
> So as I can, I wil thee comfort:
> There mayst thou ligge in a vetchy bed,
> Till fayrer Fortune shewe forth her head.
> ("September," ll. 254–57)

Though Hobbinoll's words are conventional enough, his offer of shelter seems flat in relation to either Diggon Davie's anguish of spirit or the pastoral conventions they evoke. What Hobbinoll has to offer, in fact, is sympathy but no aid. He can listen but not counsel. When confronted with bad fortune, he can only bow to events and suggest delay. What he lacks is spiritual agility, the ability to circumvent the power of fortune that, for the Middle Ages and the Renaissance, formed the core of Lady Philosophy's exhortation to Boethius in *The Consola-*

tion of Philosophy. Whereas Lady Philosophy enables Boethius, who is unjustly imprisoned, disillusioned, impoverished, and helpless, to find goods impervious to the whims of fortune and to see an underlying order to events despite what appears evidence of chaos or random spite, Hobbinoll cannot help his fellow shepherd either materially or spiritually. If his words would probably have struck the *Calender*'s first readers as philosophically inadequate, they would have seemed equally so in relation to pastoral convention. Compare, for example, the closing lines of Virgil's first eclogue, where Tityrus offers Meliboeus shelter:

> Still, you could take your rest with me tonight,
> Couched on green leaves: there will be apples ripe,
> Soft roasted chestnuts, plenty of pressed cheese.
> Already rooftops in the distance smoke,
> And lofty hills let fall their lengthening shade.[29]

Whereas Virgil's lines seem designed to effect a genuine closure, Spenser's inconclusive ending suggests a grimmer estrangement than one imposed by the physical exile of the Augustan land reforms. The still life Virgil's words conjure up mitigates the harsh reality of coming exile, of the civil injustice the eclogue itself recounts. The effect Spenser achieves in "September" is even more striking in relation to Virgil's eclogue, for "September" depicts a prodigal's return, not a farmer's unwilling exile. But "September" 's prodigal finds no feast laid on, not even Virgil's splendidly evocative pastoral meal of apples, cheese, and chestnuts. Diggon Davie comes back with nothing to find almost nothing. Despite his final couplet wishing God might repay all such friends, the renewal or reparation he seeks does not exist in the pastoral world of the *Calender,* where ideals remain theoretical and therefore irrelevant to the daily lives of its inhabitants. Nor does Diggon Davie's account of his experience seem to reach Hobbinoll, for it only reinforces his tendency to hunch his shoulders against fortune, to dissemble when necessary, and to protect himself. Hobbinoll bears an uncanny resemblance to the unfortunate Christ described in the Parable of the Talents, who, having only one talent, buried it rather than risk losing it to

29. The translation is Alpers's. See Alpers, *The Singer of the Eclogues: A Study of Virgilian Pastoral,* 15, 93–95.

investment.[30] Finally, since neither speaker has any real sympathy for the other's experience or point of view, neither can offer a remedy for the exigencies of fortune. Like Thenot and Cuddie and Thomalin and Morrel, Diggon Davie and Hobbinoll speak to one another across chasms that remain unbridged by language, the very tool man has at his disposal for establishing bonds with his fellows.

The breakdown of communication depicted in the Moral eclogues is particularly striking in "Maye" and "October," both of which concern the use of language. In "Maye" Piers seeks to dissuade Palinode from his yearnings for luxury and pleasure by telling a tale, while in "October" Piers tries—again in vain—to inspire in Cuddie a belief in the duties of the poet that would enable the young man to move beyond his own preoccupation with fortune's gifts. Whether or not it is the same Piers in both eclogues is less important than the fact that a character called *Piers* becomes a spokesman for the proper use of language. The name inevitably evokes that of Piers the Plowman, the medieval spokesman for Lady Truth, who had long since been appropriated by the English reformers as a champion of the Protestant cause. As Spenser's readers would have known, the medieval poem *Piers Plowman* ends with an especially bleak scene, for Conscience abandons the world of the poem in search of Piers, who cannot be found in an ecclesiastical hierarchy dominated by greed, corruption, and ignorance. The Piers, who in the opening scenes of the poem commands our attention with his sense of Christian mission, has little or no effect on the world he inhabits. Therefore it is no doubt significant that in Spenser's *Calender,* Piers's words fall on uncomprehending ears. Not only do Palinode and Cuddie not understand what Piers has to say, but both shepherds paraphrase Piers in such a way as to mangle two of the most coherent speeches in the *Calender.*

Both thematically and formally, "Maye" echoes the moral lessons and Chaucerian technique of "Februarie." Palinode, who sighs in "Maye" because he wishes to join the young people "girt in greene" in bringing in the May, thus acknowledges a sexual envy that Thenot seeks to conceal and finds an unsympathetic listener in Piers. Palinode, like Thenot, also looks backward to the Catholic past, when such doings

---

30. For remarks about the popularity of the moral didacticism of certain New Testament themes and stories, see Davies, 375. For a discussion of the Parable of the Talents, particularly as it relates to morality drama, see Kolve.

coincided with holy days. But Piers, the spokesman for the Protestant present, counters pastoral pleasure with pastoral care:

> Perdie so farre am I from enuie,
> That their fondnesse inly I pitie.
> Those faytours little regarden their charge,
> While they letting their sheepe runne at large,
> Passen their time, that should be sparely spent,
> In lustihede and wanton meryment.
>   ("Maye," ll. 37–42)

Piers reminds Palinode that shepherds cannot live only for themselves since the choices they make inevitably influence the well-being of those they should be protecting. In his effort to persuade Palinode of the duties of the good shepherd, Piers denounces the follies of bad shepherds and the inherent weaknesses of episcopal systems. Moreover, he advocates a form of church government that Spenser's audience would have linked to the presbyterianism of men such as Thomas Cartwright, whose presence at Cambridge while Spenser was a student caused so much controversy, as well as to literary figures like Chaucer and Langland, who had long been claimed by the Reformers as fellow-travelers.

"Maye" in more subtle ways evokes the techniques of Chaucer, for Piers, failing to win his man with a lecture on pastoral poverty, tries a fable. If "Februarie" reminds us of such characters as the Reeve, the Miller, and the Wife of Bath, Piers's fable captures the spirit of the *Nun's Priest's Tale,* an incisive depiction of human folly in the guise of a fable. The Nun's Priest describes Chauntecleer the rooster, who is aware of the warnings that dreams may impart yet ignores his own good advice and his natural sense of danger to close his eyes, stand on tiptoe, and sing before a beast whose flattery spells disaster for chickens when vanity lulls their wits.[31] Though Piers's fable does not have the happy ending of the *Nun's Priest's Tale,* his tale follows the same pattern. The kid, whose mother warns it of the end his father met at the hands of the fox, is nonetheless seduced by its fascination with baubles, bells, and the reflection of itself in a mirror. The kid disappears into the fox's capacious sack and becomes, like its father, yet another incident of woe for his mother to recite. Unlike Thenot, Piers seeks not to humiliate but to warn; he tells the fable to help Palinode, not to anger him.

---

31. For a discussion of this tale as high comedy, see Johnson (1985). The remarks in that article about the value of history are also relevant to Spenser's handling of the fable in "Maye."

Though his fable, like Thenot's, ends with a kind of justice, he does not urge upon Palinode anything except discretion. As detached as Chaucer's Nun's Priest, Piers deals in abstractions, not people, seeking to describe fraud and human folly so that his hearers may avoid the kid's unhappy fate.

Palinode's misunderstanding of the fable is a lesson to all of us who think to live by teaching. Piers tells a fable in which it would have been hard to miss the relationship between baubles and bells and the rituals of the Catholic church, especially as those rituals were described by English Protestants. First Palinode counters Piers's moral for the tale— "And such end perdie does all hem remayne, / That of such falsers freendship bene fayne" ("Maye," ll. 304–5)—with disbelief: "Truly *Piers,* thou art beside thy wit, / Furthest fro the marke, weening it to hit." ("Maye," ll. 306–7). He then adds insult to injury and wishes to borrow the tale for his priest to relate, ending with "But and if Foxes bene so crafty, as so, / Much needeth all shepheards hem to knowe" (ll. 312–13). Spenser leaves it unclear just exactly what Palinode may understand by "foxes"; it is clear, however, that Palinode did not hear the same tale we heard Piers tell. The misunderstanding, or mistranslation, goes beyond simple comedy. Spenser uses the eclogue to paint a sobering picture, for Piers's effort is not simply rebutted—as the name Palinode would suggest—it is totally misunderstood. Worse than angering Palinode, Piers does not even reach him.

As a narrator, Piers demonstrates a conscious and complex awareness of the uses of language. Whereas Thenot's language in "Februarie" reveals what he does not know about himself, Piers's reveals how well he uses what God gave Adam for the purposes of rational discourse, prayer, and praise. The most striking aspect of Piers's speech is its metaphoric flexibility: He not only uses figurative language, he uses it to create an elaborate conceit that forms a kind of counterpoint to his argument. Fittingly enough, in a group of eclogues concerning the body politic, Piers's conceit turns on the subject of economy. In arguing for a church whose priests do not grow fat and rich, he falls back on an image that pervaded earlier morality drama, the account book:

> I muse, what account both these will make,
> The one for the hire, which he doth take,
> And thother for leauing his Lords taske,
> When great *Pan* account of shepeherdes shall aske.
> ("Maye," ll. 51–54)

This passage initiates a whole series of references to barter. Palinode counters Piers's picture of the well-balanced account by advocating an approach to trade whose likely end is bankruptcy: "Good is no good, but if it be spend: / God giueth good for none other end" ("Maye," ll. 71–72). Palinode's reply seems, on the surface, to have a certain theological point. Here, as elsewhere in the *Calender,* Spenser maintains a tension between the seeming logic of an argument and its implications. Thus Palinode appears to talk of the use of good, but his subsequent remarks imply that he thinks, not of "good" (virtue or talent) but of "goods." Later, he argues for an approach to the pleasures of youth that recalls that of the Wife of Bath:

> Sorrowe ne neede be hastened on:
> For he will come without calling anone.
> While times enduren of tranquillitie,
> Vsen we freely our felicitie.
> ("Maye," ll. 152–55)

Palinode here echoes the Wife of Bath both thematically and syntactically. Dame Alyson not only moves from a general observation to a statement about her own practice, frequently referring to herself in the first-person plural, but describes a corrupt practice of trade as "use," a term that connotes a proper approach to the goods of this world. For example, she proclaims with seeming piety,

> In swich estaat as God hath cleped us
> I wol persevere; I nam nat precius.
> In wyfhod I wol use myn instrument
> As frely as my Makere hath it sent.
> (III, ll. 147–50)

She is correct in ascribing her physical self to God's creation, but, as her prologue to her tale demonstrates, she does not exactly "use" herself in a wise or selfless way. The time she thought to cheat when young remains her enemy in age. If the Wife of Bath can only lament that she now has only bran to offer, Palinode can only watch and envy the May revellers' enjoyment of the yearly ritual of youth and sexuality. Neither Palinode nor the Wife of Bath can contemplate time without envy or frustration.

By their divergent uses of the language of trade, Piers and Palinode signal their spiritual allegiances. Though Palinode casts himself as care-

free, as blithely indifferent to the future, he in fact does not trade for
nothing. Like Cuddie in "Februarie," who "won" his girl with a belt,
Palinode participates in the commerce of a world where most things
have a price. Thus Palinode does not talk of giving away; he talks of
spending, of exchanging, the good God gives him for pleasure. That
he consequently settles for easy and quick profits seems to bother him
as little as it does the Wife of Bath, who admits to trading her *belle chose*
for a cash gain. On the other hand, Piers emerges as a genuine lily of
the field, for in a long speech beginning on line 73 he describes the
world as having lapsed from a golden age, when Pan himself was any
shepherd's inheritance, to a leaden one, ushered in by complacency,
then compounded by greed and guile. He ends by describing the world
as hopelessly in debt, "This was the first sourse of shepheards sorowe, /
That now nill be quitt with baile, nor borrowe" ("Maye," ll. 130–31).
Piers's recognition of the danger of goods is a key theme of the fable
he tells. As he emphasizes, goods can lead to greed, if not fraud,
undermining a pastoral economy that should be based on spiritual
rather than material wealth. In the fable, Piers thus describes the kid as
literally engaging in bad trade: He exchanges himself for a mirror, or
for an image of himself. Describing the Damme returning to find her
son missing, Piers observes:

> All agast, lowdly she gan to call
> Her Kidde: but he nould answere at all.
> Tho on the flore she sawe the merchandise,
> Of which her sonne had sette to dere a prise.
>   ("Maye," ll. 296–99)

The words "merchandise" and "prise" emphasize Piers's moral: Don't
sell cheap. But Palinode, unwilling to recognize the nature of fraud
because he must admit his own folly, misunderstands, providing the
eclogue with its final economic metaphor:

> Now I pray thee, lette me thy tale borrowe
> For our sir Iohn, to say to morrowe
> At the Kerke, when it is holliday.
>   ("Maye," ll. 308–10)

The irony of Palinode's "borrowe" goes beyond his relatively simple
sarcasm; for *borrowe* is, of course, what he has already done. Like the

Wife of Bath, he has apparently run out of credit; the inheritance Pan had prepared for him is all squandered, exchanged for trifles.

"October," whose subject is the true poet, develops the theme of wise and foolish commerce. E.K. introduces the debate between Piers and Cuddie by pointing out that poetry is "no arte, but a diuine gift and heauenly instinct not to bee gotten by laboure and learning, but adorned with both." His words remind us that poetry is a sort of inheritance from Pan, a talent that, like any virtue, must be used—invested—wisely or it does no one any good. Since poetry is a gift, poets like Cuddie who exercise their gift only in what Piers refers to as Cuddie's "rymes and ridles" ("October," l. 5) are prodigals, wasting what is truly valuable. As Cuddie himself says, he has gained little for his efforts:

> *Piers,* I haue pyped erst so long with payne,
> That all mine Oten reedes bene rent and wore:
> And my poore Muse hath spent her spared store,
> Yet little good hath got, and much lesse gayne.
> Such pleasaunce makes the Grashopper so poore,
> And ligge so layd, when Winter doth her straine.
>   ("October," ll. 7–12)

His lament, cast in the language of the merchant, alerts us to the folly of his business ventures. Rather than blame the crowd that, naturally, paid little for its fleeting amusements, Cuddie should blame himself for selling in a lesser market. Piers therefore recommends Cuddie exchange his poetry for true fame, not empty praise:

> *Cuddie,* the prayse is better, then the price,
> The glory eke much greater then the gayne:
> O what an honor is it, to restraine
> The lust of lawlesse youth with good aduice:
> Or pricke them forth with pleasaunce of thy vaine,
> Whereto thou list their trayned willes entice.
>   ("October," ll. 19–24)

Piers here draws the distinction between true and false fame (*fama*) or between earthly fame (rumor) and heavenly praise (fame) that provided Milton with the underlying structure for his consideration of the ultimate profit of poetry in *Lycidas*. Rather than link poetry to worldly pleasures, Piers recommends to Cuddie pastoral care, the duties of a poet that Sidney so eloquently captures in the *Apology*. But Cuddie is not charmed by Piers's notion that the true poet, like Orpheus, tames hell with his song:

> But who rewards him ere the more for thy?
> Or feedes him once the fuller by a graine?
> Sike prayse is smoke, that sheddeth in the skye,
> Sike words bene wynd, and wasten soone in vayne.
> ("October," ll. 33–36)

Cuddie, like Palinode in "Maye," rejects such abstractions as honor and duty on commercial and concrete grounds, for he denies even Orpheus any tangible reward for his labors.

The dialogue reaches its nadir when each offers a radically different view of the origins of poetry. Piers first asserts the heavenly origins of poetry (ll. 83–84), then the relationship between love and poetic inspiration:

> Ah fon, for loue does teach him climbe so hie,
> And lyftes him vp out of the loathsome myre:
> Such immortall mirrhor, as he doth admire,
> Would rayse ones mynd aboue the starry skie.
> And cause a caytiue corage to aspire,
> For lofty loue doth loath a lowly eye.
> ("October," ll. 91–96)

Piers, here speaking of Colin's poetic potential, discusses inspiration as a process of platonic generation. The love-object reflects certain immortal verities that, perceived by the poet/lover, allow him to capture these same verities in poetry, which consequently functions as a mirror of truth for its readers. The relationship between the poet, the object of his regard, the poem, and the reader is one Spenser develops more fully in the addresses to Elizabeth introducing the books of *The Faerie Queene*. As Piers implies and Spenser more strongly suggests throughout his later poetry, the process is regenerative, providing lovers, poets, and readers with a means of transcending their own mortality and thus a means of return to their heavenly origins.

In contrast to Piers, who stresses the Apollonian origins of poetry,

Cuddie traces poetry to a bacchic root.[32] Cuddie first denies that the lover can ever be a poet, for Cupid's force nullifies all other drives, "where he rules, all power he doth expell" (l. 99). He then offers an alternate version of poetic generation, one that begins with bacchic excess and ends in empty dreams of verse:

> Who euer casts to compasse weightye prise,
> And thinks to throwe out thondring words of threate:
> Let powre in lauish cups and thriftie bitts of meate,
> For *Bacchus* fruite is frend to *Phoebus* wise.
> And when with Wine the braine begins to sweate,
> The nombers flowe as fast as spring doth ryse.
>   ("October," ll. 103–8)

Cuddie here describes poetic inspiration as a sort of water cycle. From the lavish cup to the wine-soaked brain to the overflowing numbers, he outlines a process that can only end with evaporation. The conventional relationship between bacchic and poetic frenzy notwithstanding, Cuddie argues for a process of generation as illusory, and ultimately as sterile, as the union he imagines between Apollo and Bacchus. Orpheus's fate at the hands of the maddened bacchantes (*Metamorphosis,* XI) illustrates all too well the genuine disharmony between true poetry and wine. In Cuddie's case, the inspiration he receives from wine—those flowing numbers—fades with the morning sun. He ends his argument for poetry with words that recall Hobbinoll's similarly helpless and futile efforts to envision a world beyond his own:

> But ah my corage cooles ere it be warme,
> For thy, content vs in thys humble shade:
> Where no such troublous tydes han vs assayde,
> Here we our slender pipes may safely charme.
>   ("October," ll. 115–18)

For Cuddie, as for Hobbinoll, the pastoral world is a realm of stasis and retreat.

In "October," as in "Maye," two characters with different values and

---

32. Willes (58) distinguished between the poet who is divinely inspired and the poet who is exalted by wine. For other views, see the comments on this passage in *The Works of Edmund Spenser* 7:389 and in Goldberg, *Voice Terminal Echo,* 63–65.

languages engage in what looks like a debate or a dialogue but remains a frame for two separate monologues. Cuddie's misunderstanding of Piers's eloquence is as devastating as Palinode's misapprehension of Piers's fable of the Kidde and the Fox. Furthermore, since both Cuddie and Palinode reject the notion of duty and therefore an economy based on long-range planning, neither is willing to entertain the substance of what Piers has to say. Piers argues for an excellence neither Palinode nor Cuddie can accept, since by accepting Piers's ideas they must renounce self and personal gain. Though Cuddie and Palinode are not evil or malicious, in terms of the pastoral world of the *Calender* the implications of their views are sobering. By arguing for self-interest, they implicitly reject the common good. Lacking priests and poets as guides, or as pastors, where shall the sheep go? Milton, of course, understanding full well the implications of such figures, linked the two concerns in *Lycidas,* where the speaker, too, wonders at the payment poets and priests shall receive. The answer Milton's narrator hears is implicit in Piers's speeches in both "Maye" and "October"—graft a new system of economics upon the old.

However, as much weight as the arguments of characters such as Piers and Thomalin receive, the fact remains that they have no effect upon their fellow citizens. In this sense, the Moral eclogues paint a dark picture, particularly if we see the world of the *Calender* as reflecting Spenser's appraisal of his own world. The Moral eclogues do so by describing not one world, but two—one, a world of abstractions where priests and poets serve their flocks and courtiers do not prey upon one another; the second, a world of actual corruption, greed, folly, weakness, malice, and waste. At no point does Spenser concentrate the two images into a single focus. Piers, like his namesake in Langland's poem, is the spokesman for values unrealized in the world he inhabits and is therefore an equally impotent agent of change. In both poems, a figure named Piers is misunderstood and mistranslated, his ideas mangled and his words misquoted by characters whose insolvency is a symptom of a materialism that can only result in bankruptcy.

As it is bankrupt economically, the world of the Moral eclogues is one where language—that other glue holding together the body politic—has ceased to be a common medium of exchange. The misuse of language is most pronounced in the "Februarie" eclogue, where Thenot uses language and the art of storytelling as a weapon. Seeking to hurt, anger, and render judgment upon Cuddie, he reaps the truly just reward for his self-serving justice; the fable of the Oak and the Briar turns on Thenot rather than his intended victim. Though none of the other characters in the Moral eclogues uses language either so maliciously or so self-consciously as Thenot, few of them seem alive to the possibilities of the language they purport to use, so they fail to communicate with or understand one another. Only Piers reveals himself as a controlled and conscious storyteller, for his fable—like that of Chaucer's Nun's Priest, which it seems designed to evoke—is a gem of narrative irony and detachment. Palinode, however, does not grasp it. Similarly, Thomalin's tales of shepherds of the past—his proper and moral use of history—does not serve as the *speculum* it should be. In the end, Morrell rejects the true mirror Thomalin offers him, choosing, instead, tales from the pagan and Catholic past. His bland rejection of Thomalin's histories is, in relation to the *Calender*'s fiction, every bit as dangerous as the Kidde's delight in the illusion created by the mirror from the Fox's pack or Palinode's refusal to admit the possibilities of fraud. The legacy of Babel seems fulfilled in "September" and "October," where the speakers talk at cross-purposes, seemingly unable to communicate with one another to any likely or useful end. Though Diggon Davie and Hobbinoll, Piers and Cuddie use the same tongue, they have no common store of concepts, narrative conventions, or figures of speech. As their "dialogues" indicate, lacking a common language— in the most fundamental sense of that word—they lack the capacity to establish common goals or envision a common good.

Conclusion: Dialogues of Re-formation

In the Moral eclogues, Spenser describes a world whose weaknesses and preoccupations are all too like the perceived dangers and weaknesses of his own age. He in fact transforms the concerns and rhetoric of preachers and pamphleteers into dramatic poetry. The jeremiad of the 1570s was directed against such evils as envy, self-interest, luxury, and covetousness that were seen as directly threatening the political and economic health of Elizabeth's England. Since the sixteenth century lacked our present sophisticated economic indices and therefore any real understanding of economics, contemporary thinkers attributed social problems to spiritual or moral diseases.[33] Preachers, politicians, and even the Queen herself in royal proclamations lamented the selfishness and envy of the age. The latter was seen as particularly damaging to the fabric of the body politic. Stephen Bateman, for example, expressed his political or moral concerns in a volume he entitled *The New Arrival of the three Graces, into Anglia, Lamenting the abuses of this present Age* (1580?). Bateman applied Seneca's emblem of three-way interdependence to the Elizabethan state, noting that the thankfulness, plenteousness, and liberality of Aglaia, Thalia, and Euphrosyne should, being "settled in man," bring forth fruit to the honor of God. He went on to enumerate persons from Old Testament history who were chastened by God and to warn England of its ingratitude for Elizabeth, the visible sign of God's goodness. Bateman sought to remind his countrymen of that principle of interdependence figured in the Graces, a principle that not only informed the political rhetoric of the day but undergirded the Elizabethan state. As Wallace T. MacCaffrey reiterates, business or professional relationships in the Elizabethan world were, in fact, personal or familial. From leading ministers to more lowly officeholders, the political society of Spenser's time was oiled by what MacCaffrey describes as "that indeterminate but ceaseless flow of gratuities, *douceurs,* and reciprocal favors."[34]

In his vignettes, Spenser implies what many of his contemporaries taught and feared, that the whole, this new creation, Protestant England, was threatened by contention, luxury, and ambitious seeking in the very members of the state who should serve as its guides, its statesmen, its churchmen, and its poets. Though we may find this same lesson in any number of works, it was particularly suited to what were considered works of moral instruction. Thus Thomas North, in his dedication of *The Morall Philosophie of Doni,* assured Leicester that the cycle of fables should be viewed as a "looking-glasse" or an "artificial memorie," elaborating upon that metaphor in the following terms:

> . . . wherein you may my Lord, see into the Court, looke into the commonwealth, beholde the more part of all estates and degrees: and the inferiour and common sort also maye learne,

---

33. White, chapter 7. For a contemporary analysis of the ills of the age, see John Foxe's "A Sermon of Christ Crucified" (1570). A Good Friday sermon in response to the Papal Bull of that year, the work is an impassioned call for national unity, particularly the final exhortation to Foxe's fellow Londoners.

34. W. T. MacCaffrey (1961), 111.

discerne, and iudge what waye is to be taken in the trade of their life: but courtyers aboue all others attending on the Princes presence. A glasse it is for them to looke into, and also a meete schoole to refourme such schollers as by any maner of deuise, practise, or subtiltie, uniustlye seeke to aspire, or otherwise to abuse the Prince.

North's words could serve as an *accessus* to the Moral eclogues. Spenser's *tableaux* underline the necessity for moral behavior toward others, more specifically for the need for loyal subjects within a state ruled by a wise prince whose wisdom manifests itself in justice. Like North's fables, Spenser's Moral eclogues are directed against deceit and illusion, for either counters truth, thereby undercutting the likelihood that a prince can rule wisely or citizens live harmoniously together. Although Thenot may be the most divisive of the characters in the Moral eclogues, Thomalin's urge to live above his fellows, Cuddie's and Palinode's yearnings toward easy living and pleasure, Diggon Davie's helpless misery, and Hobbinoll's wish to live safely are equally damaging if we see them as discordant parts that should ideally exist in harmony. Rather than relating to one another, the speakers in the Moral eclogues do not even appear to share the same language. We are left finally with a world where eloquence is perverted or misunderstood and where wisdom remains abstract, untranslatable into terms that might be relevant to those who need it most. If Elizabethans wished to see themselves as bound together—ideally or actually—by ties of personal loyalty and dependence, this is not the picture sketched by the Moral eclogues of *The Shepheardes Calender*. In these eclogues Spenser presents his age with a mirror designed to reflect the fundamental basis for human institutions since the eclogues insist that we recognize the nature of our particular talents, our individual offices, and our duties toward others. The five eclogues serve to remind us of our pastoral cares, thus inspiring us to pastoral responsibility.

Edmund Spenser
The Shepheardes Calender

Februarie.

March.

Aprill.

Maye.

June.

September.

October.

Nouember.

December.

Of Sloth.

All such as will not labour in time : but spend their dayes in idlenes:
Full soone are caught vp with the line : of sorrowe, paine, and wretchednes.

¶The signification.

HE which standeth by hys tooles, signifieth the dissēbling
labourer, who mindeth to worke no longer then his cō-
maunder standeth by, and when there is none to controle
hym, then hee loytereth as before . Of such idle labourers
there are to many.

G.s.   As

Stephen Bateman, *The Christall Glasse*

3

The Plaintive Eclogues:
Pastoral Song

n the Plaintive eclogues, Spenser moves away from the ethical and social concerns of the Moral eclogues to focus on more metaphysical subjects like alienation, destructive love, friendship, the nature and value of poetry, and, most importantly, the force time exerts on all human efforts. The eclogues revolve around a single figure, Colin Clout, perhaps the most well-known—and the most problematic—of the *Calender*'s many voices. Spenser uses Colin as a figure for his own poetic ambitions and a foil to Immerito, whose art the *Calender* itself embodies. In "Januarye," Colin complains against the cold and dreariness of winter, describing January's barren ground as a mirror for his own wretchedness. His lament, which concerns his unrequited love for Rosalind, the lesser satisfactions he now finds in his friendship with Hobbinoll, and his irresolution and lack of purpose as a poet, is one whose chords and themes reappear throughout the other three Plaintive eclogues. In "June," Hobbinoll plays Horatio to Colin's Hamlet, providing a second and decidedly subordinate voice to Colin's tale of sorrowful love and lament for the dead Tityrus, his tutor in song. In "Nouember," Thenot's request for a song for the dead Dido elicits from Colin one of the most magnificent elegies in the language. "December," like "Januarye," is a monologue in which Colin laments the waste of his own ill-spent year, for he faces winter with regret as he looks back upon the barren harvest of his life.

The Plaintive eclogues are of a noticeably different rank than the

Moral. First, the Moral eclogues are debates, *tableaux* revealing the unresolved tensions of the body politic. Despite the presence of Thenot and Hobbinoll in "Nouember" and "June," the Plaintive eclogues are more akin to soliloquies. Second, the Moral eclogues, like *The Canterbury Tales,* are composed of tales within tales; they demand that we pay attention to narrative perspective, suggesting that Spenser, following Chaucer's lead, made good use of the conventional ironies and narrative techniques of moral literature. In contrast, in the Plaintive eclogues we move from the humor, rough justice, and social criticism of *The Canterbury Tales* to the more speculative world of such works as Virgil's *Eclogues,* Ovid's *Metamorphoses,* Boethius's *Consolation of Philosophy,* and Alanus de Insulis's *Complaint of Nature.* It is primarily in the Plaintive eclogues that Spenser reveals his debt to his classical literary heritage. In Colin's speeches and poems in "Januarye," "June," "Nouember," and "December," as well as his sestina in "August," we find subtle transmutations of Virgil's handling of the problems of love, death, duty, and time. Furthermore, in his use of Colin as a foil to Immerito, Spenser demonstrates his mastery of pastoral artifice, for he uses the poem as a kind of theater where the characters serve as masks for various aspects of the self.[1]

The Plaintive eclogues also employ more elaborate verse forms and a more sophisticated style than the Moral.[2] Whereas the Moral eclogues seem designed to evoke the rhythms and forms of traditional English verse, in the Plaintive Spenser demonstrates the rare flexibility of his native tongue, in effect throwing down the poetic gauntlet in Colin's name by ringing the sorts of changes for English that poets like DuBellay and Ronsard announced across the Channel for French. It is therefore probably no coincidence that in his glosses to the four Plaintive eclogues E.K. seems rather more concerned with rhetorical forms and colors, with the French Marot and classical poetry, than he does with moral weight, historical allusions, Aesop, or Chaucer. Finally, in keeping with the more artful classical style of the Plaintive eclogues and in

---

1. For studies of the Virgilian pastoral, see Alpers, *The Singer of the Eclogues*; Leach; Otis, *Virgil: A Study in Civilized Poetry,* chapter 4; Putnam, Introduction and chapter 1. That Virgil's eclogues represent a kind of theater was a commonplace for sixteenth-century readers. For example, Michael Barth, in his commentary upon Virgil's *Eclogues* (32), linked them with tragedies and comedies in which different actors speak. Donatus even more strongly linked the *Eclogues* with theater in his *Life of Virgil.* See *Opera Virgiliana,* Aiiij and following. The technique of manifesting various parts of the self in various stances and characters is one that medieval poets like Chaucer brilliantly realized.

2. See Woods, chapter 5. See also Norbrook, 76.

contrast to the fables he creates in the Moral, Spenser in the Plaintive composes a myth. He depicts in Colin's history what can be described as an English version of the classical myth of Narcissus, a myth inextricably bound up with the interrelated problems of nascent worth, destructive love, mutability, and self-recognition. Ultimately, he uses the *topoi* associated with Narcissus as a means of hailing a new creature, the English poet.

Thematically, the Plaintive eclogues provide us with a different and highly specific perspective on the *Calender*'s pastoral world. Though both the Moral and the Plaintive eclogues describe fragmentation, dislocation, and irresolution, the Plaintive leave a different impress than the Moral. Absent from both the Moral and the Plaintive eclogues is an affirmation of the need for order, harmony, and prosperity, goods that served as touchstones for politicians, preachers, and writers of the Elizabethan age. In the Moral, we are faced with the problems of the body politic, with what should be a commonweal; in the Plaintive, however, we observe not a fragmented state but a fragmented personality, whose desires, apprehensions, and talents are never subsumed by a single creative impulse. Like the Moral eclogues, which describe a world more likely to be destroyed from within than from without, the Plaintive eclogues describe another equally tenuous microcosm, man, the victim of humors, desires, and drives that undermine the possibility of achieving true concord. Furthermore, the Plaintive eclogues describe a world at the mercy of devouring time. If the Moral eclogues touch on matters relating to ethical philosophy and are close technically, tonally, and philosophically to the social concerns thought voiced by Solomon in his first book, Proverbs, the Plaintive eclogues are closest in spirit to Ecclesiastes, which was thought to consider issues pertinent to natural philosophy such as the workings of the natural world and man's relations to a universe characterized by change.[3] In keeping with his emphasis in the four Plaintive eclogues upon nature, time, and death, Spenser illuminates both the nature of the world and man's place in that world, presenting us with eclogues that, taken together, hint at goods beyond those circumscribed by time.

3. See Cartwright, *In Librum Salomonis, qui inscribitur Ecclesiastes*; the Geneva Bible; Lok, *Ecclesiastes*; Luther, *Lectures on the Song of Solomon,* 195. On the contemporary attitude toward Ecclesiastes, see also Lewalski, 53–69. For the exegetical background, see Rupert, *In Librum Ecclesiastes,* 1198; Philip of Harvengt, *Responsio de Damnatione Salomonis,* 628; Hugh of Saint Victor, *In Salomonis Ecclesiasten,* "Hom. I"; Richard of Saint Victor, *Explicatio in Cantica Canticorum,* 409; Theodore de Beze, *Comm. in Iobus, Ecclesiastes.*

Man in Time—
The Speculative Tradition

The Plaintive eclogues are discursive explorations of problems that confront man in relation to nature and are primarily concerned with the effects of time. In "Nouember," for example, Colin seems to echo, if not the words, at least the spirit of Solomon's second book: "Now haue I learnd (a lesson derely bought) / That nys on earth assuraunce to be sought" ("Nouember," ll. 156–57). The ravages of time are especially manifest in the emphasis upon death. "June" and "Nouember" are both elegiac, one mourning the dead Tityrus ("Nowe dead he is, and lyeth wrapt in lead" ["June," l. 89]), and the other the dead Dido (*"Dido* my deare alas is dead, / Dead and lyeth wrapt in lead" ["Nouember," ll. 58–59]). "Januarye" and "December" testify to the fleeting nature of time, to the brief span man is given to live, love, and write poetry. They also testify to Colin's bad government. In "Januarye" his sheep are dying through his carelessness, while in "December" he mourns his wasted resources. By abrogating his responsibility, Colin has abused time and can only lament its swift passing. The general effect of the Plaintive eclogues is to impress us with the finitude of life and the fragility of human efforts in the face of mutability. Like Solomon's Ecclesiastes, they point to the transitory nature of the world and implicitly affirm an attachment to the nonmutable and nontemporal, the only true refuge from the tyranny of time.

Spenser's decision to explore time and its use must have struck a particularly resonant chord in the minds of his contemporaries. As Protestant Englishmen, they were intensely aware of the power of time. From Elizabeth's response to the fourth pageant in her coronation procession, "Time hath brought me hither," through Foxe's belief that time and progress had culminated in Elizabeth's accession to the throne, to the equally pervasive sense that England's happiness and prosperity, figured by its unmarried and thus childless queen, were all too vulnerable to time, sovereign and subjects alike reckoned all achievements against time's inevitable triumph. Thus in *The Laws of Ecclesiastical Polity,* Richard Hooker, in the inimitably evocative prose of the sixteenth century, first defined time and then placed man against its rigidly finite measure:

> For time considered in itself is but the flux of that very instant wherein the motion of the heaven began, being coupled with

other things it is the quantity of their continuance measured by
the distance of two instants. As the time of a man is a man's
continuance from the instant of his first breath til the instant of
his last gasp. . . . we must of necessity use the benefit of years,
days, hours, minutes, which all grow from celestial motion.[4]

Though he speaks of the quantity of continuance, Hooker's words also
suggest that quality may be even more important than quantity. The
one is merely a measure of flux, the other the rule of eternity. We find
similar warnings about the necessity of using time well throughout the
period. Sometimes, as in the case of Jan van der Noot's *Theatre for
Voluptuous Worldlings,* which in places consciously evoked the language
of Ecclesiastes, a writer's sense of time could result in a tone more
usually associated with the jeremiad.

The subject of time touches each element of the created universe.
Even the most untrained eye can observe that everything is subject to
time, that man shares with plants and trees an existence that can be
measured by the "distance of two instants." The subjects, then, of man
and of the physical and natural sciences were grouped together under
the heading of natural philosophy, disciplines associated with meta-
physics and speculative thought. Just as Lucretius in *De Rerum Natura*
noted that his poem detailing the elements, the order of the universe,
and the laws of nature was written to convert men from fear of death
by causing them to contemplate the structure of the universe, so writers
of works of science or mathematics frequently justified themselves by
stressing the philosophic importance of their disciplines, their useful-
ness as means of acquiring wisdom. In his Preface to Euclid's *Elements of
Geometry* (London, 1570), for example, John Dee stressed the essential
utility of the work, stating that "a knowledge of mundane and divine
truth may be obtained through a knowledge of numbers" and that "a
study of the multiple beings in nature can only lead to our belief in an
underlying unity pervading all things." Dee's Preface, an *apologia* for
the study of numbers, differs only in its rare eloquence and erudition
from many other works of the period. Various sorts of almanacs,
anatomies, and herbals all sought to link a study of the physical world
to an increased understanding of the spiritual. Thus John Woolton

---

4. Hooker in *Works* 2:382. Hooker here perhaps echoed Bartholomeus Angelicus's com-
ments on the properties of time. See *Bat[e]man vppon Bartholome, his Booke, De Proprietatibus
Rerum,* Bk. VIII.

entitled a book of spiritual instruction *A Newe Anatomie of Whole Man, Aswell of his Body, as of His Soule* (1576). In the Epistle Dedicatorie, he referred to Solomon as having moved us to behold the glory of God by describing his "handy workes," most especially man, whose body Woolton described as of a "straunge and almost divine composition."[5]

From a recognition of mutability comes knowledge, itself a means of passage for the exile. Caxton eloquently expressed the belief in the value of knowledge that was echoed throughout the sixteenth century. In his Prologue to *The Mirror of the World*, Caxton stressed the work's utility, observing, "that we may lerne, and that learned to reteyne, and that reteyned so that we may haue so parfyght scyence and knowleche of God, that we may get therby the helthe of our sowles" (8). Caxton reiterates one of the educator's most cherished ideals, that knowledge may indeed be one way back to ourselves, to our lost Eden. Thus, when seeking to position humanity within the cycle of time, the men who planned the thirteenth-century cathedral of Chartres, along with the sequence of the physical Labors of the Months, a convention whose traces can be detected in both *The Shepheardes Calender* and *The Mutabilitie Cantos,* included the intellectual labors, one other means of passage available to fallen humanity.

For the Renaissance, as for the Middle Ages, the figure of man, his labors, maladies, physique, histories, or ambitions, was superimposed on that great figure for time, the circle of the zodiac. Discussions of time thus tended to have two related points of reference. First, a study of time and natural causes, in piling up evidence for transience and mutability, should impel humanity to an attachment to what is immutable. Spenser's *Mutabilitie Cantos* develop just such a case for and against the triumph of mutability.[6] Second, the very relentlessness of time should suggest the necessity of using time wisely. Since man, like

---

5. Even the author of the *Arcandam* (London, 1568), a book of physiognomy, denied that the discipline is inimical to the doctrine of free will. Insisting upon a metaphysical use for his "natural science," he pointed out that physiognomy allows a man to "know where he inclines." See also Boker; Williams, 69. Natural philosophy was thought to exercise the reason and help develop the powers of understanding. Otherwise, the study of natural philosophy would be worse than useless since knowledge could contain its own snares. As Peter Boaistuau put it in the dedicatory epistle to his popular *Theatrum Mundi*, "man knows natural science but remains ignorant of himself." (The volume was first published in 1566 [?] and issued again in 1574 and 1581; I quote from the edition of 1581.) What a reader will see if he gazes into Boaistuau's mirror are *tableaux* of mutability, describing not only natural causes, but the infirmities and miseries that beset the smaller world, man. On the importance of the scientific poem for the intellectual life of the English Renaissance, see Schuller.

6. See Hawkins.

nature, is bound by time, he can only do two things to free himself from its constrictions: He can learn to live harmoniously within it, and he can align himself with eternal principles and realities. In his efforts to come to terms with time, man must rely on his rational faculties. Having moved beyond childhood—a state without a sense of time—man arrives at an awareness of his own finitude as he learns more about the natural world. In other words, he deduces his own eventual death from the evidence around him. He is then faced with the necessity of using time wisely, of neither hoarding it nor spending it foolishly; otherwise, he risks facing harvest, with its scales of balance, empty-handed.

Spenser, however, rather than offering a general meditation upon the threat of time to human efforts, treats mutability by focusing on a single figure, Colin Clout. By doing so, Spenser seems to reveal his admiration for Virgil, who had recognized that the abstract might best be manifested through the actual as he anchored the conventions of the more disembodied and supremely artful Greek pastoral to the conditions—sometimes harsh—of Augustan Italy. Virgil thereby insisted that we consider such abstractions as time, love, injustice, and human potential in relation to individuals who, in turn, must be seen as parts of a larger frame—the Augustan Age, its glories, possibilities, and, naturally, miseries. Virgil, however, did not stop with joining the abstract to the actual, but from that fusion created a third and symbolic world at once relevant to the conditions of its specific age and the conditions of all ages. That third world is the world of the pastoral eclogues, whose very familiarity, or verisimilitude, heightens its value to us as a symbol. Spenser's Plaintive eclogues at once reveal his awareness of Virgil's strategies and his keen appraisal of the temper, exigencies, and expectations of his own age. If, in tribute to Chaucer and other masters of moral literature, he creates in the Moral eclogues fables and dialogues that in numerous details and turns of phrase bespeak their parentage, in the Plaintive he uses Colin Clout to embody a myth, specifically the myth of Narcissus. Like the histories of many of the figures in *The Faerie Queene,* Colin's story in *The Shepheardes Calender* owes its iconographic details to classical mythology while nonetheless proclaiming itself as sixteenth-century and English. Colin demonstrates all too well the pathos, the folly, and the waste of youth, beauty, and talent that figured in the myth of Narcissus, but he does so as a native Englishman, speaking the language of Chaucer and Langland. The fact that Colin shares with Edmund Spenser certain traits, avocations, and associations gives him ballast as a character. By giving Colin the credentials of an Elizabethan shepherd-poet, Spenser establishes two perspectives on the issues explored in the Plaintive eclogues, thus teaching us more than Colin alone can adduce about the nature of the universe and man's place in it.

"My Plenty Makes Me Poor": Colin Gazing in Narcissus's Well

Ovid's richly textured account of Narcissus, the son of the nymph Lyriop and the river Cephisus, is a tale of blight. Even at birth Narcissus's beauty is so striking that Lyriop begs Tiresias to tell her if her son will have a long life. In his answer ("yea full long, so that him self he doe not knowe"),[7] Tiresias announces one of the central themes of the myth. Tiresias's words about the dangers of knowing the self seem nonsense until Narcissus grows to adolescence and begins to demonstrate a fatal self-involvement. At sixteen, between boyhood and manhood, his beauty begins to disturb others; both young men and maidens pursue him. But Narcissus, disdaining to be touched by any and taking pride in his own inviolate beauty, devotes himself to hunting, moving deep into the woods well beyond the society of his fellows. One of Narcissus's suitors is Echo, a nymph whom Juno had bereft of any power of independent speech, and who can therefore only woo Narcissus by repeating his words back to him. He is at first charmed by the echo of his own voice, but upon discovering that the voice masks yet another suitor for his love, he grows cruel and flees. Rejected, Echo pines away, becoming disembodied. Finally, one young man prays that Narcissus should feel the same pangs of unrequited love that he has aroused in so many others, a plea that Nemesis grants. Thus, one day weary from hunting, Narcissus stoops to quench his thirst in a clear spring. From the spring, as Ovid says, he gets an even greater, and unquenchable, thirst, for he falls in love with the face he sees leaning up to him in the water. Although he finally comes to recognize that

7. *Shakespeare's Ovid, Being Arthur Goldings Translation of the Metamorphoses*. Since the language Spenser employs in his handling of Colin Clout has many similarities to Golding's translation of the story of Narcissus, all quotations from Ovid's *Metamorphoses* refer to this edition and will be cited in the text by book and line number unless otherwise noted. For another, though later, English Ovid, see *Ovid's Metamorphoses, Englished, Mythologized, and Represented in Figures*.

face as his own, he is unable or unwilling to wrench himself away from the pool, starving to death and leaving behind him nothing but the spring flower that bears his name. His final complaints are echoed by the unhappy nymph who watches him suffer the same pangs and the same privation that she suffered for love of him.

The tale itself was well known in the sixteenth century. Spenser knew Ovid in both the original and in translation. Arthur Golding's English translation of the first four books of the *Metamorphoses* appeared in 1565, and Golding's translation of the complete poem appeared in 1567. Both volumes were dedicated to the Earl of Leicester. Golding's was not the only contemporary translation of Ovid's tale; in 1560 an anonymous verse translation, *The fable of Ovid treting of Narcissus,* also appeared. Both Golding and the author of *The fable* indicate that the story of Narcissus was considered one of the most important tales in the third book of the *Metamorphoses.* Spenser probably also knew Pausanias. Whereas Ovid places a great deal of emphasis upon Narcissus's awareness that the face he loves is his own (and thus upon Narcissus's fatal moment of self-recognition), Pausanias offers an alternate version, or explanation, of Narcissus's fixation: "it is said that Narcissus had a twin sister; they were exactly alike in appearance, their hair was the same, they wore similar clothes, and went hunting together. The story goes on that Narcissus fell in love with his sister and when the girl died, would go to the spring, knowing that it was his reflection that he saw, but in spite of this knowledge finding some relief for his love in imagining that he saw, not his own reflection, but the likeness of his sister."[8] Although Pausanias seeks to provide a more logical explanation for Narcissus's fixation, both Pausanias and Ovid stress his consciousness of his own folly in choosing a world of images.

Both medieval and renaissance attempts to explain the story of Narcissus focus on Narcissus's inability to free himself from what he knows is a fixation upon the shadow world of images, a world symbolized by the pool in which he gazes.[9] Narcissus was treated as a figure of pride and sloth, as an example of regression and waste or extraordinary self-

8. Pausanias IX, 31:311.
9. For allegorical treatments of the legend of Narcissus, v., "Narcissus," see Alciati; Bacon; Comes; Estienne; Fraunce, *The Third part of the Countesse of Pembroke's Yuychurch*; *Integumenta Ovidii,* 49–51; Ovid, *Metamorphoses* (incl. glosses of Piette Bersuire); *Ovide Moralisé,* 327–31; Philostratus; Pontanus 1; Reynolds, "The Tale of Narcissus"; Sabinus; Cartari, v., "Pluto" and "Echo." For scholarly discussions of the legend of Narcissus, see Bergman; Bush 48–49, 112, 137, 195, 241, 284; Goldin; Harley; Hollander; Lemmi, 184.

involvement and, interestingly enough, as an artist enclosed within his own self-reflective art.[10] The pool itself naturally received a good deal of attention; like an antitype of the mirror traditionally linked to the figure of Contemplation, its depths induce self-involvement rather than prompt self-knowledge. The pool was also used as a trope for the lover's fixation since, as every sixteenth-century sonneteer knew well, the beloved's eyes could easily become a mirror of the self, a mirror that held the looker captive in the imagined rather than the actual world. Most commentators also remarked the fact that the narcissus blossom, the only memorial the young man leaves behind him, cannot withstand summer's heat and blooms only in spring, serving as a token of Narcissus's arrested development, his fascination with the insubstantial and illusive. Frequently, commentators used metaphors relating to the natural cycle in their attempts to discuss Narcissus as an emblem of waste and lost promise.

The details of Colin's legend that are scattered throughout the *Calender,* together with the iconographic details of the woodcuts for "Januarye" and "December," strongly suggest that Spenser drew upon the *topoi* of Narcissus in creating his shepherd-poet. Spenser does not duplicate the myth but instead uses it as a kind of analogue, selecting those elements that point up the themes of mutability, destructive love, self-involvement, and wasted promise that inform the Plaintive eclogues as a group. The connection between the Ovidian myth of Narcissus and the themes of the eclogues gains additional strength if we consider Golding's dedicatory verse epistle to his translation of the *Metamorphoses,* where he describes Ovid's poem in language that could also describe works grouped under the rubric of natural philosophy. Golding links Ovid to Moses since both evince an intimate knowledge of natural causes, suggesting that an understanding of natural law and the cycles of human history should turn our eyes to what is changeless. He then points out the lesson inherent in the story of Narcissus: "Narcissus is of scornfulnesse and pryde a myrror cleere, / Where beawties fading vanitie most playnly may appeere" (ll. 105–6). Golding here plays upon the tale's central image, describing Narcissus himself as a mirror in which a reader may find reflections of human vanity and decay. In *The Shepheardes Calender,* Colin Clout functions as a similar mirror, wherein

---

10. Compare the pictures and comments for Olympe and Narcissus in Philostratus's *Les Images.* See also Callistratus's *Descriptions in Philostratus the Elder, Imagines,* 395, where Callistratus describes Narcissus as a pastoral musician, holding a syrinx.

we may see the decay of talent, of youth, and of beauty. Seen thus, Colin serves as a powerful warning of the effects of time.

We come to Colin through the woodcut for January. The woodcut itself seems carefully designed to function iconographically since each of its details combines to suggest that Colin's year is, from the beginning, threatened by infertility. There is a striking resemblance between this woodcut and the picture of Sloth in Stephen Bateman's *A Christall Glasse of christian reformation,* published in 1569 (see figures).[11] Though the verses that accompany Sloth in *A Christall Glasse* describe only literal sloth, or idleness, the figure itself, leaning against a tree, legs crossed, tools abandoned, strongly suggests the conventional associations between sloth and melancholy, or *accidia*.[12] The woodcut in the *Calender* for "Januarye" differs in its obvious details—since Colin is a shepherd and a poet, there are sheep in the background, and, instead of builders' tools, his broken and cast-off instrument lies in front of him. Colin's figure is also slightly more central than the figure for Sloth. Such differences, however, do not alter the essential affinity between the two pictures, for both depict single figures, standing idle before a background of houses and bare trees, with the outlines of a city in the far landscape. The city depicted would probably have evoked sixteenth-century woodcuts of Rome, a *topos* firmly linked in the minds of contemporary readers with the theme of mutability.[13]

More important yet are the implements of trade in the center foreground of both woodcuts. The figure for Sloth has abandoned those very tools by which cities are built: the compass, axe, and pick. Colin has not simply abandoned but actually broken his pipe, the symbol of his poetic vocation. The woodcut, however, suggests a particularly complicated form of *accidia*; for, unlike the other pipes pictured throughout the *Calender,* the one in "Januarye" is a bagpipe, an instrument whose association with male genitalia is obvious from the woodcut alone.[14] If we translate Spenser's picture into words, we might say that the woodcut depicts an act of castration, for by destroying the tools of his trade as a poet, Colin dooms himself to the powers of time. Like getting a child, making a poem allows Colin to cheat time of some of its power since both acts extend a person beyond the constrictions

11. Luborsky (1981) has also noticed the resemblance (28).
12. For a discussion of the iconography of Melancholy, see Strong (chapter 2).
13. See Luborsky (1981) 24; Russell (1972). On "Januarye," see also Durr (1957); Hamilton (1956); Moore (1975).
14. On bagpipes, see Robertson 128–33; Winternitz, chapter 4.

of mortality. Narcissus not only cuts short his own life by refusing to love another and, later, by fixing upon his own image, he also destroys the possibility that he might live in another form through an heir. Like Narcissus, Colin chooses to work against his own literal and figurative longevity. Because he cannot possess it, Narcissus starves and mutilates the face he loves (see *Metamorphoses,* III, ll. 588ff.). Wishing to feel neither love nor frustration, Narcissus is committed to working against himself. Colin's broken bagpipes signal just such an act of self-mutilation:

> Wherefore my pype, albee rude *Pan* thou please,
> Yet for thou pleasest not, where most I would:
> And thou vnlucky Muse, that wontst to ease
> My musing mynd, yet canst not, when thou should:
> Both pype and Muse, shall sore the while abye.
> So broke his oaten pype, and downe dyd lye.
> ("Januarye," ll. 67–72)

Colin here addresses his pipe, the symbol for his trade, and his Muse, the disembodied inspiration for every poem, blaming both for his misery. Though the pipe pleases Pan, the god of shepherds, it does not please Rosalind. Because the pipe does not please Rosalind, the act of composing poetry does not please Colin. He will therefore break the pipe, the instrument through which his Muse speaks. He thereby breaks the circuit through which the ideal manifests itself in the actual world, for the pipe is not simply a musical instrument but a conduit between celestial and sublunary worlds. Colin's reasons for falling silent are as irrational as Narcissus's reasons for scarring his own fair face: Neither likes the effect produced by beauty or song and, rather than reconsider the nature or use of beauty or of poetic talent, both choose death. Narcissus embraces a literal death while Colin chooses a figurative one.

The woodcut for "December" depicts the "fruit" of January's action by depicting only barrenness and dejection. Colin no longer stands, he sits. His shoulders have a dejected stoop; he stares vacantly at the ground before him while behind him water gushes from a four-sided fountain. What may be a broken pipe lies near his right foot. Though the landscape is filled with sheep and a house appears in the far left-hand background, the artist has suggested a theme of isolation by enlarging Colin's figure and placing it to the right of the picture. The sheep grazing around him seem to belong to another picture, for the woodcut lacks depth or perspective. While the cut may simply be the work of an unskilled or unsophisticated artist, it may also have been intended to convey Colin's isolation and self-absorption. Again, these ideas are strongly linked to the iconography of Narcissus, who was conventionally depicted as staring downward into a pool or fountain. In the cut for "December," the figure stares at the ground, but the otherwise incongruous detail of the quadrilateral fountain seems firmly linked to the figure before it, as though the artist intended the figure of dejection and the fountain as components of a single emblem. Narcissus was similarly portrayed as isolated from his fellows. Alciati not only depicted Narcissus as alone, as literally self-involved, but heightened our sense of his alienation by scattering hints of civilization in the background of the emblem. As in the woodcut for "December," the two parts of the composition seem not to belong to the same picture, for the evidence of life throws Narcissus's torpor into high relief, while beside him already blooms the flower that symbolizes his lassitude, sterility, and death.

If the woodcuts for "Januarye" and "December" hint at an association between Colin Clout and Narcissus, the details of Colin's story even more strongly suggest that Spenser used the classical figure as an analogue for his English poet. Like Narcissus, Colin not only shows a good deal of early promise but rejects the love he awakens in others:

> It is not *Hobbinol,* wherefore I plaine,
> Albee my loue he seeke with dayly suit:
> His clownish gifts and curtsies I disdaine,
> His kiddes, his cracknelles, and his early fruit.
> ("Januarye," ll. 56–59)

Colin here speaks against himself. His use of the word *disdain* to describe his attitude toward Hobbinoll's gifts does not imply disinterest but rejection. Moreover, Colin rejects the pastoral world conjured up by Hobbinoll's simple offerings of *kiddes, cracknelles,* and *early fruit.* These three words function as a trope, as a synecdoche for an interdependent pastoral world that Colin rejects in favor of his grief over Rosalind. Colin's reaction seems as extreme as that of Narcissus, whom Golding describes as fleeing not so much from the love of others as from contact with them. "That to be toucht of man or Mayde he wholy did disdaine" (*Metamorphoses,* III, l. 442). What Ovid describes here is not simply a young man's disinclination to love any of those who pursue him, but a state of mind that is "anti-Eros," that is, opposed to love.[15] His self-absorption precludes any sympathy for others; from the beginning, Ovid implies that Narcissus is incapable of truly fruitful love.

Spenser's initial portrait of Colin is informed by the themes of isolation and sterility associated with the figure of Narcissus. Though Colin describes himself as a lover, the evidence in "Januarye" points toward his attitude of rejection. The links between Colin and Narcissus may also explain E.K.'s curious comment about this speech of Colin's. In his discussion of Colin's scorn for Hobbinoll's gifts, E.K. goes on at great length about the benefits of male friendship, insisting that he praises a platonic bond between members of the same sex and not "horrible sinnes of forbidden and vnlawful fleshlinesse" ("Januarye," "Glosse," 1. 59). The remark may be intended to trigger an association between Colin and Narcissus early enough in the *Calender* to influence our response to Colin Clout in the succeeding eclogues.[16] Ovid notes that both boys and girls seek out Narcissus for his beauty and that a youth makes the fatal request to Nemesis. If Narcissus runs from the effect his beauty has upon others, Colin runs from the love his talent awakens, rejecting what he himself has inspired.

The section in the "December" eclogue in which Colin describes his spent youth also seems designed to link the English figure with the classical. Colin describes himself in boyhood as devoted to the woods, as wandering freely without fear, and as a skilled hunter:

> I wont to raunge amydde the mazie thickette,
> And gather nuttes to make me Christmas game:
> And ioyed oft to chace the trembling Pricket,
> Or hunt the hartlesse hare, til shee were tame.
> ("December," ll. 25–28)

Once more, Colin's description of himself evokes the legend of Narcissus, whom Golding describes as "dryving into toyles the fearefull stagges of flight" (*Metamorphoses,* III, 1. 446) when Echo first sees him and falls in love with his beauty.

15. Goldin, 42.

16. That Spenser is drawing upon a classical myth in his treatment of Colin has been suggested by both Berger (1983) and Cain (1971). Berger follows Cain in linking Colin to the figure of Orpheus, but Berger stresses the negative aspects of the association. Berger has also (1983) stressed the narcissistic quality of Colin's love for Rosalind. For a reading of the "Januarye" eclogue that explores Spenser's handling of the issue of homosexuality, see Goldberg (1989).

Not only does Colin, like Narcissus, spend much of his youth hunting, heedless of the demands of time and the dangers of mortality, but he, too, receives his fatal love wound in late boyhood or early manhood. Ovid is quite specific about the age at which Narcissus first becomes desirable to others, "For when yeares three times five and one he fully lyved had, / So that he seemde to stande beetwene the state of man and Lad" (*Metamorphoses* III, ll. 437–38). Spenser draws upon the calendrical metaphors that inform his poem and denotes summer, when the sun reigns in Leo, as that fatal moment when Colin fell in love with Rosalind. Just as Ovid notes that Narcissus's wound is Nemesis's reward for the pride he takes in his own beauty, Colin sees his plight as the result of vengeance, as a sign of Pan's jealousy:

> But ah such pryde at length was ill repayde,
> The shepheards God (perdie God was he none)
> My hurtlesse pleasaunce did me ill vpbraide,
> My freedome lorne, my life he lefte to mone.
> ("December," ll. 49–52)

The pride to which Colin refers here is the pride he took in his talent: "For if the flocking Nymphes did folow *Pan,* / The wiser Muses after *Colin* ranne" ("December," ll. 47–48). His wording suggests that he still takes pride in the memory of his abilities, for the first and dependent clause of this sentence is qualified by the second. Thus, *wiser Muses* implicitly disparages the subject of the first clause, *flocking Nymphes,* just as *ranne* downplays the verb *folow,* used to describe Pan's drawing power among his nymphs. Once more Colin aligns himself with his mythic analogue, for Narcissus's dying lament at once bemoans his fate and folly and catalogues his still-fatal beauty.

Finally, like Narcissus, Colin admits his folly and fixation even as he observes his own demise. Colin's two monologues in "Januarye" and "December," though confessional in tone, are ultimately passive. In "Januarye," Colin readily admits the source of his misery:

> A thousand sithes I curse that carefull hower,
> Wherein I longd the neighbor towne to see:
> And eke tenne thousand sithes I blesse the stoure,
> Wherein I sawe so fayre a sight, as shee.
> Yet all for naught: such sight hath bred my bane.
> Ah God, that loue should breede both ioy and payne.
> ("Januarye," ll. 49–54)

Colin first curses, then blesses, then admits futility, concluding with the hardly profound lament that love should engender both joy and pain. Colin's emphasis here upon sight, together with his description throughout "Januarye" of nature as a mirror for his own plight, links him to the sort of destructive and introverted fixation that informs the story of Narcissus. Colin is similarly detached about, and therefore helpless before, the seriousness of his situation. Thus Colin's description of himself in "December" merely elaborates on a condition already well advanced in "Januarye":

> And thus of all my haruest hope I haue
> Nought reaped but a weedye crop of care:
> Which, when I thought haue thresht in swelling sheaue,
> Cockel for corne, and chaffe for barley bare,
> > Soone as the chaffe should in the fan be fynd,
> > All was blowne away of the wauering wynd.
> > > ("December," ll. 121–26)

This speech is disarming, for Colin admits that his year has come to nothing, that he has reaped nothing but weeds from what looked a rich harvest. Despite his admission, he seems as incapable as Narcissus of creative change or growth. Compare, in fact, Narcissus's complaint as he leans over the face he has come to love:

> It is my selfe I well perceyve, it is mine Image sure,
> That in this sort deluding me, this furie doth procure.
> I am inamored of my selfe, I doe both set on fire,
> And am the same that swelteth too, through impotent desire.
> What shall I doe? be woode or wo? whom shall I wo
> > therefore?
> The thing I seeke is in my selfe, my plentie makes me poore.
> O would to God I for a while might from my bodie part.
> This wish is straunge to heare a Lover wrapped all in smart,
> To wish away the thing the which he loveth as his heart.
> My sorrowe takes away my strength. I have not long to live,
> But in the floure of youth must die. To die it doth not grieve,
> For that by death shall come the ende of all my griefe and
> > paine.
> I woulde this yongling whome I love might lenger life obtaine:
> For in one soule shall now delay we stedfast Lovers twaine.
> > > (*Metamorphoses* III, ll. 582–95)

Golding's translation captures the chaos and fundamental absurdity of Narcissus's predicament. He recognizes himself, admits that his own image deludes him, that he burns with impotent desire, and that he already has (or is) that which he seeks, capping this series of admissions with the oxymoronic "my plentie makes me poore," a tag that Spenser borrows for Diggon Davie's Embleme in "September." Fittingly enough, E.K. is at great pains to explain that the tag "Inopem me copia fecit" is "the saying of Narcissus in Ouid." He not only goes on to recount the story of Narcissus in his gloss on the Embleme, but ends by suggesting that the tale was an important one to Immerito, "This poesie I knowe, to haue bene much vsed of the author, and to such like effecte, as fyrste Narcissus spake it." The "poesie" of Narcissus, as Golding demonstrates, is one that proclaims a process of reasoning as thoroughly irrational as the situation in which the young man finds himself, for his admission that he is impoverished by his own wealth initiates a series of illogical statements. He sees death as the only remedy for his misery, for death will blot out the fatal image. If more conventional sixteenth- and seventeenth-century lovers wish for a metaphoric "death," Narcissus wishes for one that will *literally* ameliorate his physical discomfort. He is supremely and futilely self-aware, for he uses his knowledge of himself and his obsession not to free himself from his self-imposed bondage, but to justify his own untimely and unnecessary death. Narcissus's final words, words that are "rebounded" by the similarly helpless Echo, " 'Alas sweete boy belovde, in vaine, farewell,' " have their own ironic echo in the final lines of the "December" eclogue of *The Shepheardes Calender,* as Colin bids his love goodbye, " 'Tell *Rosalind,* her *Colin* bids her adieu.' "

Though the final speeches of both figures are indeed marked by a confessional tone and stance, neither figure seems prepared to follow confession with action. Both Ovid and Spenser create a curious and complicated effect in their handling of these figures' final moments since each speech demands our sympathy while awakening our judgment. We are therefore aware of the tragic waste of each life but equally alert to the absurdity of that waste since the remedy for the situation is implicit in each figure's description of his predicament. Like Narcissus, Colin's ability to see himself does not enable him to help himself. The lessons his legend holds, like those of Narcissus's myth, serve as warnings of time's power and man's folly: Choosing a realm of images, the soul, introverted and alienated, will finally starve unless it finds within itself the power to transfer its love and allegiance from the insubstantial to the actual. Otherwise, like Colin, we become fixed in a world that has become a mirror of the self. Colin's complaints, which he sees as briefs against Rosalind and circumstance, are further evidence of his narcissism and passivity. While he insists on seeing himself as the plaintiff, Spenser implies that we see him as the defendant; for like Narcissus, Colin brings a case against himself.

Plaintive Colin's Plaintiff Plaints

It is in Colin's poetry that we arrive at Spenser's most profound recasting of the legend of Narcissus. The distinction between Colin's understanding of his poetry and Spenser's use of it helps us understand the difference between a sterile and a creative art. Such a distinction rests, at least in part, upon sixteenth-century treatments of the figure of Echo, the nymph whose unrequited passion for Narcissus precipitates her ruin. The nymph enjoyed a certain vogue throughout the sixteenth and seventeenth centuries, whether appearing as an actual acoustical effect, as a poetic game such as Gascoigne's in the festivity of Kenelworth, or as the genuine full-voiced echoing refrain that signals harmony between human affairs and celestial motions in Spenser's *Epithalamion*. Echo was interpreted in two ways. In relation to Narcissus, Echo was allegorized as boasting (*iactantia*), the fitting companion for self-love.[17] However, like Syrinx, Echo was a nymph beloved of Pan; therefore she was also linked to truth and celestial harmony. Allegorically, the union between Pan and Echo signaled the union between sound and natural philosophy, a subject with a good deal of significance for Spenser's purposes in the Plaintive eclogues.[18] As Reynolds noted in the discussion of the myth of Narcissus that was appended to the *Mythomystes,* Narcissus's rejection of Echo symbolizes his denial of intellectual beauty, for Narcissus exchanges the possibility of immortality, or of true fame, for the transitory delights, the *otium,* of a world of images and shadows.[19] As reductive as all such allegorizations may seem, the difference between a poetry that echoes the self and a poetry that echoes principles of universal harmony lies at the heart of the implicit

---

17. See Comes IX, xvi; Estienne 195; Reynolds, "The Tale of Narcissus," 26; Sabinus III:103; Bush, 49.

18. Thus, in "Aprill," Colin declares Elisa the offspring of the union between Pan and Syrinx, offering his lay as an echo of Elisa herself. On the union between Echo and Pan, see Cartari, v. "Pan"; Estienne 195; Reynolds, "The Tale of Narcissus," 27; Hollander, 9–15.

19. Reynolds, "The Tale of Narcissus," 27.

distinction in the *Calender* between Colin's plaints and Spenserian complaint.

In using the term *plaintive* to describe the eclogues for January, June, November, and December, E.K. hints at the various perspectives they afford for the problem of mutability. *Plaintive* was in use by 1579, but does not appear to have been used in precisely the way Spenser employed it in the *Calender*. Thus, though Spenser did not coin the term, he seems to have invented a new context for it. First, as a noun, *plaintive* was used legally as *plaintiff* is today to describe one who brings a case or an injury to a court of law. Second, as an adjective, *plaintive* could mean mournful or complaining. Third, the word suggests *complaintive*, used as an adjectival form of the noun, complaint. From certain of his later remarks, it is clear that Spenser linked what were three separate connotations for the term. For example, in his prefatory remarks to *Virgil's Gnat*, published appropriately enough by Ponsonbie in a gathering entitled *The Complaints* (1591), Spenser cast himself as a plaintiff and described his tone as complaining:

> Wrong'd, yet not daring to expresse my paine,
>   To you (great Lord) the causer of my care,
>   In clowdie teares my case I thus complaine
> Vnto your selfe, that onely priuie are. . . .
>   (*Virgil's Gnat*, Dedication)

He styled Leicester, to whom the poem is dedicated, as at once the defendant and the adjudicator in the case, going on to characterize the Gnat's speech, which constitutes the bulk of the poem, as a complaint: "But what so by my selfe may not be showen, / May by this Gnatts complaint be easily knowen." Furthermore, Ponsonbie's Epistle to the Reader, which introduces the entire volume, suggests that the complaint itself was firmly tied to the sort of considerations likewise found in the Book of Ecclesiastes: "I haue by good meanes gathered togeather these fewe parcels present, which I haue caused to bee imprinted altogeather, for that they al seeme to containe like matter of argument in them: being all complaints and meditations of the worlds vanitie; verie graue and profitable." (*Complaints*, "The Printer to the Gentle Reader"). The nine poems that follow, beginning with *The Tears of the Muses* and ending with *The Visions of Petrarch*, explore the theme of time and mutability and the vanity of man's frequently foolish and sometimes disastrous efforts to find any lasting good in a post-lapsarian world.

In *The Shepheardes Calender,* Spenser employs the complaint as a mode of address in two ways. First, Colin, who seems most comfortable with the idea of himself as a plaintiff, brings his private complaint before us for judgment. He accuses Rosalind and Pan of unkindness and jealousy, using his life as his evidence of the irreparable injury he has suffered. But he uses the complaint only as an opportunity for complaining, for augmenting his own pain, as he himself suggests in the lay inserted into the August eclogue:

> Hence with the Nightingale will I take part,
> That blessed byrd, that spends her time of sleepe
> In songs and plaintiue pleas, the more taugment
> The memory of hys misdeede, that bred her woe.
>   ("August," ll. 183–86)

Colin inadvertently speaks against himself: Aligning himself with Philomela and her unceasing misery, he vows to sing "plaintive pleas" as a means of publishing Rosalind's cruelty and thereby recalling his own pain.

On the other hand, Spenser uses the Plaintive eclogues as a means of exploring man's position within a natural cycle of birth and death, and ultimately as a forum for an extended complaint upon mutability. Like the later *Mutabilitie Cantos,* the four Plaintive eclogues seem to describe time's triumph but, in fact, adumbrate eternity's victory over change and time. In contrast to the *Mutabilitie Cantos,* there is no narrative voice to deduce a consolatory lesson from what appears to be overwhelmingly damning evidence, but the Plaintive eclogues nonetheless suggest a remedy for the constrictions of time. In particular, Spenser employs Colin Clout, not only as the focal point of the eclogues, but as a foil to Spenser or Immerito. Moreover, he uses Colin's own song, his elegy for Dido in "Nouember," as the implicit remedy for the *Calender*'s complaint upon mutability and for Colin's complaining case. Though Colin seems incapable of availing himself of this remedy, remaining as plaintive in "December" as he is in "Januarye," the lessons time has for Spenser are of a different order than those time offers Colin. While Colin shows only evidence of waste, Spenser deduces permanence from such exhibits of mortality.

As a plaintiff, Colin casts himself as the victim of love and change, an estimate E.K. passes on in his Arguments for "Januarye," "June,"and "December." E.K. introduces Colin in "Januarye" by pointing up the eclogue's implicit suggestion that we see Colin as an unsatisfied plaintiff whose "carefull case" inspires him to break his pipe, the symbol of his poetic abilities: "In this fyrst AEglogue Colin cloute a shepheardes boy complaineth him of his vnfortunate loue. . . . he compareth his carefull case to the sadde season of the yeare. . . . And lastlye, fynding himself robbed of all former pleasaunce and delights, hee breaketh his Pipe in peeces, and casteth him selfe to the ground." ("Januarye," Argument; Cf. "Januarye," l. 80). E.K. continues the implied comparison between Colin's case and that of an unlucky merchant in the Argument for "June":

> This AEglogue is wholly vowed to the complayning of Colins ill successe in his loue. For being (as is aforesaid) enamoured of a Country lasse Rosalind, and hauing (as seemeth) founde place in her heart, he lamenteth to his deare friend Hobbinoll, that he is nowe forsaken vnfaithfully, and in his steede Menalcas, another shepheard receiued disloyally. And this is the whole Argument of this AEglogue. ("June," Argument)

E.K.'s legalistic tone and charged use of language might well serve as opening remarks in a court of law; he heavily weights the "Argument" in Colin's favor by describing him as the victim of fickleness, infidelity, and disloyalty. Finally, in the Argument to "December," E.K. describes the eclogue as Colin's "complaynte" to the God Pan. Following his initial plea in "Januarye" and the evidence for his desolation introduced by other characters in the *Calender,* the "December" eclogue serves as Colin's final plea for a merciful adjudication.

Though his voice is compelling, Colin's argument is less coherent than moving. Since Spenser gives Colin the *Calender*'s opening and closing statements, it is hard to ignore the fact that Colin's complaint is static. Rather than the change and growth that calendrical structure might lead us to expect, his complaint in "Januarye" merely serves as the preamble for a longer complaint upon the same subject in "December." From first to last, Colin sees the annual cycle as dominated by death, notwithstanding E.K.'s remarks in the "Generall Argument" that the cycle from January to December is a "memoriall" to Jesus Christ and the everlasting life he offers man. Colin, however, finds in each aspect of the created world a memorial to his own sorrow. Thus, though in the circular rotation of the months we have evidence of the earth's fruitfulness and heaven's stability, in Colin, who serves as the *Calender*'s zodiacal man, we have a token of the restlessness, the dissatisfaction, and the decay that accompany man when his fixations cause him to turn inward on himself.

With the exception of the lay in "Aprill" and the elegy in "Nouember," Colin's poetry reflects his alienation from his world. By depicting Colin as increasingly solitary, Spenser implicitly opposes him to not only the ideals but the poetics of the Elizabethan age.[20] Like Narcissus, who moves deeper into the woods and away from his fellows, Colin gradually shrugs off his pastoral companions till in "December" he is described as sitting "in secreate shade alone," a solitary figure of dejection, idleness, and introversion. Similarly, his attitude towards his art becomes increasingly narcissistic. His remark in "June," "I play to please my selfe, all be it ill" ("June," l. 72), is best understood in relation to sixteenth-century conceptions of man and his duties to his world. Thus, in his translation of Giraldi's *Dialogues,* entitled *A Discourse of Civill Life* (1606), Lodowick Bryskett, who belonged to Spenser's circle of literary acquaintances in Ireland, stressed the underlying rationale for the ideal of duty, whether civic or artistic, by affirming that man "is not borne to himselfe alone, but to ciuill societie and conuersation, and to the good of others as well as of himselfe" (208). Colin's decision to please only himself—"one if I please, enough is me therefore"[21]—thus constitutes a decision to remove his art, as well as his person, from the constrictions and responsibilities of his pastoral world.

For this reason, again setting aside "Aprill" and "Nouember," Colin's poetry is static since he uses it as a mirror for his own melancholy. His complaint in "Januarye," his brief song in "June," the doleful lay that Cuddie repeats in "August,"and his more elaborate complaint in "December" all revolve around the same subject, his unrequited love for Rosalind. Not only does he sing the same song, but the songs themselves share similar images of barrenness, waste, and disorder, indices of Colin's own character and art.

Spenser hints at the static nature of that art in "Januarye," where Colin addresses Pan, asking him for sympathy, "And *Pan* thou shepheards God, that once didst loue, / Pitie, the paines, that thou thy selfe didst proue" ("Januarye," ll. 17–18). Colin here is probably alluding

---

20. Cullen (86–90) has remarked that Colin's life traces a movement away from society. For comments about the issue of the poet's relation to society, particularly as it relates to Spenser, see Helgerson, chapter 2.

21. On this line, see Cullen, 94–95.

to Pan's unrequited love for Syrinx, a story to which he directly refers in "Aprill" by calling Elisa the child of Pan and Syrinx. As the "Aprill" laye makes clear, however, Pan's love for Syrinx, though unrequited, was nonetheless fruitful. As Ovid tells the story, Pan's pursuit of Syrinx left him only with some reeds, since the nymph preferred chastity and metamorphosis to Pan. From those reeds came Pan's pipe; losing Syrinx, he gained music, the means to express those universal principles of nature that Pan embodies. In contrast, losing Rosalind, Colin will devote his music only to his love for Rosalind or to himself. The many attempts to identify Rosalind with a real person point up the solipsistic nature of Colin's verse. Other than the fact that she is linked to a town rather than the countryside and loves someone else, Colin's songs tell us nothing pertinent about her. Rather than a real woman, she is an abstraction, the cruel lady whose disdain for her lover is a conventional feature of sixteenth-century love poetry. Not Rosalind but Colin is the subject of his poetry, poetry that he sees as his presentation of his plaintiff's case.

That Colin views his poems as briefs against Rosalind is clear from the statements he makes about the purpose, and hence the utility, of his own verse. First, in "Januarye" he hopes to win pity from Pan, in effect asking Pan to judge the situation in Colin's favor. In "June" he also discusses his poetry, juxtaposing himself with the dead Tityrus. He eulogizes Tityrus in language that recalls the classical, medieval, and renaissance aesthetic, whereby poetry at once delights its hearers and instructs them in wisdom:

> He, whilst he liued, was the soueraigne head
> Of shepheards all, that bene with loue ytake:
> Well couth he wayle hys Woes, and lightly slake
> The flames, which loue within his heart had bredd,
> And tell vs mery tales, to keepe vs wake,
> The while our sheepe about vs safely fedde.
>   ("June," ll. 83–88)

Though he praises Tityrus's ability to laugh at himself and thereby relieve his own pain and help others with his wisdom, Colin goes on to say that if *he* had such a gift, he would use it as a means of vengeance:

Then should my plaints, causd of discurtesee,
As messengers of all my painfull plight,
Flye to my loue, where euer that she bee,
And pierce her heart with poynt of worthy wight:
As shee deserues, that wrought so deadly spight.
And thou *Menalcas,* that by trecheree
Didst vnderfong my lasse, to wexe so light,
Shouldest well be knowne for such thy villanee.
                    ("June," ll. 97–104)

As this stanza suggests, Colin sees poetry as complaint, as a plaintiff's
bid for reparation. Significantly, the entire stanza is cast in the subjunc-
tive. He makes clear his sense of injury in the first line, referring to his
poems as "plaints" bearing witness to Rosalind's discourtesy. These
poems would then serve as Cupid's arrows, piercing Rosalind's cruel
heart "as she deserues." Colin appears torn between a desire for mercy
and a wish to see justice enacted. Although he seems to hope to turn
her pity to his own advantage, line 101 raises the spectre of justice,
leaving his reaction to her pity somewhat in the dark. Colin's vengeful
feelings are more apparent in the last three lines, where he avows a use
for this fancied gift of poetry that would transform it into a weapon of
slander. Like Thenot in "Februarie," whose abuse of the fable of the
Oak and the Briar likewise transforms a potential emblem of concord
into a cause of discord, Colin's words suggest an ignoble metamorpho-
sis. Though Colin comes out of his dangerously solipsistic daydream,
where he is the adjudicator rather than the suppliant, his self-absorption
persists:

But since I am not, as I wish I were,
Ye gentle shepheards, which your flocks do feede,
Whether on hylls, or dales, or other where,
Beare witnesse all of thys so wicked deede.
                    ("June," ll. 105–8)

The shift here from the subjunctive to the objective mood signals
Colin's return to the exigencies of present time. But he continues to
dwell on his sense of injury. He thus uses the dependent clause of this
sentence to restate his position as a plaintiff, then, in the independent
clause, uses the imperative "beare witnesse" to suggest what he sees as
the just outcome of his complaint: Since he cannot, others should

publish Rosalind's cruelty. Hobbinoll closes the eclogue by saying that he laments Colin's "case," thereby echoing Colin's legalistic language, including the "beare witnesse" of the poem's final line.

Colin's self-absorbed appraisal of his own poetic gifts is once again revealed in the song inserted into the "August" eclogue. Fittingly enough, Colin is absent, apparently silent and withdrawn, but the song, informed by those very ideas, devices, and images that are central to the legend of Narcissus, proclaims Colin's tendency to see the world as a mirror for his misery. In many ways, the song looks forward to Spenser's handling of the natural world in the *Epithalamion*. There he describes the world as a vast echo chamber for the harmonies figured by his own marriage. For example, in stanza 8, the joy of the coming wedding is transformed to the boy's shout of "Hymen," which is, in turn, transformed to the shout of the rejoicing crowd, whose "noise" is carried by the echoing woods up to heaven, whose harmony is, of course, manifested in the wedding pair, themselves the genesis of the original cry from the troop of boy messengers. Perfectly circular, the music of the *Epithalamion* suggests in more than one way the fundamental harmony of the universe by employing Echo as one of its most important poetic devices.[22] Similarly, in Colin's "Aprill" lay for Elisa, he captures the universal harmony manifested in Elisa and, through her, to the pastoral world by drawing upon echoing devices and thus suggesting that the earthly realm is most real when it serves as a mirror for the celestial. Colin's lay in "August" is reflective in a more deadly way, for what he describes is a world that echoes or reflects his own "carefull cryes":

> Ye wasteful woodes beare witnesse of my woe,
> > Wherein my plaints did oftentimes resound:
> > Ye carelesse byrds are priuie to my cryes,
> > Which in your songs were wont to make a part:
> > Thou pleasaunt spring hast luld me oft a sleepe,
> > Whose streames my tricklinge teares did ofte augment.
> > > ("August," ll. 151–56)

The end words in Colin's elaborately wrought sestina form a litany of desolation—woe, resound, cryes, part, sleepe, augment. *Woe* and *sleep* relate to Colin's despairing frame of mind, while *resound, cryes,*

---

22. See Hollander, 15.

part, and *augment*—words that he skillfully employs as both verbs and nouns—mimic the cacophony that he perceives Rosalind's cruelty as having created. If the "Aprill" lay and the *Epithalamion* seem the spirit of music, the sestina in "August" seems untuned, as strident, over-wrought, and arrhythmic as Colin himself. Rather than describe the microcosm as a reflection of the greater harmonies of the macrocosm, harmonies reflected, in turn, by humanity's music, Colin reverses the ratio and describes the world as a reflection of the self. Music, then, magnifies what can only be called chaos. He justifies his isolation in the forest by saying that the forest is "fitter to resound / The hollow Echo of my carefull cryes" ("August," ll. 159–60). Colin's own words betray him since he rhetorically places himself in the "part" of Narcissus, whose self-absorption was broadcast by Echo herself, hollowed out by care and pain.

Colin's attitude toward poetry has become equally solipsistic:

> Hence with the Nightingale will I take part,
> That blessed byrd, that spends her time of sleepe
> In songs and plaintiue pleas, the more taugment
> The memory of hys misdeede, that bred her woe:
> ("August," ll. 183–86)

He no longer aligns himself with Pan, whose pipes serve as a kind of compensation for the loss of Syrinx, a loss transmuted into divine music. Colin instead links himself to Philomela, whose lurid tale of rape and mutilation was conventionally used to underline the dangers of overviolent love. Philomela herself, changed into the nightingale, became a figure for poetry and the solitary life.[23] That Colin associates himself with the victim of this tale suggests just how far he has descended into himself. If he is Philomela, Rosalind can only be Tereus, the brother-in-law by whose hand Philomela suffered. But nothing in the *Calender* warrants such a view of Rosalind. In fact, there is little evidence that she is anything but the object of Colin's fixation. Colin here appears to be caught up in an invented reality, a narcissistic transformation that has also altered his poetic purpose. He intends hereafter to use poetry as a memorial to his pain, or as a means of augmenting Rosalind's

23. See Goldberg, *Voice Terminal Echo,* 11–13. In "The Warbling Pipe: The Bird as an Orphic Emblem in *The Shepheardes Calender*," a paper read at the 1989 session of Spenser at Kalamazoo, Patrick Cheney suggested that the reference to the nightingale linked Colin to the Orphic poet.

misdeed. Moreover, Colin's plaintive cries seem no longer even directed at Rosalind but at a pastoral world that will echo back to him the sound of his own misery, as he suggests in the final lines of the sestina, "And you that feele no woe, when as the sound / Of these my nightly cryes ye heare apart, / Let breake your sounder sleepe and pitie augment" ("August," ll. 187–89).[24]

The "December" eclogue, which Colin uses to summarize his case before Pan, describes a life whose natural creativity and development has been halted. The eclogue may be the most haunting of the twelve, for Spenser allows his awareness of the year, of the facts and labors of each month and season, to inform Colin's account of his personal year so that the calendrical revolution, its real and metaphoric meanings, and the figure of Colin himself seem to form one figure and to speak with one voice of the brevity of time. At once lucid and opaque, the eclogue is difficult. Like Narcissus, Colin takes a confessional stance, adopting a candid tone for his account of an ill-spent life. His willingness to accuse himself gains our sympathy, at least until we discover that he is not entirely honest. Though he is physically old, appearing to have gained some sort of wisdom from his wrinkles and crow's feet, his words belie his appearance. He looks like December, but speaks like May, arrested in a perpetual adolescence. By proportioning his life to the four seasons, Colin brings evidence against himself, for he adumbrates a natural cycle whose orderly revolution exposes his own lack of development.

The convention that provides Colin with the scaffolding for his complaint in "December" is one whose roots go far back into the literature and iconography of Western culture. They need not be traced, since the tendency to associate each stage of human life with a particular season—its weather, its labors, its perils—seems a natural one.[25] There is ample evidence throughout sixteenth-century literature that renaissance man continued to find the figure of the annual cycle a meaningful metaphor for the revolutions of his own life. The figure was intimately,

24. Here particularly does Spenser seem to suggest his fundamental understanding of Virgil's art. Eclogues 2 and 8, which Brooks Otis has paired, both contain complaints of unrequited love in which the speakers oppose themselves to the ethos of the pastoral world. Eclogue 8 is an especially resonant one: The first speaker's self-absorption, his inability to move beyond *amor indignus*, renders him, like Narcissus (whose legend informs Eclogue 2), an alien and finally a suicide.

25. For a discussion of the iconographic conventions of the seasons and months, see Tuve, *Seasons and Months*. For a discussion of Spenser's handling of the natural cycle in relation to the "December" eclogue, see Alpers (1972).

and logically, tied to the theme of mutability. For example, the Prologue to the *Kalender of Shepherdes* reminded its readers of mortality, saying that the calendar before them provided everything necessary for this life and the next. A few pages later, the author remarked a model for human finitude in the year, proportioning man's life to the four seasons, beginning with the three months of spring—February, March, and April. As the *Kalender of Shepherdes* implied, man's relationship to the annual cycle should provide him with a means of using time. Since inactivity comes with winter, man should work during the good months to provide for it. The authors of devotional manuals also drew upon the four seasons as a means of heightening the lessons of mutability. Thus the *Preces Privatae* (first published in 1564 and frequently reprinted, the edition of 1573 being the best known) contained prayers for each of the four seasons. Each prayer exploited appropriate figurative language in an implicit comparison between an agricultural cycle and mortal life. The prayer for autumn gave thanks to God, maker of sky and earth, for bringing the year to its maturation, asking for an abundant harvest through grace. The emphasis throughout was on fruitfulness, in keeping with a time of year where the earth's fruit is harvested, weighed, and laid aside for winter. Correspondingly, the prayer for summer emphasized good gardening, addressing God as "sol noster, sine quo nec lucidum est quicquam in animis nostris" (390). The prayer for Spring focused on water, the earth's beauty, and flowers, the harbingers of summer's labor and autumn's fruitful harvest.

Colin's account of the seasons of human life makes it clear that he is aware of the duties of each season and the idea of justice or reckoning implied by such a figure. He thus divides life into seasons that reflect humanity's evolution from hunters to builders to rulers. He begins with Spring, a time for heedless wandering, nut-gathering, and hunting. It is during this period that Colin learns the rudiments of song. With summer come more mature occupations. Colin learns the arts of constructing sheepfolds and baskets, as well as how to read the sky, a branch of the natural science. Autumn he associates with harvest and winter with cold and death. The cycle Colin describes is one that was thought to be the natural pattern of man's development. Man begins his life heedless and without a sense of time; thus his "labors" resemble pastimes rather than actual labors. Like a true Arcadian, man lives by gathering and hunting; in other words, he does not think about what he will eat or do tomorrow but satisfies his wants each day. It is at this stage that he learns to sing, a sign that poetry is a token of our primordial

harmony with nature. From the less complicated duties and relation-
ships of youth or spring, man passes to a more complex season, summer.
He then absorbs the elements of natural science, learns how to provide
for tomorrow's hunger or bad weather by learning how to build. More
complicated yet, man in summer begins to keep company with the
opposite sex and to fall in love. Summer's heat and activity naturally
lead into autumn's harvest, into its labors of measuring and storing.
Winter must find its nourishment in autumn's storage barns, its shelter
in what was built in summer's heat.

Though Colin uses the rotation of an entire year as the *figura* for his
account of his life, his complaint reveals that his own year is composed
of only two seasons, spring and early summer. His words also suggest
that his unchecked desires are the cause of his blighted cycle. His
description of his spring idyll thus prepares us for the more obviously
destructive summer that follows:

> Whilome in youth, when flowrd my ioyfull spring,
> Like Swallow swift I wandred here and there:
> For heate of heedlesse lust me so did sting,
> That I of doubted daunger had no feare.
> I went the wastefull woodes and forest wyde,
> Withouten dreade of Wolues to bene espyed.
> ("December," ll. 19–24)

Colin characterizes his spring in terms of motion, thereby signaling
a restlessness that initially lacks an object. Thus he wanders aimlessly,
impelled by the "heate of heedlesse lust." It is not necessary to invest
"lust" with any sexual connotations in order to be aware of Colin's
sexual vulnerability, for his very lack of motivation makes him particu-
larly vulnerable to obsessive love.[26] Like Narcissus, with whom he
shares his fondness for hunting, sense of fearlessness, and inherent
selfishness, Colin's very lack of attachment seems to foreshadow a
passion as rooted and fixed as his youthful freedom was unrooted and
unfixed. His subsequent references to his youthful "libertee," to "looser
yeares," and to his own sense of timelessness fill in the outlines of a
portrait whose details hint at its vulnerability to the very time its youth
and freshness seem to deny. In relation to the figure of the annual cycle,

26. This is the same pattern that underlies Chaucer's handling of Troilus in *Troilus and
Criseyde*: Troilus first sees Criseyde and falls in love when he is restless, heedless, and objectless.

Colin's account of his spring "labors" describes the buds and flowers that will become autumn's harvest. Given Colin's own spring, we can only hope there is neither a late frost nor a hot summer; for his flowers seem as fragile, as inherently sterile, as his harvest will be barren.

Colin's description of his summer is more problematic. Rather than acknowledging the natural progression from spring to summer, or from boyhood to manhood, Colin blames Pan for the loss of his spring. He insists that his piping rivaled Pan's, so Pan repaid Colin's pride with love:

> But ah such pryde at length was ill repayde,
> The shepheards God (perdie God was he none)
> My hurtlesse pleasaunce did me ill vpbraide,
> By freedome lorne, my life he lefte to mone.
>   Love they him called, that gaue me checkmate,
>   But better mought they haue behote him Hate.
>   ("December," ll. 49–54)

Colin's language here is conventional enough. Like all heirs of Guillaume de Lorris's Amant, Colin sees himself as conquered by a stronger party, wounded, and lacking his former freedom of motion. He even goes so far as to use the language of chess to describe his condition, linking himself to such venerable figures in the literature of love as the Black Knight in Chaucer's *Boke of the Duchesse*.[27] Furthermore, Colin's words suggest a helplessness, a fatalism, that characterizes him throughout the *Calender,* for at no point does he seem to see that his melancholy is his to banish, that the despairing and passive, like Narcissus, must inevitably fade away to nothing.

Colin's second effort to describe the advent of summer strengthens the impression of fatalism left by his first attempt:

> Tho gan my louely Spring bid me farewel,
> And Sommer season sped him to display
> (For loue then in the Lyons house did dwell)
> The raging fyre, that kindled at his ray.
>   A comett stird vp that vnkindly heate,
>   That reigned (as men sayd) in *Venus* seate.
>   ("December," ll. 55–60)

Colin's language here is particularly significant, for the stanza signals

---

27. According to the *MED,* "Checkmate" was frequently used to describe the discomforts of love or the inequalities of certain relationships. For a discussion of Troilus's "extraordinary passivity," see Wetherbee, 65ff.

the shift from activity to passivity that marks Colin's life. Before falling in love, in Spring, he uses active verbs to describe his movement. Beginning with line 49, with his description of Pan's vengeance, he begins to use passive verbs more frequently, thereby indicating his sense of helplessness and ultimately his refusal to take responsibility for his own year. Thus, in the stanza above, he describes himself as stationary, as a still landscape that is visited by seasons. In other words, he endures the arbitrary motion of outside forces, for Spring "bid me farewel" and Summer "sped him to display." In one sense Colin is right, for time acts on everything. But though time moves independently of human actions, human actions in time are nonetheless a matter of choice. Colin rules out any possibility of choice, linking passion's heat to Venerian influences. In the following stanza, he underlines his own now circum-scribed motion by saying, "Forth was I ledde, not as I wont afore, / When choise I had to choose my wandring waye" ("December," ll. 61–62). Both explicitly and implicitly, the lines reveal his fatalism; the passive verb of the first line serves as a preamble for the more explicit denial of freedom of choice. If he begins in a state of random motion, he moves into an orbit whose path is—though he does not see it that way—determined by his own fixation. If heedless lust once inspired that early motion, now genuine and frustrated desire impels him. Both sorts of motion have their origins in the self.

Like Narcissus, he becomes a captive of the self, moving deeper into the forest, away from all signs of communal life. He thus characterizes himself in the past as having sought out the honey bee, "Working her formall rowmes in Wexen frame." ("December," ll. 68); now he dwells where toadstools grow (l. 69) and owls shriek (l. 72). In the very season when he should be emulating the bees, whose orderly industry served classical, medieval, and renaissance writers as a trope for communal harmony and purpose, Colin recedes into a world of darkness and isolation. With their emphasis on isolation, night, and death, his words here bear out the evidence of the "June" eclogue and the lay inserted into "August"; for the "ghastlie Owle" of "December" echoes the shrieks of the "banefull byrds" he describes in the sestina capturing his own chaotic state of mind (see "August," ll. 173–74). Colin not only becomes his own prisoner in summer, he also fails to avail himself of the lessons he links to that season. He learns the lessons of the natural world—the motions of the stars and the healing properties of herbs— but cannot apply them to himself, "But ah vnwise and witlesse *Colin cloute*, / That kydst the hidden kinds of many a wede: / Yet kydst not ene to cure thy sore hart roote" ("December," ll. 91–93).

Colin's pitiful helplessness, his persistence in disease, and his oxymoronic language underline the destructive nature of his passion. Ultimately, as Spenser implies, Rosalind matters less than Colin's fixation upon her:

> The fragrant flowres, that in my garden grewe,
> Bene withered, as they had bene gathered long.
> Theyr rootes bene dryed vp for lacke of dewe,
> Yet dewed with teares they han be euer among.
>   Ah who has wrought my *Rosalind* this spight
>   To spil the flowres, that should her girlond dight?
>   ("December," ll. 109–14)

This and the preceding stanza describe waste, linking Colin to agricultural infertility. In the preceding stanza, Colin speaks of boughs laden with blossoms, promises of "timely fruite"; but now the boughs are left both bare and barren, the fruit having rotted before it could ripen. In the stanza above, Colin chooses to elaborate upon flowers rather than boughs, describing once fragrant flowers as dried up for lack of water. The ironies of both stanzas go well beyond Colin, who uses such metaphors as boughs and flowers dramatically but not logically. The answer to the question in lines 113 and 114 is, of course, Colin himself, who has blasted his harvest and spilled the flowers, flowers that, like the memorial Narcissus leaves behind him, wither in summer's heat. The very rhetoric Colin uses so powerfully and evocatively subverts his argument. By juxtaposing his seasons to those of the natural year, or the course of human life, Colin unwittingly throws into high relief the violence he has committed upon his own potential harvest. He can only starve to death once winter truly comes.

Spenserian Complaint

Perhaps the most damning piece of evidence against Colin is his lay in "Nouember" for the dead Dido, which points up the weaknesses and illogic of his complaint to Pan in "December." Where Colin's life and poetry for Rosalind suggest incompletion or truncation, his elegy for Dido implicitly resolves the questions and problems posed by the other three Plaintive eclogues. In Colin's lay, Spenser made stunning use of the classical and Christian conventions that had accrued around the pastoral elegy, thus pointing the way for the young Milton in *Lycidas*.[28] The lay is also central to the themes and concerns of the Plaintive eclogues, for in "Nouember" Spenser suggests the possibility of triumphing over mutability. Furthermore, the eclogue brings the figure of Colin Clout into sharper focus, for here, as in the "Aprill" eclogue, he fulfills himself by fulfilling his duties as a poet and a steward.

Rather than the solitary Narcissus-like figure who sings for himself alone and uses the world as a mirror of the self, Colin in "Nouember" takes his subject from Thenot's suggestion, sings for someone else, and uses the world as a means of transcending the world's sorrows. The problems outlined in the discussion about poetry between Piers and Cuddie in "October" are alleviated by Colin's fulfillment of his role in "Nouember." Piers and Cuddie lament the lack of patronage for poets; although Thenot in "Nouember" (with his offer to repay Colin's song with a "Kidde or a Cosset") is no Maecenas, he nonetheless gives Colin his subject matter and offers the orphaned lamb in payment at the end of the eclogue. Where Piers argues for a poetry that teaches wisdom and is thus intimately tied to the good of the body politic, Colin eulogizes Dido, who served as a figure for the common good, a eulogy that affirms her everlasting triumph over earth's imperfections and decay. Thenot, Colin's patron and audience, underlines Colin's success by observing at the elegy's close, "Ay francke shepheard, how bene thy verses meint / With doolful pleasaunce, so as I ne wotte, / Whether reioyce or weepe for great constrainte?" ("Nouember," ll. 203–5). Whereas Thenot begins by referring to "deathes dreeriment," Colin's song moves him beyond the stark fact of mutability. Finally, Piers argues for a poetic that leads man back to his heavenly origins, outlining a circular orbit of descent and ascent for poetry as well as for men. Colin's elegy likewise suggests a circular orbit, for he describes Dido as having descended into the earth and its clay with death, but as having triumphed over her own clay. Colin's voice in "Nouember" is an Orphic one, celebrating man's release from infernal darkness into life and light.

Like his lay in "April," Colin's elegy in "Nouember" is visionary. Indeed, both poems represent Colin's attempt to capture in verse a private revelation. Thus, in the third stanza of the "Aprill" lay he urges upon us his own vision of Elisa, enthroned as Queen of shepherds. The lay contains a series of verbs and nouns such as "saw," "see," "sight,"

---

28. For a recent study of the elegy, see Sacks, chapter 1 and 40–51.

or "gaze" and other terms like "compare," "show," and "amaze," all of which underline the wonder and majesty of Elisa's presence in this pastoral world. Colin describes Elisa as the focal point of this world and his sight of her as a revelation; he thus assumes the role of the visionary poet, the medium through which universal laws or truths are transmitted to those of us lacking the particularly keen sight of the poet or *vates*. Colin's revelation is, however, put to the test in "Nouember." If "Aprill" celebrates Elisa as, like the sun, the principle of life for her world, "Nouember" describes the effect of a sun's eclipse on the world in which we live. Both poems celebrate persons of the highest rank—the one Elisa, the other Dido (whose other name, as every literate English man would have known, was Elisa)—and both treat the figure in remarkably similar ways, as the center of the pastoral world, as a principle of light, order, stability, music, and growth.[29]

Like "Aprill," "Nouember" evokes the figure of the poet as seer, as the intermediary between our insufficiencies of sight and the blazing reality and beauty of natural law. In fact, if "Aprill" captures Colin's sight and sudden comprehension of Elisa's powers, "Nouember" traces his gradual awareness of natural laws previously unknown. "Nouember" charts Colin's own reorientation, his vision of a cosmos ruled not by death but by life, as abundant, as stable, as the new heaven and earth he sees and communicates to us. In "Aprill," Colin celebrates Elisa's rising up (see "Aprill," ll. 145ff.); in "Nouember" he suggests that we, too, may begin to imagine our own individual uprisings. Colin begins in darkness and ignorance, saying in the second stanza of the elegy that not only does Dido's death constitute a blot in nature, but that by her death the earth is plunged into night:

> Shepheards, that by your flocks on Kentish downes abyde,
> Waile ye this wofull waste of natures warke:
> Waile we the wight, whose presence was our pryde:
> Waile we the wight, whose absence is our carke.
> The sonne of all the world is dimme and darke:

29. I link Dido to the Queen; see 174–78; 199–201. The fact that Spenser adapted Marot's elegy for Queen Louise to the "Nouember" eclogue indicates the association he drew between the elegy and the idea of royalty. See Patterson, *Pastoral and Ideology*, 106–32, and Prescott, *French Poets and the English Renaissance*, 11–12. For remarks about Dido as a cover for Elizabeth, see McLane 47–60. For another view about the identity of Dido, see Cullen 92 n.29.

> The earth now lacks her wonted light,
> And all we dwell in deadly night,
>   O heauie herse.
> Breake we our pypes, that shrild as lowde as Larke,
>   O carefull verse.
>   ("Nouember," ll. 63–72)

This stanza evinces the problems Colin poses in his elegy. He first describes the shepherds' grief, the emptiness in the pastoral community caused by Dido's death, a death he describes as a waste of nature. In the second sentence, he broadens the implication of Dido's death, describing a world whose natural rhythms are interrupted by a variety of solar winter. Whether he refers here to an eclipse or to a prolonged period of night, he describes her absence as both unnatural and catastrophic. The catastrophe, or man's perception of nature's discord, destroys man's attempts at harmony, causing him to break his pipes and thereby silence his music.

Though he here suggests a correspondence—albeit negative—between man and nature, he goes on to stress the disjunction between man and his world. In the third stanza he describes death as fading or destroying the fairest flower in "our gyrlond," following up the metaphor by comparing nature's cycle of recurring life with man's lamentable half-cycle:

> Whence is it, that the flouret of the field doth fade,
> And lyeth buryed long in Winters bale:
> Yet soone as spring his mantle hath displayd,
> It floureth fresh, as it should neuer fayle?
> But thing on earth that is of most availe,
>   As vertues braunch and beauties budde,
>   Reliuen not for any good.
>   ("Nouember," ll. 83–89)

The question he poses concerns the disproportion between the human and the natural cycles: If winter in nature serves to usher in spring and new life, then why do "vertues braunch and beauties budde" fade, not to return? Through the eleventh stanza, Colin's song describes his own anguished appraisal of earth's laws of mutability, concluding: "Now haue I learnd (a lesson derely bought) / That nys on earth assuraunce to be sought" ("Nouember," ll. 156–57). If the lay were to end here, it would illustrate only the negative lessons we find in "December," for Colin offers us the only logical deduction he can draw from his observation of natural law. From his initial perspective, earth's laws of motion are those by which man is ground down to nothing.

Colin resolves the problems posed by the first part of his elegy by gaining a new vantage point upon the natural world, one that allows for a broader and therefore more accurate perspective from which he apprehends the nature of motion. Spenser's handling of the idea of motion probably owes a good deal to the scientific speculations and pronouncements he would have encountered at Leicester House. The important English Copernican, Thomas Digges, was but one of a number of thinkers who suggested that the stable center of the universe was the sun and not the earth, which, fittingly enough, Digges referred to as "this orb of decay." Furthermore, Digges not only affirmed a heliocentric universe but an infinite one as the frontispiece to his revised edition of his father's popular *Prognostication* implies with its depiction of a universe that appears without boundaries. He included in this edition an essay, which is a translation of key chapters in Book 1 of Copernicus's *De Revolutionibus,* which argued that the older and incorrect theory of geocentricity owes more to our misunderstanding of perspective than it does to scientific observation: The citizens of this moving planet only think it stable and the heavens mobile, but our own motion precludes us from recognizing heaven's stability. Earth, in company with the other planets, performs its course around a stable center.[30] Colin's elegy for Dido embodies that perception, which he arrives at in two stages. The first part of the elegy demonstrates, to Colin's growing anguish, that what he perceived as stable is mutable. The final part of the elegy, however, ascends from his recognition of Dido's mortality as Colin envisions a circular motion about a stable center. His ability to understand mortality allows him to see that the laws of motion are not necessarily the laws of decay; what he thought the downward arc of human life is, in fact, but one half of a circle.

Stanzas 11 and 12 juxtapose Colin's old and new understanding of these laws of motion. In stanza 11, after learning the hard lessons of earth's instability, he underlines the empirical basis for his deduction: He knows there is no stability in earth because he has *seen* (line 161)

30. See also Johnson and Larkey (1934); Johnson, *Astronomical Thought in Renaissance England,* chapter 5; Meyer.

the bier on which her body was borne. He thus communicates to us his own sight of Dido's burial, the evidence for mortality, an emblem of the inherent futility of all mortal efforts: "O trustlesse state of earthly things, and slipper hope / Of mortal men, that swincke and sweate for nought, / And shooting wide, doe misse the marked scope" ("Nouember," ll. 153–55). The "earthlie mould" (l. 158) of which Dido is composed offers assurance only of decay. Colin comes close here to affirming chaos since he seems lost in a cosmos that lacks a stable center. What he thought of as stable is even more vulnerable to time than the most ordinary bush or flower. The poem, however, turns with the first line of the following stanza:

> But maugre death, and dreaded sisters deadly spight,
> And gates of hel, and fyrie furies forse:
> She hath the bonds broke of eternall night,
> Her soule vnbodied of the burdenous corpse.
> ("Nouember," ll. 163–66)

These lines, with their crisp syllables, strong alliteration, and simple verbs gain additional force in relation to the preceding stanza, which is dominated by sibilance, assonance, compound verbs, and a series of qualifying phrases. The one laments the constrictions of the flesh, the other announces a newly perceived and infinite universe.

The allusions in stanza 12 to the death and resurrection of Christ are unmistakable. Like Christ, Dido denies the gates of hell their power, breaks through the constrictions of darkness, her soul unbodied and hence lighter. Returning from hell triumphant, she now reigns a goddess among the saints, her orbit returning to its place of origin in the skies. What appeared to be linear motion is, in fact, circular; Dido's course, patterned on that of Christ, offers us a pattern of circular, or redemptive, motion, suggesting a new way of understanding the nature of the universe. As the elegy affirms, Dido's motion—her death—is supremely natural, not the blot on nature it first appears; she now inhabits a celestial realm. Colin thus testifies, "I see thee blessed soule, I see, / Walke in *Elisian* fieldes so free" ("Nouember," ll. 178–79). He can now testify to resurrection; he can actually see her in a new realm. Colin draws two conclusions from the new evidence he discovers. First, he redefines death as but the nadir of a circular orbit, "We deeme of Death as doome of ill desert: / But knewe we fooles, what it vs bringes vntil, / Dye would we dayly, once it to expert" ("Nouember," ll. 184–

86). In the last stanza of the elegy he hints at the final and blessed use
of Dido's revolution:

> *Dido* is gone afore (whose turne shall be the next?)
> There liues shee with the blessed Gods in blisse,
> There drincks she *Nectar* with *Ambrosia* mixt,
> And ioyes enioyes, that mortall men doe misse.
> ("Nouember," ll. 193–96)

Implicitly, Colin here applies the lesson of Dido's death to himself, thus
bringing to an end the chain of analogues that binds the elegy together:
What appears solar motion is, in fact, evidence for earth's rotation about
a stable and life-giving center. Thus Christ offers humanity a pattern
for redemptive motion, the course that Dido follows, offering Colin
and his fellows in turn a pattern that reflects the underlying order of
the universe. The final stanzas of the elegy signal Colin's own acceptance
of and assent to motion, a point underscored by E.K. in his gloss on
the emblem for "Nouember," where he likens death to harvest, echoing
Chaucer's Parson by calling it the "grene path way to lyfe."

The theme of resurrection also informs Spenser's handling of Colin
in the "Nouember" eclogue. While he sings, he ceases to function as a
figure for Narcissus. Not only does he sing of something other than his
own despair, his song brings together man and nature in one harmoni-
ous chorus. Like the echoing effect that Colin achieves in the "Aprill"
lay to Elisa, and that Spenser achieves in the *Epithalamion,* the elegy
suggests a world whose correspondences and harmonies are fundamen-
tal and essential. The measured pace of Colin's verse in the first eleven
stanzas of the elegy echoes or reflects the effect of death. Just as the
earth grows dim and lifeless, Colin's verse slows down, while the refrain
"O heauie herse. . . . O carefull verse" gives each stanza a weight that
is lifted when the refrain is altered with Dido's resurrection. Corres-
pondingly, the imagery shifts from the dark winter landscape of the
first part of the elegy to the eternally lush spring landscape of the Elysian
fields that Dido now inhabits. Like a true son of Pan, or an Orpheus,
who could cause all nature to move in concord and whose music broke
hell's bounds, Colin causes nature to sing in harmony with his song,
piping Dido out of earth and into realms of pure light and love.
Moreover, by proclaiming Dido's resurrection, Colin brings about
Thenot's renewal of spirits. His song is thus catalytic, providing its
audience with tidings of a new realm of eternal life. Though Spenser

does not include any explicitly religious details, thereby maintaining the eclogue's pastoral fiction, he invests the elegy with characteristics and patterns that cannot help but evoke the Gospels' accounts of Christ's resurrection. He thereby informs the elegy with a joy that for his audience was inextricably tied to that central message of Christianity, "Why do you weep . . . Whom are you seeking . . . He is not here. He has risen." Finally, Dido provides Colin with a means of achieving in verse what he cannot do in life. Poetically, he has played Orpheus to himself.

Formally, Colin's elegy in "Nouember" is his only complaint that can be described as complete. His complaint in "Januarye" breaks off in line 71, when he breaks his pipe, leaving Spenser with the task of completing the stanza. In "June," Colin not only maintains his silence, he defends a poetic that locates its subject and its audience in the self:

> Nought weigh I, who my song doth prayse or blame,
> Ne striue to winne renowne, or passe the rest:
> With shepheard sittes not, followe flying fame:
> But feede his flocke in fields, where falls hem best.
> I wote my rymes bene rough, and rudely drest:
> The fytter they, my carefull case to frame:
> Enough is me to paint out my vnrest,
> And poore my piteous plaints out in the same.
>
> ("June," ll. 73–80)

In relation to sixteenth-century poetic theory, Colin's argument here is particularly disturbing, for he disavows any reality except the self, describing his task as a poet solely in terms of his misery as a lover.[31] He sees his verse only as a *plaint* for his *carefull case*.

The poetic narcissism of Colin's *apologia* is even more apparent in the remaining four stanzas of the "June" eclogue, which constitute a badly disjointed, rhetorically chaotic elegy for the dead Tityrus, Colin's mentor. Like a conventional elegy, the stanza falls into two parts. The first part can be described as a compression of the first eleven stanzas of the lay for Dido in "Nouember." In "June," Colin begins by announcing that Tityrus, who taught Colin "to make" (l. 82), is dead, going on to praise Tityrus for his wisdom:

---

31. For a differently directed discussion of Spenser's handling of this convention, see Helgerson, chapter 2.

He, whilst he liued, was the soueraigne head
Of shepheards all, that bene with loue ytake:
Well couth he wayle hys Woes, and lightly slake
The flames, which loue within his heart had bredd,
And tell vs mery tales, to keepe vs wake,
The while our sheepe about vs safely fedde.

("June," ll. 83–88)

The ironies of his encomium seem lost on Colin himself, for Tityrus used poetry as a means of compensation and thus as a remedy for the woes of love. Colin does not credit Tityrus with complaints, but with the poetry of assuagement and with "mery tales." Furthermore, he underlines Tityrus's position as a figure of the common good, as a poet whose art was bound up with the pastoral community. Colin follows up this stanza of praise by returning to the subject of death, using turns of speech that are recast in the elegy in "Nouember." However, in contrast to "Nouember," where Colin draws upon the figure of the annual cycle to envision an eternal spring after Dido's winter and death, his verse in "June" is fixed by his own misery. He makes no attempt to turn a lament into an elegy, seemingly unable to lift his verse or his memories of Tityrus beyond the boundaries of his own sorrow. Colin's fixation is both literal and metaphoric: Fixed upon Rosalind, the object of his desire and his pain, his poetic, like his physical freedom, is circumscribed by what he has made the center of his being.

More seriously yet, Colin subverts the ongoing life that Tityrus might have in his poetic heirs by saying that he would use his own poetic skill to complain about Rosalind and to publish her cruelties. In terms of elegiac convention, Colin—in sharp contrast to Spenser—denies Tityrus any immortality. First, Colin sings only for himself, silencing not only his song but those he learned from Tityrus. Second, Colin's use of poetry is, in reality, an abuse. Since he sees poetry only as a brief for the self, he denies the possibility of teaching others, of lifting man away from earth to heaven. Thus Colin's elegy for Tityrus wanders off into complaining, circling ceaselessly about his own sorrow, and never achieving the turn by which the lay for Dido shifts direction and turns descent into ascent.

Just as the elegy in "Nouember" throws the illogic and solipsism of Colin's complaint in "June" into high relief, so his final complaint to Pan in "December" appears even more inadequate in relation to the preceding eclogue. Like his complaints in "Januarye" and "June," Colin's account of his year in "December" may be described as truncated. Though Colin achieves the semblance of a completed form by comparing his life to the four seasons, the order inherent in that conceit is undermined if we look at the eclogue as the "complaynte" E.K. says it is. Spenser's own *Complaints,* published in 1591, but probably written over a period of several years, suggest that he, like his medieval forebears, saw the complaint as a poem in which the speaker seeks relief for some problem. Chaucer's burlesque of the mode in "Complaynt to his Purse," though different in tone from Alanus de Insulis's important *Complaint of Nature,* sketches in miniature the conventions of the form. Chaucer directs his complaint to an empty purse, identifying its lightness as the source of his heaviness. He wishes to hear the purse chime and to see it shine with gold, hoping it to be heavy so that he can be light. He ends with a stanza to the king, asking him to hear his supplication. As Chaucer's witty complaint implies, the notion of a remedy was implicit in the mode itself. For example, Puttenham's discussion of "The Forme of Poeticall Lamentations" suggested that when a poet turns his hand to the lament, he acts as a physician for the reader; Puttenham then described fit subjects for the lament such as deaths and burials, as well as adversities of wars or "true love lost or ill bestowed" (62). Spenser in his *Complaints* dilates upon the effects of mutability in a way that suggests—either explicitly or implicitly—a remedy for time and decay. A better known example of Spenser's handling of the complaint is in *The Mutabilitie Cantos,* where the narrator, in recognizing the case for mutability, comes to see that mutability is but the earthly manifestation of permanence. Whether resolved directly or indirectly, the complaint moves naturally towards an affirmation of ongoing life in whatever terms are meaningful to the subject, the poet, and his audience.

There is, moreover, an important distinction between Colin's use of the complaint and Spenser's. Since Colin casts himself as a plaintiff, "December" serves as his final statement of injuries. While his complaint certainly presents evidence of injury in the wasted Colin, starved by his own bad management, it is unclear what Colin expects from the statement. What possible reparation can there be for a blighted life, and how might Pan grant Colin equity? Colin himself seems to expect little from the case, for his complaint trails off into lament. Whereas his descriptions of his spring and summer are fairly concrete, depicting the activities appropriate to each season, with late summer he falters and is able to describe only what might have been:

Thus is my sommer worne away and wasted,
Thus is my haruest hastened all to rathe:
The eare that budded faire, is burnt and blasted,
And all my hoped gaine is turnd to scathe.
    Of all the seede, that in my youth was sowne,
    Was nought but brakes and brambles to be mowne.
("December," ll. 97–102)

Colin's use of passive verbs here suggests a fatalism that the remainder of the eclogue does not counter since "is burnt" and "is turnd" relieve Colin of the responsibility of saying "I burned" and "I blasted." In the remaining stanzas, Colin describes himself as active only once, "Here will I hang my pype vpon this tree" ("December," l. 141). Appropriately, his final action is a negative one; he will hang up his pipe, or cease singing. As a plaintiff, Colin prepares a case without a solution. In his passivity, he cannot help himself, so it is hard to see how either Pan or Rosalind can help him. As a poet, he complains; he does not write complaints.

Conclusion: A Finished Form

Spenser, however, reveals himself as thoroughly aware of the demands and strategies of the complaint. If we see "December" as the final movement in an extended meditation or complaint upon the subject of mutability, we recognize that the Plaintive eclogues, like *The Ruines of Time, Muioptomos,* or *The Visions of Petrarch,* suggest remedies for time, folly, and decay even as they describe waste. As Colin's own elegy for Dido reiterates, man can use earth and its cycle of change as a means of transcending earth. Rather than bow to winter and death, man can graft himself onto an eternal pattern whose course around a stable center was first run by Christ. The pattern of descent and ascent that Colin suddenly perceives in Dido's death and rebirth is one that each person can choose for himself. Though Colin's complaint in "December," truncated like his life, reads like the first part of Ecclesiastes, reminding us that all is vanity, that man withers as the grass, and that all human endeavors end in disillusion, the Plaintive eclogues as a whole suggest a remedy for mutability.[32] Spenser's use of Colin as a figure who destroys his gift of song just as Narcissus destroys his gift of beauty gains added power from the poetry of Colin's interspersed throughout the *Calender*. Colin's is a prodigious talent, as Spenser's career bears out. For Cuddie to settle for "dapper ditties," as he says in "October," is one thing; it is quite another for Colin to choose an audience of one.[33] Colin's isolation from his fellows breeds an artistic isolation whose end is silence. Through Colin's fragmentation and passivity, Spenser demonstrates the need for mastery over those discordant elements of the self that threaten a potentially and naturally creative order. He also demonstrates the positive relationship between the poet and his society, for the poet ideally mediates between the actual world and an ideal realm. If the poet denies his responsibilities to either sphere, he alters the function, and hence the form, of his art. As Colin's legend suggests, the poet's most insidious enemy is himself. The very emblem Spenser gives to Colin in "Januarye," "Anchôra Speme," suggests the fundamental difference between the poet and his fictional creation.[34] For Colin's adoption of the emblem represents an abuse of an emblem conventionally linked to true stability; Colin uses the tag to describe his hopes for attaining Rosalind, herself doomed to death. On the other hand, Spenser uses earth—its cycles, its lovers, its symbols, its very finitude—as elements in a complaint that argues for awareness, responsibility, and wisdom, lest we face our dark days alone—hungry, passive, and lamely sorry.

32. Thus Henry Lok saw the underlying strategy of Ecclesiastes. Of the works of Solomon, Lok writes:

> But this his large discourse was chiefly ment,
> To teach the world to know how farre they stray,
> That do by earthly helpes a meane inuent
> To leade their liues vnto a happie day,
> Since nature wholy doth the same denay (115)

33. In *The French Academy*, Pierre de la Primaudaye wrote: "We are not onely borne (saith Cicero) for our selues, but our countrie, parents, and friends both will and ought to reape some commoditie by our birth . . . no man liueth more disorderly, than he that liueth to himself, and thinketh on nothing but his owne profit" (89).

34. Since hope was conventionally depicted as the anchor the soul needed in the world's tumult, the emblem is possibly a pun; *anchôra* (still) inescapably conjures up *ancora* or *anchora* (anchor).

4

The Recreative Eclogues: Pastoral Loves

ith the three Recreative eclogues, we move from the contemplative to the pleasurable life, from Athena to Venus, from the concerns and techniques of the Virgilian pastoral and Latin poetry to those of even more ancient pastoral sources, the Greek idyll and the biblical epithalamium. Each eclogue focuses on the figures of Venus and Cupid, those twin forces of chaos or cohesion that underlie human institutions. "March" and "August" are imitations of what Spenser and his contemporaries conceived of as the Greek pastoral, attempts to describe the powers of Cupid and Venus in the mythic language and amoeban dialogue of a Theocritus or a Bion.[1] In "March" Thomalin recounts his recent misadventure with Cupid, and in "August" Perigot and Willye engage in a singing contest, the subject of which is an unlucky encounter with a rural Venus. Cuddie ends the "August" eclogue by singing Colin's sestina, the echo of Colin's disastrous passion for Rosalind. In "Aprill," Spenser drew upon the strategies, imagery, and themes of the biblical

---

1. For a discussion of Spenser's relation to Greek poetry, see Hughes (1923). As Hughes demonstrates, Spenser's attempts to imitate the Greek idyll reflect the literary fashions of his day—in other words, the sixteenth-century sense of what Greek poetry was—rather than actual Greek poetry. See also Braden; Greg 18 n. 1; *Sixe Idillia, That is, Sixe Small, or Petty Poems, or AEglogues, chosen out of the right famous Sicilian Poet Theocritus, and translated into English Verse* (1588). This translation of Theocritus is particularly interesting since it is an imitation of *The Shepheardes Calender*. The volume thus suggests the degree to which Spenser had insinuated himself into the company of Greek poets, so much so that a translator of Theocritus felt it necessary to nod to Spenser in passing.

epithalamium, epitomized for the Middle Ages and the Renaissance by
the Song of Solomon, a book Spenser, like many of his contemporaries,
might have referred to as the *Ballette of ballettes*. Gervase Markham went
so far as to entitle his translation of the book *The Poem of Poems, or Sions
Muse, Contayning the diuine song of King Salomon, deuided into eight
Eclogues* (1596?). He dedicated the volume to Elizabeth, the daughter
of Sir Philip Sidney. In his Canticle, Solomon, under the name of *Idida*
or "Beloved of God," was thought to have achieved the highest form
of poetry, for the book was usually seen as celebrating the raptures of
spiritual union. Martin Luther, however, reflecting the protestant habit
of identifying the Church with the elect nation, read the book as an
elaborate encomium of the state.[2] This interpretation may well have
influenced Spenser's decision to use the imagery and structure of the
Canticle in the only truly re-creative of the three recreative eclogues,
for in "Aprill" he fused the all too often separate considerations of love
and beauty in his description of Elisa, the figure in the *Calender* who
most fully embodies the idea of fruitful love.

The difference between the handling of love in the Recreative and
the Plaintive eclogues lies at the heart of Spenser's strategy for each of
the three *ranckes*. In the Plaintive eclogues, Spenser treats love in a
highly specific way: Colin is the focus of the four eclogues, rather than
any abstract consideration of love or beauty. Thus it is Colin's obsession
with Rosalind that interrupts his life's normal development, not Colin's
encounter with a winged Cupid or an anonymous "Bellibone," the tag
Perigot uses to designate his rural beauty in "August." In "March" and
"August," Spenser adopts a tone that at once undercuts the seriousness
of the poems and distances us from the protagonists and their problems.

2. For the exegetical tradition, see Saint Ambrose, *Comment. in Cantica Canticorum*,
1853ff.; Paschasius Radbertus, "Expositio in Ps. XLIV," 1010; Hugh of Saint Victor, *In
. . . Ecclesiasten*, Hom. I; Richard of Saint Victor, *Explicatio in Cantica Canticorum; Glossa
Ordinaria*; Saint Bernard, *Sermones in Cantica Canticorum*; Philip of Harvengt, *Cantici Canti-
corum Explicatio*; Thomas of Perseigne, *Comment. in Cantica Canticorum*; Alanus de Insulis,
Expl. in Cantica Canticorum; Martin Luther, *Lectures on the Song of Solomon*. For a study of
medieval interpretations of the Song of Solomon and their relation to poetry, see E. Faye
Wilson (1948). For the more popular tradition, see the preface to the Song of Solomon in
the 1535 edition of the Bible and the 1568 edition, or Bishops' Version. In the sixteenth-
century translation of the Solomonic literature, *Here begynneth the Proverbs of Salomon* (1540),
the Song of Solomon is called *Ballettes*, celebrating the love song of Christ and the Church.
Barclay similarly linked his "ballade" with the "fruitful clauses" of Solomon. See *The Eclogues
of Alexander Barclay* "Eclogue IV," 167. In *The Monument of Matrones*, 8, Thomas Bentley
referred to the Song of Solomon as the "Ballat of ballats." For discussions of Solomonic
poetry, see Campbell, *Divine Poetry and Drama in Sixteenth-Century England*, 57–63; Lewalski
53–69.

The love wound of "March" is not different from Colin's in "Januarye," but Cupid's wounding of Thomalin seems less compelling than Rosalind's wounding of Colin. Both protagonists are plunged into grief, but Colin's is more immediate. Similarly, the Emblemes for these two months, while addressing a similar problem, have different effects. "Anchôra Speme" is linked with Colin's individual experience of grief and dislocation, but the Petrarchan tag of "March," likening love to an unequal mixture of honey and gall, is general and bears no genuine relation to Thomalin himself. By generalizing and formalizing his handling of love, Spenser undercuts its pathos. The contrast between his two treatments of love is most apparent in "August," which juxtaposes Perigot's "bonnibell" with Colin's Rosalind. Although the subject of the two poems in "August" is the same, the concerns of the singing match appear trivial compared with the chaotic grief of Colin's lament. Metrically, Spenser also undercuts any sense of tragedy in "March" and "August." Whereas the sophisticated iambic pentameter of Colin's laments in "Januarye," "June," and "December" and the complicated stanzas and meter of his elegy in "Nouember" reinforce the philosophical tone of these poems, the simple meter, the lack of secondary and tertiary stresses, and the short lines of "March" and "August" prevent us from taking Thomalin's or Perigot's problems very seriously.[3] Spenser's reasons for employing such techniques in "March" and "August" become more clear when we consider them, along with the metrically complicated "Aprill," as an exploration of the force love exerts on human efforts. What he treats dramatically in the Plaintive eclogues he treats abstractly in the Recreative, for love is Accident in the Plaintive eclogues; here, it is Substance.

Spenser's interest in and handling of the subject of love may also be understood as a natural outgrowth of concerns, both national or political, and literary, of the seventies, especially the last few years of the decade. These concerns focused on the Queen, who then had finally to decide whether to marry or remain single. Politically, the decade's preoccupation with national identity and stability, especially in relation to the Protestant cause, gave force to the various and oftentimes, to our eyes at least, extreme reactions to Elizabeth's proposed marriage to the Duc d'Alençon. From the festivities of Kenelworth and Woodstock,

---

3. We can see a similar contrast if we compare Virgil's treatment of love in Eclogue 10 with Bion's Idyll, number 4, from which the story of Cupid in "March" is drawn. Virgil used Gallus to dramatize the pain and the destructiveness of obsessive love; we see in Gallus the effects of what is treated abstractly in Bion's Idyll.

through Sidney's *Lady of May,* to John Stubbes's *Gaping Gulf* and Sidney's *Foster Children of Desire,* the nation and the court debated, to Elizabeth's growing distaste, the possibility of the Queen's marrying and bearing a child. The subject brought in its train a whole range of related subjects—many of them prompted by accounts of Mary Stuart, since 1568 the confined "guest" of her English cousin—such as a sovereign's right to satisfy personal desires or to seek self-fulfillment at the possible expense of a people's security and happiness. The issue of the Queen's marriage bore perhaps its most lasting fruit in the various literary efforts to depict, or chastise, Elizabeth that characterized the last years of the decade. If we can see the beginning of such efforts in the pageants of Woodstock and Kenelworth, we can see the "Aprill" eclogue as a fusion of a number of previously disparate elements into a logical and coherent whole, one that served as the primary source for such later treatments of Elizabeth as Peele's *Arraignment of Paris,* Blenerhasset's *Reuelation of the True Minerva,* and Drayton's *Shepheardes Garland.*

Elizabeth: The Triumph of Chastity

It was on the subject of the Queen's proposed marriage to the Duc d'Anjou, or Alençon, that the various issues and concerns of the seventies converged. The decade began innocuously enough—perhaps even hopefully—with Baif's Academy, chartered in 1570 by Charles IX, auguring a reign of international humanism rather than provincialism and prejudice. But the tensions between Catholic and Protestant and among Protestants began to escalate. The events of 1572 disrupted the conciliatory mood of the sixties, severely straining the international relationships between French and English men of letters.[4] In August of that year, only four months after the signing of the Treaty of Blois, Catherine de Medici and her son Charles IX gave either tacit approval or active support to French Catholics, who joined forces in the Saint

---

4. See van Dorsten, *Poets, Patrons, and Professors*; Yates, *The French Academies of the Sixteenth Century.* For a more intimate sense of the syncretic and pan-European mood of the early period of Elizabeth's reign, see *Letters and Memorials of State . . . written and collected by Sir Henry Sidney, Sir Philip Sidney, Robert, Earl of Leicester, and Viscount Lisle,* ed. Collins, in addition to the letters of Sir Philip Sidney collected in *The Complete Works of Sir Philip Sidney* 3:73–183.

Bartholomew's Day Massacre. That event was witnessed by Sir Philip Sidney, the guest of Sir Francis Walsingham, the ambassador to France. The slaughter not only claimed the lives of such notables of international Protestantism as Peter Ramus, but reawakened in England the active distrust of all Catholic institutions that had characterized the first generation of Elizabeth's political leaders and advisors, the former Marian exiles.

A new generation had begun to dominate Commons in the seventies, a generation of political leaders whose Puritan sympathies were well matched by their political acumen.[5] Well organized, they had learned the lessons of statecraft so thoroughly that they were able to use the existing political system in order to get a majority in Commons. With Walsingham occupying a major part in the government (he was named as one of the two principal secretaries in 1572), a Puritan majority in parliament, and the economic stability that, ironically, so often provides the ideal climate for political restlessness, we can fairly describe England as ready—if not anxious—for change. For many of England's leaders, at least, that change was seen as Puritan or Progressive, a movement to establish England as the New Jerusalem, the very center of European Protestantism. To this new generation, the Saint Bartholomew's Day Massacre inspired an increased interest in the nature of monarchical power and the delicate balance between the divine right of kings and the power, stability, and health of the people, since the events of that day destroyed the mutual faith of prince and subject.[6] In a flood of publications on both sides of the Channel, political leaders questioned the rights and responsibilities of sovereigns. Though many were impatient with Elizabeth's lack of action and eager for her to assume leadership of international Protestantism, Englishmen were nonetheless able to distinguish between the chaos in foreign countries and the peace the Queen had brought to England. Thus in 1575–76 Edward Hake, drawing upon a pastoral language whose roots go deeply into Protestant and classical sources, opposed the peace, fertility, and civilization of England to other countries, which he described in antipastoral language as chaotic and barren.

5. On the early Elizabethan parliaments, see Neale, *Elizabeth 1 and Her Parliaments, 1559–1581.*

6. I am indebted to Robert P. Adams (1977) for a shrewd assessment of this period. For the text Adams discusses, see Junius Brutus (pseud.), *A Defense of Liberty Against Tyrants* (London, 1579; Trans. 1689). See also Charbonnier; Pineaux; M. C. Smith (1969).

England's sense of its blessings notwithstanding, Elizabeth's marriage negotiations with the younger brother of the King of France awakened a number of writers who, publicly and privately, explicitly and implicitly, began to question the relationship between sovereign power and the rights of subjects.[7] If we use 1578 as a point of reference—when Elizabeth reopened, and more seriously this time, marriage negotiations with Alençon—we can detect a difference between remarks about and directed to the Queen before and after that year. For example, there was a genuine difference in tone and focus between the festivities prepared for the Queen during her progresses in the summers of 1575 and 1578. In 1575, Elizabeth made an extensive progress into Northamptonshire, Warwickshire, Staffordshire, Worcestershire, and Oxfordshire. During this royal journey, the magnificent festivities at Kenelworth and Woodstock were arranged by Gascoigne and probably shaped by Leicester, Gascoigne's patron and the close friend of Sir Henry Lee, tenant of Woodstock.[8] The pageants at Kenelworth and Woodstock are important in the history of English literature for a number of reasons; as early attempts to work out a program of praise and entertainment for Elizabeth, their use of Arthurian legend, pastoral apparatus, and classical myth all contributed to the more elaborate and coherent encomia of the nineties.

But in relation to the political atmosphere of 1575, the two pageants can be read as Leicester's praise of the Queen since both extol her beauty, her virtue, her justice, and her bounty, making her a symbol of life, harmony, and rectitude for the pastoral worlds redeemed by her visit. Moreover, both pageants reveal Leicester's continued attempts to suggest the benefits of the Queen's marrying, while the pageant at Kenelworth strongly suggests his own continued suit to his sovereign.[9] The subject of her marriage had been unwelcome to Elizabeth since she acceded to the throne; it is thus probably no coincidence that one of the pageants in the Kenelworth festivities, in which Iris, Juno's messenger, conquered Diana, was canceled. The reason given for the cancellation was bad weather, but Iris's final words, a message from Juno to Elizabeth, may well have prompted an even more stormy response from the Queen:

7. See Adams (1977); W. T. MacCaffrey (1979).
8. See Nichols I:418ff.
9. See also Leicester's rather anxious letters to Burghley, written just before the royal visit, particularly the third letter. In Nichols I:524–26.

That where you now in princely port
A world of wealth at wil,
In weded state, and therewithall
The staffe of your estate;
Yet never wight felt perfect blis,

have past one pleasant day,
you henceforth shall enjoy,
holde up from great annoy;
O Queen, O worthy Queen,
but such as wedded bene.[10]

The bold hints that "wedded state" is more worthy, more potentially bountiful, than the chaste single state acquire the ironic resonance only history can provide, especially in relation to the festivities accompanying the Queen's extensive progresses in the summer of 1578. Early in the season, the Queen had gone to Wanstead, the seat of the Earl of Leicester, where she had been entertained by *The Lady of May,* the work of Sir Philip Sidney. Later in the summer, she traveled through Suffolk and Norfolk, where she was entertained by Thomas Churchyard's elaborate festivities in a six-day visit to Norwich. Since the French Ambassador seems to have accompanied this progress, the weight given to the side of chastity in the debates and dramas was probably strategic.[11] Thus, in a masque prepared for the Privie Chamber on Thursday night, August 21, after the Olympian gods entered to honor the Queen, Mercury spoke, apologizing for those who were absent. Some, he said, such as Ceres, Baccus, and Pomona could not attend because of the yearly labors of harvest. But, "only Himeneus denyeth his good-will, eyther in presence, or in person! Notwithstanding, Diana has so countre-checked him therefore, as he shall ever hereafter be at your commaundement."[12] Later in the evening, Cupid presented Elizabeth with his golden shaft, saying that the arrow's effectiveness lay in Elizabeth's will, not in Cupid's power. The entertainment seems deliberately ambiguous: On the one hand, Diana has checked Hymen, on the other, Elizabeth may string her own bow.

The more public show of Tuesday was less oblique. In it Cupid was despoiled by Chastity, who then presented Cupid's weapons to Elizabeth, "bycause (said Chastitie) that the Queene had chosen the best life, she gave the Queene Cupid's bow, to learn to shoote at whome she pleased, since none coulde wounde hir Highnesse hart, it was meete (said Chastitie) that she should do with Cupid's bow and arrowes what

10. Nichols I:514–15. On Elizabeth's aversion to the subject of marriage, see Bevington 8.

11. For accounts of these festivities, see Nichols II.

12. Nichols II:159.

she pleased."[13] Churchyard underlined the force of his endorsement of Chastity by giving Cupid Riot and Wantonness as companions and by ending the show with an explicit praise of chastity. The first two stanzas of the song tell us much about the popular mood of the summer of 1578:

> Chast life lives long, and lookes on world and wicked ways;
> Chast life for losse of pleasure's short, doth winne immortall
>   prayse;
> Chast life hath merrie moodes, and soundly taketh rest;
> Chast life is pure as babe new borne, that hugges in mother's
>   breast.
>
> Leawd life cuttes off his dayes, and soone runnes out his
>   date,
> Confounds good wits, breeds naughty bloud, and weakens
>   man's estate.
> Leawd life the Lord doth loath, the lawe and land mislikes,
> The wise will shunne, fonde fooles do seek, and God sore
>   plagues and strikes.[14]

The verses praise chastity as a sort of wedded state. First, by opposing the lewd life to the chaste life, the song from the beginning slants the argument in favor of what is not lewd. Second, chastity is praised for its immortality. Chastity thus "lives long," and deserves "immortal praise," a theme developed in the final stanza, "Chast life a pretious pearle, doth shine as bright as sunne; / The fayre houre-glasse of dayes and yeares, that never out will runne." But Leawd life "runnes out his date," engenders chaos, lives alone "In hollow caves" and "walkes with muffled face" (stanza 4). Those very goods that throughout the sixties and early seventies were used as arguments for the Queen's marriage—continuity, stability, fruitfulness, peace—in the late seventies were used to praise the single life.[15]

13. Nichols II:189.
14. Nichols II:197.
15. Throughout the Middle Ages, Chastity was linked with fruitfulness, an association that Spenser himself made in *The Faerie Queene*. These remarks from the late seventies were, however, more pointed. Compare the conference notes from 1570 about the subject of the Queen's marriage. Printed in Collier, *The Egerton Papers*, 50–59. The notes, in the hand of Sir Walter Mildmay, are divided into four headings, "Considerations of hir Mariage," "Discommodities," "Answeres to the Obiections," and "The Commodities that mighte ensue upon the mariage with the Duke of Anjou." As these headings suggest, the tone of the conference was rather mild, and the benefits of the match seemed to outweigh the possible objections. This conference is also printed in *Calender of State Papers*, Domestic Series, XIX:328–32.

Sidney's *Lady of May* is less explicitly opposed to marriage but far more skillful in affirming the idea of order implicitly figured in the chaste life. First, he jockeys Elizabeth into a position as adjudicator. Though the Queen was normally the focus for civic and courtly entertainments, Sidney's use of her seems designed to force her into an especially self-conscious position. Walking in Wanstead gardens, she found herself suddenly in the midst of a literary pastoral, a debate between two suitors, Therion, a forester, and Espilus, a shepherd, for the hand of the May Lady. The Lady herself cannot decide between their suits. As she tells the Queen:

> I like them both, and love neither, *Espilus* is the richer, but *Therion* the livelier: *Therion* doth me many pleasures, as stealing me venison out of these forrests, and many other such like prettie and prettier services, but withall he growes to such rages, that sometimes he strikes me, sometimes he railes at me. This shepheard *Espilus* of a mild disposition, as his fortune hath not bene to do me great service, so hath he never done me any wrong, but feeding his sheepe, sitting under some sweete bush, sometimes they say he records my name in dolefull verses. Now the question I am to aske you faire Ladie, is, whether the many deserts and many faults of *Therion*, or the verie small deserts and no faults of *Espilus* be to be preferred.[16]

The conundrum is at once simple and wickedly complex: Should the Lady choose liveliness, pleasure, and abuse or decide upon mildness, wealth, and stability? Sidney thus presented the Queen—and at a particularly ticklish point in her own life—with a choice between heart and head. A modern judge might choose Therion; Elizabeth knew better and chose Espilus. Sidney said nothing about chastity, nothing against marriage, but instead presented Elizabeth with a situation in which she must play the part of judge: Does she emulate Paris or Astraea? The lesson is nicely hidden in the masque's pastoral hilarity, but it nonetheless informs the various speeches and songs, for, in the end, the masque counsels clear vision, a true sense of human nature, and the willingness to choose tomorrow's stability over today's amusements. The latter must have seemed a particularly hard point, for even today, four hun-

---

16. For *The Lady of May*, see Sidney, *Works* 2:329–38. For another reading of *The Lady of May*, see Orgel (1963). Orgel sees the piece as an examination of pastoral convention or a debate between Action and Contemplation. According to Orgel, Elizabeth picked the wrong suitor.

dred years later, it is clear from contemporary accounts how much fun Elizabeth seemed to have had with the French prince and his agent, Simier.[17] Ultimately, the *Lady of May* argues for self-control, establishing a dialectic as heavily weighted in favor of chastity as Churchyard's later entertainment in August of that same summer.

George Puttenham's *Partheniades*—probably presented to the Queen on New Year's Day, 1579—placed a similar emphasis upon Elizabeth's might and worth, those aspects of her person that allowed her to control rather than be controlled by circumstances. Puttenham drew upon classical myth, the Song of Solomon, English history, and current events in an effort to praise Elizabeth as the "paragon" of her age. Her beauty, wisdom, justice, scholarship, and power all combine to make Elizabeth the prize of Europe, the object of all princes' desires. Early in the poem, Puttenham remarked that the Queen had a number of gifts impervious to time, such as youthful beauty, a noble heart, regal estate, friends, and honor, but that she lacked two joys: "A Cesar to her husband, a Kinge to her soone- / What lackt her highnes then to all erthly blisse?" (ll. 57–59).[18] Later on, however, he was careful to stress that Elizabeth retained the power over her own emotion:

> A constante mynde, a courage chaste and colde,
> Where loue logget not, nor loue hathe any powres;
> Not Venus brandes, nor Cupide can take holde,
> Nor speeche prevayle, teares, plainte purple or golde
>   (ll. 203–6)

As Puttenham continued, comparing Elizabeth to Athena, Juno, and Venus, and to the bride of the Song of Solomon, it must have become abundantly clear that she lacked nothing. Unlike other women, she need not look to Cupid or Hymen to guarantee her immortality since she possessed in herself virtues enabling her to outlive herself and thus to transcend mutability.

The conversation of elaborate compliment and veiled advice engaged in by writers like Churchyard, Sidney, and Puttenham became more explicitly focused upon the issue of marriage after January, 1579, when

---

17. See, for example, Neale, *Queen Elizabeth I*, chapter 15.

18. For a slightly different discussion of Puttenham's politics in relation to "The Partheniades," see Norbrook 78. In chapter 3, "*The Shepheardes Calender*: Prophecy and the Court," Norbrook offers a number of insights into the religious and political atmosphere of the decade, discussing figures like Puttenham and Harvey and the early pageants for the Queen.

Simier, Alençon's agent, arrived in England. In August, the Duke himself paid Elizabeth a visit. From the tone of a document recording a conference on the subject of the Queen's marriage, endorsed in 1579, the subject was clearly one that Elizabeth's subjects saw as touching upon their own rights as Englishmen. The agenda involved four major areas of concern: what must be done to assure Elizabeth of peace and physical safety; what perils might grow out of her marriage; what commodities might come from the marriage; and what perils might ensue from breaking off marriage negotiations. The shortest of the agenda items was the third. Considerations regarding England's autonomy and its status as a Protestant nation seem to have dominated the discussions, in addition to fears that England had already committed itself to the alliance and that breaking off negotiations might bring more perils.[19] What was at stake was England's security, her responsibilities to Protestant countries and factions, and her relations to European, Catholic powers. The document held up Mary Stuart, that other significant female sovereign of the age, to Elizabeth. Needless to say, Mary's example was not one that Elizabeth's commissioners wished to see their own queen follow, for Mary's imprudence had thrown her state into jeopardy. Since Elizabeth was not only England's head but the symbol of its own permanence and glory, it was crucial that she not be threatened or devalued. The latter possibility came to dominate English thinking on the subject of the Queen's marriage, for in John Stubbs's *Gaping Gulf* and in Sir Philip Sidney's letter to the Queen, both written in 1579, the Queen was held up to her self—the woman to the symbol—and warned of the dangers of devaluing a currency she herself had so recently stabilized.[20]

The full title of John Stubbs's publication is *The Discoverie of a Gaping Gulf Whereunto England is Like to be Swallowed By an other French Mariage, if the Lord forbid not the banes, by letting her Maiestie see the sin and punish ment thereof.* As the title suggests, Stubbs donned the mantle of an Old Testament prophet and, like John Knox thundering at Mary Stuart, did not hesitate to point out the dangers to the country should Elizabeth marry the Duc d'Alençon. He justified his argument, first, by affirming his love for queen and country and, second, by identifying the country with the true Church and Elizabeth with both. He then proceeded—with true Protestant zeal—to point out the disastrous con-

19. Collier, *The Egerton Papers*, 78–80. See also Murdin, comp., 319–42.
20. For discussions of this period, see Adams (1977); Judson 58; Greville 63–69; W. T. MacCaffrey, *Queen Elizabeth and the Making of Policy*, 265ff.

sequences of what he called "contrary couplings." He held up the figure of King Solomon for Elizabeth's contemplation, a figure to whom she was frequently and favorably compared as having completed the temple envisioned by her father "David." But, as any Elizabethan child would have known, the figure of Solomon might also afford a less flattering example since in his old age Solomon married foreign women and forsook the worship of the one true God. Stubbs pointed out the weak character of Elizabeth's French suitor, the evil consequences of having Catharine de Medici as a mother-in-law, glanced at the fate of Elizabeth's sister, Mary Tudor, and speculated gloomily on the nature of and English control over any children who might bless this proposed marriage. He then touched upon a particularly significant issue—the concept of the Queen's two bodies. As queen, she was sovereign and immortal, but as wife her mortal body would be subject to her husband. In effect, Stubbs pointed out the genuine impossibility of the Queen drawing a sharp distinction between her two identities, especially considering sixteenth-century views of the nature of marriage. Stubbs ended by raising the spectre of Mary Stuart, whose ties to France were the continual object of English scrutiny. At no point did Stubbs mince words; his eighty-four-page warning can be read, as Elizabeth apparently did, as a barely veiled threat: God will turn from Elizabeth as he did from those Old Testament leaders who turned from him. For Stubbs the visible sign of heavenly disfavor was a country whose citizens' love and obedience were transformed into wrath and disloyalty. He made it clear that only Elizabeth herself could set such a chain of events in motion.

Sir Philip Sidney's Letter to the Queen on the subject of her marriage made many of the same points that Stubbs made in *Gaping Gulf*, but in less space and with far greater shrewdness. The letter was not published, so Sidney could not, like Stubbs, be accused of crimes against the state, but the letter seems nonetheless to have enjoyed wide circulation; certainly it would have been known to Edmund Spenser.[21] Sidney began, as he began *The Lady of May*, by placing Elizabeth in the role of adjudicator, throwing himself not upon her mercy but upon her judgment. After affirming his unfeigned love for his queen and his care for her safety, he stated the thesis of the letter, "Herein I will now but onely declare what be the reasons that make me thinke the mariage of Monsieur unprofitable for you." He organized his argument around

21. For Sidney's letter, see *Works* 3:51–60.

two major considerations. First, he emphasized Elizabeth's real and metaphoric wealth—she lacked nothing that marriage would supply, save, perhaps, children. But the potential gains of bearing a child need not, as Sidney said, depend upon such as Alençon. Second, he assessed the nature of Elizabeth's power by comparing her force to a knot: "Your inward force. . . . doth consist in your subjectes generally unexpert in warlike defence, and as they are divided into two mighty factions & factions bound upon the never ending knott of religion" (52). This metaphor is critical, for Sidney used it to imply that Elizabeth's domestic tranquility was a delicately achieved tension. The presence of Alençon as consort would unravel the knot by giving Protestant impatience a cause and Catholic disaffection a focus. Like Stubbs, Sidney noted that the loss of her people's love would result in the loss of England's peace, the balance Elizabeth had so painstakingly achieved between opposed factions and interest groups. Sidney, too, cast aspersions upon the character of Alençon, accusing him of inconstancy, ambition, and weakness of character. Sidney ended his letter by saying, "doe not raze out the impression you haue made in suche a multitude of heartes" (59), urging Elizabeth to make the true religion her only strength, to realign herself with the cause for which she and England stood.

In radically different ways both Sidney and Stubbs revealed English reactions to Elizabeth's marriage negotiations. Sidney's concern is cast in the clear and elegant prose of an educated man, a courtier, and an astute political observer, while Stubbs's piece falls within the tradition of the Protestant jeremiad. However different in tone, the two works not only evince similar rhetorical structures, but imply that, in agreeing to this French marriage, Elizabeth would be tarnishing her own image by becoming like other women. One of the things at stake in 1579 was the Queen's image or myth, a myth twenty years in the making, whereby Elizabeth, as England's Judith or Deborah, reigned supreme in chastity, the actual token of her devotion to her people.[22] The issue of Elizabeth's virginity as a significant component of the royal image becomes even more obvious if we compare reactions to Elizabeth's proposed marriage to the earlier reactions to the ill-advised marriage of her cousin, Mary Stuart, the figure most often held up as the threat to Elizabeth's sovereignty. As James E. Phillips notes, "following her marriage, at the close of 1565 her [Mary's] beauty and courtly graces (the same qualities that were subjects of all but universal eulogy a few short years before) are

22. W. T. MacCaffrey, *Queen Elizabeth and the Making of Policy*, 265.

seen as the cause of her undoing and of Scotland's."[23] Such works as
Thomas Jeney's "Maister Randolph's Phantasey: a breffe colgulacion
of the procedinges in Scotland from the first of Julie to the Last of
Decembre," which was never printed in the sixteenth century but had
a wide manuscript circulation, suggest just how fragile the image of a
female sovereign was.[24] The poem purported to be an account by
Thomas Randolph, Elizabeth's ambassador in Scotland, of a dream in
which Mary revealed to him the true circumstances of the Darnley
marriage. Both this poem and John Pikeryng's *Horestes*, a play presented
at the English court late in 1567, only a few months after Mary's
enforced abdication, emphasized the disastrous effect on a state of
self-interest in a ruler, particularly of the dangers of giving in to the
temptations of love or *luxuria*.[25] The subject of Mary's political crimes
and fleshly laxitudes was, of course, taboo around Elizabeth, but she
could hardly have been unaware of the fact that her marriage to Alençon
would provide yet another example of the inherent weakness of the
female flesh. Her position as a member of the weaker sex made her all the
more vulnerable to certain types of political observations, particularly
during a period when politics, morality, and theology were so closely
interrelated. As contemporary expressions of concern over her negotia-
tions with Alençon implied, the real issue was self-control, or the
sovereign's just rule not only over the body politic but over her own
mortal body.

Elizabeth's response to such attitudes can be seen in the proclamation
she issued on September 27, 1579. The proclamation was apparently
written by Elizabeth herself and was, as Frederic A. Youngs remarks,
the only time in her reign when she used a royal proclamation "to refute
rather than merely to suppress a dissident religious book."[26] She did
so, I believe, because she saw it as an opportunity to reaffirm certain
aspects of her official personality that were being obscured or ques-
tioned by those who opposed her marriage. The proclamation was to
the point. She began by maintaining her identity as a Christian prince,
chosen by God, a prince whose peaceful realm was a sign of her people's
love and God's favor. These twin benefits she gladly acknowledged.

---

23. Phillips, *Images of a Queen: Mary Stuart in Sixteenth-Century Literature*, 35.

24. This piece is quoted and discussed in Phillips, *Images of a Queen*, 35–36. On the
fashioning of female figures in the Renaissance, see Beilin; King (1985).

25. Phillips, *Images of a Queen*, 46.

26. Youngs, 208. This proclamation is also printed as Appendix I of Stubbs's *Gaping Gulf*,
ed. Berry. All references to the proclamation refer to Berry's edition.

She accused Stubbs of malice, of irritating foreign princes, of alienating the love of her people, and of awakening their fears for the future. In the bulk of the proclamation she defended her care for her country, stressed her awareness of her role as Christian prince, and proclaimed her eagerness to secure for England a stable future in a "peaceable succession, either with her marriage, or without her marriage"[27] She ended by emphasizing her reliance on her people's love, the advice of her councillors, and the will of Parliament, accusing Stubbs of libel.

The argument between Elizabeth and her concerned subjects appears less about her marrying Alençon than about the power of kings and the rights of subjects.[28] It was a subject of vital importance to Elizabeth, whose reaction to Stubbs's publication was extreme. The statute whereby Stubbs lost his right hand for his act was one Elizabethan authorities found among the statutes of Philip and Mary. Lawyers who questioned the legality of using a statute technically void upon Mary's death were imprisoned. Furthermore, Stubbs's punishment was staged as high drama, a drama in which Stubbs, like a good Elizabethan, played the starring role.[29] Later, in the eighties, Elizabeth followed up this show of sovereign might by allowing Whitgift, her new Archbishop of Canterbury, to establish rigorous censorship laws, thereby guaranteeing a sort of domestic tranquility, certainly not an equilibrium of the sort Sidney described in his letter. The issue would, of course, reappear, though not in Elizabeth's lifetime; but the arguments that occupied political thinkers during the last years of the seventies and the first years of the eighties would recur in the reign of Charles and find their final expression in the motion of the headsman who decapitated an English king.[30]

The subject of Elizabeth's courtship with Alençon preoccupied the group around the Earl of Leicester; it is thus a subject that could not but have occupied Spenser at the point when he was completing *The Shepheardes Calender*, a poem designed as a mediation of the political issues and political mood of its time. That the mood was less than euphoric is not surprising considering the domestic and

27. Elizabeth wickedly pointed out (150) that many of the same arguments once used to advance her marriage were now being used to dissuade her from it.
28. Adams (1977), 80.
29. See Adams (1977), 82. See also Camden, 137–38.
30. For a discussion of these arguments, see Harold J. Laski's introduction to Brutus's *A Defense of Liberty Against Tyrants*.

foreign tensions of the decade, along with the fact that England had now enjoyed twenty years of Elizabeth's peace and prosperity. This is not to say the country tired of its queen but that, inevitably, the novelty had dissipated. For example, Arthur Golding's pamphlet on the earthquake of 1580 conveyed the sense that England was past its prime. "For peace, health, and plentie of al things necessarie for the life of man, we have had a golden worlde aboue all the rest of oure neyghbours rounde about us . . . We haue growen in godliness as the moone doth in light when she is past the full."[31] Golding followed up the implicit connection between England's glory and the waning of the moon by pointing out the luxury and ambition of the age and the "want of love in al states one towardes another." His use of the word love is critical; for the Elizabethan age, as for the medieval, love was seen as the glue holding societies together, as Elizabeth's many proclamations and speeches stressing the love (usually maternal) she bore her subjects suggested. Love is the creative force that maintains opposing forces in balance. It is this force whose potential Spenser explores in the Recreative eclogues, supplying his poem and his age with both a lesson and an ideal, Spenser's remedy for the frustrations, prognostications, and hopes of the age. That remedy is a new image of the Queen—not as Deborah or Judith, but as Elisa, whose fruitful virginity manifests itself as pastoral harmony.

2.   Recreate or Re-create

Spenser's strategy in the three eclogues E. K. refers to as Recreative ("which conceiue matter of loue or commendation of special personages") turns on the word *recreative*. His use of *recreative* as a critical or formal term does not exactly constitute a new usage but should nonetheless be seen as an example of Spenser's etymological *legerdemain*. Thus, while the word was used with rather more resonance than today, Spenser employed it in a way that captures both its associations with the light poem and the concept of re-creation, refreshment, or

---

31. Golding, "A Discourse upon the Earthquake that hapned throughe this Realme of England . . . the first of April, 1580," in Golding, 193. In his analysis of the period, Braden (9) also cites this passage.

restoration.[32] In the three Recreative eclogues, each of which considers the nature of love and beauty, Spenser allows the eclogues themselves to suggest the distinction between recreation and re-creation. We are implicitly urged to place the sterile pursuit of the earthly Venus—the subject of the eclogues for March and August—against the promise of the celestial Venus praised in "Aprill," where Spenser offers both the Queen and the country a new and potentially glorious identity.

Whereas "March" and "August" are indebted, if not directly to Theocritan pastoral, certainly to the contemporary idea of Theocritan pastoral, "Aprill" emerges directly from the ideals and rhetoric of Elizabethan protestantism, which cast Elizabeth as the Bride of the Canticle and England as the pastoral paradise made possible by her accession. The distinction helps to explain the radically different quality of the three eclogues. "March" and "August" seem, even on a first reading, inferior, theory-bound, perhaps, certainly artificial in ways that probably do not charm most modern readers. There is also some question as to whether they charmed the poem's original audience, for both poems contain stances and techniques already somewhat shopworn by 1579.[33] On the other hand, "Aprill," though rooted in the conventions of the past, rings with genuine originality. Spenser achieves his effect in the "Aprill" eclogue by fusing a number of interrelated traditions and rhetorical stances. The eclogue reflects the pastoral traditions of classical literature, the language of the popular broadside of Tudor England, and the elaborate modes of address to the Queen of both the courtly and civic pageantry of the decade. It also plays on a series of associations that informed the ideals of English Protestantism in the early period of Elizabeth's reign. Thus, in order to celebrate Elizabeth as a principle of harmony whose virtue manifests itself in national peace and prosperity, speakers frequently addressed Elizabeth as an English Solomon whose virtue and wisdom had created a pastoral paradise.

Efforts to associate Elizabeth and Solomon created an elaborate series of metaphors for both England and Elizabeth. England was frequently compared to the vineyard, or garden, of the Song of Solomon, the

32. Thus in *The Arte of English Poesie*, I, x, Puttenham linked recreation with solace. More important, Jude Smith in his translation of the Song of Solomon, entitled *A misticall devise of the love between Christ and the Church* (London, 1575), drew on the association between the Canticle, the idea of recreation, and the concept of spiritual revival or resurrection: "For Salomon had great delite in the makinge of these, to recreat and reuyue his spirits, and called them by this name, Canticum canticorum" ("To the Reader"). Smith signified his sense of the Canticle as poetry by arranging his translation as verse drama.

33. See Hughes (1923).

most fully realized example of biblical pastoral poetry. Elizabeth herself, prince of this kingdom, was compared not only to Solomon, but to the pure bride of the Song of Solomon. As an Elizabethan expression of pastoral harmony, Spenser's "Aprill" eclogue reflects the metaphors of its time. More striking than the metaphors themselves, however, are the ideals behind the comparisons. By choosing to praise her in a specific way, Spenser implicitly suggests that Elizabeth, and the country's love of her, are remedies for discord. Although he celebrates Elizabeth as both prince and bride, the backdrop to his encomium is the distraught pastoral world of *The Shepheardes Calender*. An exploration of the Solomonic metaphors linked to Elizabeth in the sermons, prayers, speeches, and prefaces of the time reveals the fears and ideals of the period; it also suggests that Spenser's eclogue plays off the ideal of the Protestant bride and prince against those forces opposing the realization of this ideal. As it praises, the eclogue also teaches its readers about the dangers that threaten England's new world.

The tensions and problems of the period perhaps reinforced Protestant England's sense of itself as an elect nation. Much of the national and/or religious rhetoric of the period is a result of what can only be called an "exile mentality." As self-styled martyrs for religion, the Marian exiles left England; both their flight and their years in Geneva, Zurich, Strasbourg, Frankfurt, or Basel inevitably affected their expectations for England on their return.[34] John Bale had written that Geneva was a Paris, a London, and a new Frankfurt, containing and superseding those cities; and the special Genevan sense of history accompanied the English exiles on their return to their own country.[35] John Foxe wrote that November 17, the day of Elizabeth's accession to the throne of England, "brought to the persecuted members of Christ rest from their careful mourning."[36] That the exiles longed to translate the ideals of Geneva into their native tongue is clear from Robert Fills's translation in 1562 of *The Lawes and Statutes of Geneva*. The book, dedicated to "Lord Robert Duddeley," bore the colophon, "Except the Lorde kepe the Citie, the keper watcheth in vayne. Psal. 127." In the Epistle Dedicatory, Fills expressed the hope that in these laws, Englishmen "may beholde as in a glasse, a Christian reformation, and employe them

34. See, for example, Bale, *The Image of Both Churches*. Bale began the Preface by saying, "Into the desert sendeth the Lorde hys church . . ." For studies of, or relating to, the Marian exiles, see Droz, Garrett, Goyau, Martin, Kingdon.

35. See Dufour, 63–95.

36. Foxe, *The Acts and Monuments*, 8:624.

selves to the imitation as farre forthe as they see best for them, as shal be most convenient."

The identification of Elizabeth and the English Church formally began with her coronation procession. In one of the pageants of the procession, Truth gave a book to a child, who then presented it to Elizabeth. The book was, of course, the Bible in English, and Elizabeth symbolically linked herself with the English Church by kissing the book and vowing to cherish it forever. The sign for the final pageant read "Debora the iudge and restorer of the house of Israel," a rubric that likened both Elizabeth and her people to the elect of God. Later, in 1563, John Foxe wrote to Queen Elizabeth after her visit to Cambridge, asserting that she restored "the country in a manner to itself." He admonished her as to her duties to the English Church, urging "that you illustrate and promote the temple of God and the glory of evangelical doctrine."[37] Foxe's sense of mission is much more clearly defined in the Preface to his *Acts and Monuments*. He addressed the Preface to "the True and Faithful Congregation of Christ's Universal Church" and stressed the historical vitality of the "true" Church in spite of centuries of Catholic oppression, making a continual plea for the pervasive antiquity of the *English* true church. Foxe asserted that his history is "a new history for a new land," offering in his work a "new Kalender, filled in with English martyrs."[38] In his account of the Princess Elizabeth, he included John Hales's oration to the Queen, wherein Hale linked Elizabeth's restoration of the Church to Solomon's building of the temple.[39]

The association between Queen Elizabeth and King Solomon is relevant to many features of the Elizabethan myth. Solomon was not only known for his wisdom (I Kings 3), but also for his extraordinary wealth, the national peace and prosperity of his reign, his justice, and his attention to true religion.[40] By comparing Elizabeth to Solomon, the speaker could thus address himself to her wisdom, the prosperity and peace of her kingdom, and her care for the state of the church. The latter provided the translators of the Geneva Bible with the subject of their Epistle to the Queen. There they exhorted Elizabeth to become a second and better Solomon by building the spiritual temple in England.

37. See Strype 1.2:110, 111.
38. Foxe, *The Acts and Monuments* 1:xvii, xxiii, xxix.
39. Foxe, *The Acts and Monuments* 8:678. See also Strype 2.2:597–99. Strype includes two prayers composed by Pilkington, afterwards the Bishop of Durham, in which he alluded to the English restoration of the Temple.
40. For an Elizabethan account of Solomon, see Grafton 41.

The compliment seems to have gained popularity with the visit, from September 1565 to April 1566, of the Swedish princess Cecilia Vasa. Her amazing trip from Sweden to England was compared to Sheba's visit to Solomon. In fact, at Christmastime, the Westminster Boys performed a play, *Sapientia Salomonis, Drama Comico-tragicum*, before Elizabeth and Cecilia.[41] The tag gained currency, and there were variants on it: "as a woman journeyed to see a man, so now men journey to see a woman" was the most common turn of phrase. The association acquired further significance when applied to Elizabeth's role as head of the Church: For many, Elizabeth had continued the work of her "father David" by carrying out his plan for the house of God.[42] The analogy between Elizabeth and Solomon thus reinforced England's sense of election—a people in exile have returned home, have found a ruler, and now worship God in a special sense and a special place.

The references to Elizabeth as an English Solomon reflected the intimate association between national peace and prosperity, true religion, and Elizabeth herself. For example, in his sermon comparing Elizabeth to Solomon, John Prime asserted:

> Israel reaped mutual helpe ech of other, but the sun, the generall light, the streames, the foundation, the root of their blisse and whole repose . . . depended altogether and rested most in having Salomon to be their prince. Under him, their peace and plenty was more than wonderfull . . . (B2v)

Not only was Solomon, and through him Elizabeth, identified with peace and plenty, but Edmund Bunny felt that the story provided Englishmen with a pattern for behavior and thus an assurance of national prosperity:

> . . . any state that followeth the same, may conceive of the undoubted protection of God. Which being alreadie fully perfourmed in Iesus Christ, the more that we find among ourselves

41. Bell, 37.

42. See Foxe, *The Acts and Monuments* 8:678; Prime, "A Sermon Briefly Comparing the Estate of King Solomon and his Subiects togither with the condition of Queene Elizabeth and her people," Preface; Bentley 261–72; Bunny, *Certeine prayers and other godly exercises, for the seventeenth of November*, "Epistle Dedicatory"; "A Meditation wherein the godly English giveth thanks to God for the Queene's Majesties prosperous government hitherto, and prayeth for the continuance therof to God's glory," in *Harleian Miscellany* IX:136–39.

his kingdome aduanced, and the ruines of his Temple repaired:
(which God be thanked, by the gouernement that nowe is estab-
lished, we finde to bee done in comfortable maner) . . . (Diir)

The intimate bond between a prince and his state that is so pervasive
a feature of medieval and renaissance political rhetoric underscored
England's sense of grace in having Elizabeth as ruler.[43] Her state was
an emanation of herself: The harmony, health, and prosperity of En-
gland was considered a manifestation of Elizabeth's wisdom, virtue,
and piety. Like Solomon, Elizabeth was a guarantee of order. In a
sense, then, it was natural that many writers adopted the metaphors of
Solomon in describing their queen and country. The Song of Solomon
was traditionally interpreted as an epithalamium celebrating the mar-
riage between God and the soul and/or church, an interpretation that
remained common during the Renaissance.

For England, Elizabeth was both virgin and queen, mystically linked
with both deity and country, and the metaphors of spiritual marriage
were thus applied to her person and situation. Thomas Bentley in *The
Monument of Matrones* not only referred to Elizabeth as Solomon, but
identified her with the bride of Christ, or the Church. Bentley included
an extraordinary section entitled "The Kings Heast, or Gods familiar
speech to the Queene," in *The Monument*. God's speech to Elizabeth
strongly suggested her role as both queen and church: "And as I was
present of old, when thou returnest out of the Egypt, and bondage of
the spirituall Pharao . . . I will bring to passe that thou shalt enioie a
stable peace, and sure tranquillitie, and that thou shalt see Jerusalem
flourishing so long as thou doest liue."[44] Here Elizabeth was addressed
as the elect nation of Israel, espoused of God, whose prosperity depends
upon God's favor. Bentley used the traditional language of the pastoral
to describe Elizabeth's present state: Peace, tranquility, and fruitfulness
are signs of her election. Bentley's account of the Queen's answer to
God's speech continued the metaphor of espousal or marriage, though
he no longer identified Elizabeth as the bride of Christ but as the
intermediary between her people and God. She rejoices that on Novem-
ber 17 God "begot" her as a daughter and anointed her as His minister

43. See, for example, the long entry under Elizabeth in William Patten's *A Calendar of
Scripture* (London, 1575). Patten linked the name *Elizabeth* with the number seven, or the
"seventh of my God." Langham (64) also referred to Elizabeth as the "seauenth of my God."
Cf. Nohrnberg 52.
44. Bentley, 316. For Elizabeth as Solomon, see 264, 272, 279.

and Queen. Therefore November 17 is the day when an "unmarried" and hence unfruitful country is made potentially fruitful, decked by Elizabeth for marriage: "Go to now therefore I beseech you, let us altogether praise the Lord, as we are bounden; let the whole companie of us virgins plaie upon the Timbrels on euerie side and corner of the citie Zion, one exhorting and answering another by course, and that with new and excellent songs of praise to the glorie of God."[45] Elizabeth then leads the virgins in celebrating the marriage of Jerusalem, or England, to God. Implicit in the analogy is Bentley's belief that the peace and prosperity of Solomon's Jerusalem would reappear in England, whose ruler figured forth the true wisdom of the Old Testament king.

In relation to Elizabeth, the language of ardent Protestantism and the language of the classical pastoral converged; Englishmen spoke of their country as a garden, a garden made possible by the wisdom of their queen. For example, in the Epistle to the Queen which prefaced *The Monument of Matrones*, Bentley thanked God who had loved England in setting Elizabeth on the throne. His description of England resonated with biblical allusions:

> This long and blessed peace wherein we your loiall subiects doo presentlie liue . . . euerie man sitting under his uine and figtree throughout all your dominions . . . that in you our zealous Hezechias, Isaie, we may still remain in happie peace, and haue an hiding place from the wind, and a refuge from storms and tempests, and riuers of waters to quench our thirst, and temperate shadows to shrowd us from parching heate in a drie lande.[46]

The peace (both real and metaphoric) that Elizabeth offered to England received pastoral treatment. She was the Isaie, the Hezechias of her people, providing them with a new covenant and a golden age.

Bentley's pastoral and biblical description of Elizabeth and England is another example of a tradition that began when Elizabeth acceded to the throne. Londoners expressed their hopes for their new queen in her coronation procession. One of the pageants that she saw that day

45. Bentley, 341–43; citation from page 342.
46. The Old Testament lessons for November 17 linked Elizabeth with these figures. Cf. Clay 548–54.

depicted two hills: One hill was rocky and contained a withered tree; the other hill was green and flourishing and contained a fresh, green tree. The first hill was called *Ruinosa Respublica* and the second *Respublica bene instituta*. After seeing this tableau, Elizabeth received the Bible in English, being assured that she could avoid the barrenness of the one hill by taking the book. In 1570, Thomas Drant used a similar image in a sermon at St. Mary's Hospital in London. In the prayer before the sermon, he prayed for the Queen: "That her scepter may growe greene, and florishe like a Palme tree well and moystly planted, and that her seate may never totter, or nodde, but stand stedy as the seate of Solomon and fayre as the sunne" (Biir). The subject of the sermon was the Song of Solomon, and Drant utilized the metaphors of his text in describing his queen. The peace and prosperity of England were linked with the wisdom of its queen, and both queen and state received decidedly pastoral descriptions.

The "garden" of England was not simply a metaphor for prosperity; it was also a way of describing a spiritual state. Thomas Bentley underlined the spiritual dimensions of the "garden" in the Epistle to *The Monument of Matrones*. He addressed the Queen and spoke of the pastoral peace she had made possible, a peace that found popular expression in devotion: "God has been so good that each man goes to temple to return something to God. This work is his gift of loue to God & countrey."[47] Bentley thus suggested that the pastoral paradise made possible by Elizabeth must be protected by the thanksgiving of her subjects. God had graced England, and England must return thanks to God. England's awareness of its duty in regard to Elizabeth was manifest in Accession Day prayers, court pageantry, and the popular celebrations that greeted her progresses.[48] The responsibility of maintaining the garden was seen as a double one. The decade abounded with advice to Elizabeth as protector of the faith, queen, and royal virgin, describing her duties to God and people. But there were as many injunctions to the people to live in peace and thankfulness lest popular

47. Bentley, Epistle. See also the two Accession Day sermons (1557 or 1558) by Edwin Sandys in *Sermons*, 56–81. Sandys's text was drawn from the Song of Solomon. He described England as the vineyard and the enemies (the "little foxes") as those whose spiritual ingratitude threatened the vineyard.

48. See Clay, 463, 544, 556–61; Nichols II:158; "A prayer and also a thanksgiving vnto God . . . in giuing and preserving our Noble Queen Elizabeth to liue and reigne over us . . ." in Collier *Broadside Blackletter Ballads*, 16–20.

restlessness endanger England's golden age.[49] To borrow the metaphors of Elizabethan England, God in his grace had given England a new Solomon whose wisdom was visibly manifest in peace and plenty, who had, in fact, made the land fruitful. Solomon's own pastoral language described both queen and country: As a woman and a virgin, she resided in the garden as the daughter of God, or bride; as a queen she fructified the land, creating a garden that became an emanation of her spiritual properties. The language of what was considered a biblical epithalamium was a fit vehicle for the ideals of English Protestantism, especially since the ideals of the biblical poem were considered spiritual. The garden was a metaphor for spiritual harmony, and England's outward peace and prosperity were therefore visible signs of an invisible peace.

In his "Aprill" eclogue, Spenser used the metaphor of the garden to describe the spiritual harmony contained in and emanating from Elizabeth. Within the context of his poem she is both pastoral Elisa and royal Elizabeth. By hinting at her dual role as both Solomonic bride and maker of the garden, he at once compliments his queen and points out the duties of her subjects who dwell in the garden she has made. In Colin's lay, Spenser adumbrates the ideals of the Golden Age by praising "fayre Elisa, Queene of shepheardes all" in a manner that suggests her identification as bride or daughter of God. He thus reinforces the theme of the golden age that undergirds the lay by linking Elisa with the pastoral harmony of true marriage, an ideal most notably found in the Song of Solomon. In fact, the lay celebrates a "decking of the bride" preliminary to marriage; however, the harmony of the marriage is implicit and, in a sense, unfulfilled in either the eclogue or the poem as a whole. The lay is a statement of an ideal that is only potential, even within the closed world of the "Aprill" eclogue.

After an invocation, Colin praises Elisa's real and metaphoric purity. This second stanza is important because it establishes certain things about his poetic subject and prescribes the way in which Spenser wishes us to consider the queen:

> Of fayre *Elisa* be your siluer song,
>   that blessed wight:
> The flowre of Virgins, may shee florish long,
>   In princely plight.
> For shee is *Syrinx* daughter without spotte,

49. See John Foxe's prayer, recorded by Strype, Appendix II, 638–39; Bat[e]man, *The New Arival of the three Graces into Anglia*, "To the Reader"; "A Thanksgiving and prayer for the preservation of the Queen and the Realm," in Clay, 544–45.

Which *Pan* the shepheards God of her begot:
    So sprong her grace
    Of heauenly race,
No mortall blemishe may her blotte.
                (ll. 46–54)

The first reference is relatively uncomplex—she is the "flowre of Virgins." In explaining what he means by the term, however, Spenser adds that she is "*Syrinx* daughter without spotte." The phrase "without spotte" is one with very definite associations for a sixteenth-century audience, an exact translation of the Latin phrase *sine macula*, used in Song of Solomon 4:7 (Cf. Geneva Bible, Psalm 14, Revelations 19:5) to describe the bride of that poem. That Spenser intends the phrase to trigger those associations is clear from the last line of the stanza, where Colin insists that she has no "mortall blemishe," thus completing the tag "without spot or blemish."[50] What appears a simple description of purity is charged with associations linking Elisa to the pure bride of the Song of Solomon.

Spenser underlines his point by saying that she is "begotten" upon Syrinx by Pan, a statement that E. K. feels supports Elisa's heavenly origins. E. K.'s gloss, however, contains more than simple classical information. He first tells the story of Pan and Syrinx in a way that suggests Elisa's relation to the harmony of music. Syrinx was virtuously changed to a reed long before Pan caught her. The only possible issue from their union is music.[51] E. K. continues his discussion by saying that Pan not only designates Henry VIII, but "kings and mighty Potentates: And in some place Christ himselfe, who is the verye Pan and god of Shepheardes." ("Aprill," Glosse, l. 50) Although the information is relevant to the entire *Shepheardes Calender*, it appears misleading, perhaps blasphemous, in relation to Elisa's parentage. Within the context of the Song of Solomon and the pastoral metaphors of the seventies, however, it becomes apparent that Spenser is addressing Elizabeth as bride and daughter of God. The way that he describes her virginity and her origins links her with the allegorical bride of Solomon's song.

The next five stanzas expand on Elisa's beauty, majesty, and virtue as principles of harmony. Spenser places her within the pastoral world as its crowning jewel, describing her effect on mortal eyes. The description becomes more cosmic when Colin (ll. 73–81) asserts that Phoebus

---

50. For the theological implications of this phrase, see Peter Lombard, *PL* 191:168.
51. Cf. Cullen, 114.

himself is amazed by Elisa's glory: "He blusht to see another Sunne belowe . . ." (l. 77). In majesty, Elisa confounds the sun, in beauty, the moon (l. 84). Both Pan and Syrinx may rejoice that they have been graced in their child. If Spenser also had in mind the conventional Renaissance interpretation of Pan as the universal efficacy of nature, his description of Elisa becomes even more allusive.[52] Elisa's association with the bride, or daughter of God, inevitably links her with grace. As Pan's daughter and "the flowre of Virgins," she embodies the evolution from nature to grace, and is, metaphorically, the fair flower of nature's potential creativity, music, or grace. This suggestion perhaps illuminates the realm of nature within *The Shepheardes Calender*. As virgin and bride, Elizabeth harmonizes the realm of nature with that of grace.

In "Aprill" Spenser establishes Elisa's nonmutable qualities in the bridal gifts she receives as Colin describes a cosmic "decking of the bride" (l. 100). Calliope and the Muses bring "Bay braunches" (l. 104), the graces add her to their number, and Chloris and the ladies of the lake present her with an olive coronal. Their gifts are outward, or metaphoric, signs of her inward properties. E. K. thus specifies that "Bay branches be the signe of honor and victory" ("Aprill," Glosse, l. 104); that the Graces denote "al bountie and comelines" ("Aprill," Glosse, l. 109); and that olives, first planted by Athena, are signs of "Peace and quietnesse . . . a nurse of learning, and such peaceable studies" ("Aprill," Glosse, l. 124). In this manner, Elisa receives signs of herself—honor, beauty, and peace, or power, beauty, and wisdom.[53] Decked with these tokens, she stands ready to receive the accolades of shepherds and shepherdesses.

Colin then turns to Elisa's human attendants, urging them to pattern themselves on her example. Her attendants must all be virgins, and their chastity must be signified by an outwardly modest appearance. The shepherdesses then deck Elisa with flowers, many of them iconographically associated with Elizabeth,[54] and the song ends with Colin singing, "Now ryse vp *Elisa*, decked as thou art, / in royall aray . . ." (ll. 145–46). The Elisa of the end of Colin's song is a figure who now

52. For interpretations of Pan, see *Ovid's Metamorphosis, Englished, Mythologized, and Represented in Figures*, 658; Abraham Fraunce, *The Countesse of Pembrokes Yuychurch*, 11; Estienne, 333.

53. Cain (23) has suggested that by linking Elisa with the "flowre Delice," the "chivisaunce," and the pansy, Spenser conceals a reference to the *triplex vita*. Such a reference is more explicit in Elisa's association with the bay, the olive, and the beauty of the Graces.

54. For a discussion of flowers iconographically associated with Elizabeth, see Strong 50, 68–71.

wears outward signs of inward virtues. Colin's tribute to her poetically captures the pastoral ideals that play so great a part in the Solomonic language of the period—peace, plenty, and beauty all bear witness to the wonder of her reign.[55]

The pastoral paradise depicted in the woodcut to "Aprill" differs from that sketched in Colin's lay. In fact, the scene the woodcut depicts is at sharp variance with either the eclogue or Colin's song. Whereas Colin sings pastoral Elisa sitting upon "the grassie greene" and crowned with flowers, the woodcut contains a regal figure carrying orb and sceptre—signs of princely identity. Colin describes the Muses as playing violins (l. 104), but in the woodcut we can clearly see a harp, a cello, a lute, and a flute. The poem mentions the Graces dancing and singing, but they do not appear in the woodcut. Finally, Thenot sets the scene for Colin's song by asking Hobbinoll to sing it "The whiles our flockes doe graze about in sight, / And we close shrowded in thys shade alone" ("Aprill," ll. 31–32). Though the woodcut shows sheep, the scene Thenot describes does not appear.

Although the woodcut to "Aprill" appears unrelated to the eclogue, it establishes Elizabeth as the focal point of the pastoral world. In the woodcut she is queen rather than bride, and the harmonies of the woodcut emanate from her figure much as the harmony of Israel under Solomon was felt to emanate from his person. The spatial composition of the woodcut underlines the harmony proceeding from the Queen. She stands in the exact center of the picture. To her left are six muses and behind them the sun. To her right are three Muses and Chloris, who carries olive branches. Beyond these four figures is a group of three, presumably Thenot and Hobbinoll, carrying staves that point downward like the sides of an equilateral triangle. At the apex is a third figure, Colin, who pipes as he faces the queen. Each figure in the woodcut turns the eye toward its center, the Queen. Thus the woodcut provides us with a visual emblem of the hierarchy and harmony proceeding from Elizabeth. The scene is pastoral, but far more formal than the eclogue suggests. Elizabeth's princely figure is the key to this picture—

---

55. That Spenser is praising Elizabeth as a bride is borne out by comparing Colin's laye to the first part of *The Epithalamion*, which not only follows a similar progression but resonates with the language of the Song of Solomon. *The Epithalamion* celebrates an actual marriage as a manifestation of cosmic harmony; the "Aprill" eclogue stops short of marriage, but, in presenting Elisa as bride, as a manifestation of natural and cosmic harmony, Spenser establishes an ideal of fruitful love. To this end, the emblems for "Aprill" link Elisa with Venus, as Wind (*Pagan Mysteries in the Renaissance*, 77–78) has pointed out.

the peace and plenty of the golden age flow from her, and the landscape
is an emanation of her majesty.

The harmony in the woodcut and the lay contrast with the lack of
harmony in the "landscape" of the eclogue as a whole, and Colin's song
comprises the major portion of an eclogue that sketches a less-than-
harmonious pastoral world. Thenot opens "Aprill" by asking Hobbinoll
if a wolf has eaten his lambs, if his bagpipe has broken, or if his girl has
left him. He finally guesses that Hobbinoll is merely in harmony with
the year, and the tears that stream down his cheeks reflect the showers
of April. Hobbinoll's reply alerts us to his mental state:

> Nor thys, nor that, so muche doeth make me mourne,
> But for the ladde, whome long I lovd so deare,
> Nowe loues a lasse, that all his loue doth scorne:
> He plonged in payne, his tressed locks dooth teare.
>
> Shepheards delights he dooth them all forsweare,
> Hys pleasaunt Pipe, whych made vs meriment,
> He wylfully hath broke, and doth forbeare
> His wonted songs, wherein he all outwent.
>   ("Aprill," ll. 9–16)

Colin's love of Rosalind has broken the bond of friendship, made
Hobbinoll miserable, and halted Colin's own poetry. Once Hobbinoll
has sung Colin's song, and we return to the actual pastoral world,
Thenot underlines the present state of affairs by commenting:

> And was thilk same song of *Colins* owne making?
> Ah foolish boy, that is with loue yblent:
> Great pittie is, he be in such taking,
> For naught caren, that bene so lewdly bent.
>   ("Aprill," ll. 154–57)

Thus love for Rosalind and praise for Elisa appear mutually exclusive.
The one destroys verse, the other inspires it: The one is the work of
Cupid "with a deadly darte," the other brings recognition of the divine
Venus.

The issue of thankfulness is central to both the ideal pastoral paradise
of Elizabethan England and to Spenser's vision of it in the "Aprill"
eclogue. In his translation (1578) of Seneca's *De Beneficiis*, Arthur

Golding asserted that the work is directed against the vice of unthankfulness. In fact, Golding's title points out what he considered the moral message of the work, *The Woorke of the excellent Philosopher Lucius Annaeus Seneca Concerning Benefyting, that is too say the dooing, recyuing, and requyting of good Turnes*. *De Beneficiis* is, of course, the *locus classicus* for the Renaissance treatment of the Graces, who figured, as Seneca said, the gracious triadic motion of true thankfulness. The Graces, or *Charites*, were thus a metaphor for ideal social and spiritual relationships and were inescapably tied to man's existence as a social being. E. K.'s discussion of the Graces underlines their relevance to human relations:

> . . . they make three, to wete, that men first ought to be gracious and bountiful to other freely, then to receiue benefits at other mens hands curteously, and thirdly to requite them thankfully: which are three sundry Actions in liberalitye. ("Aprill," Glosse, l. 109)

The motion of giving, receiving, and gracious requiting is the triadic progression that ought to characterize man's relation to his fellows and to his God.[56] Bentley's assertion that in Elizabeth's England men return thanks to God hinted at a similar progression of thankfulness. The devotion men return to God completes the pattern initiated by God in giving England such a queen. In "Aprill" Spenser likewise intimates a triad of thankfulness in his presentation of Colin's lay. Colin made the song, and Hobbinoll will sing it; the song itself magnifies neither Colin nor Hobbinoll, but Elizabeth. In effect, the "motion" of the poetry echoes that of the graces: Colin "gives" the song to Elizabeth; she receives, and gives back again, the gracious harmony of her rule and love.[57]

The pattern is both redemptive and fruitful, and it is significant that only a hint of the pattern appears in "Aprill." Colin no longer composes lays to Elisa, and the gracious pattern of friendship between Hobbinoll and Colin is broken. Spenser introduces his pastoral world in "Januarye" by having Colin describe what can only be a broken triad of giving.

56. See Wind's discussion of the Graces in *Pagan Mysteries of the Renaissance*, 36–80.

57. For a similar "motion" of thankfulness, also associated with the Queen and a poet praising her, see Eglog 111 in Drayton's *Idea, The Shepheards Garland*. After Rowland's praise of Beta, Perken thanks him for the *Roundelay* and blesses Beta. Rowland "requites" Perkins's thanks by promising Beta his first lamb, or his "first-fruit." The Eglog ends with harmony between the two shepherds, united by their mutual love of Beta, or Elizabeth.

Hobbinoll loves Colin and gives him gifts; "Colin them gives to *Rosa-lind* againe" ("Januarye," l. 60), who scorns all—gifts, poetry, and love. The harmonious motion of the *Charites* is one of interdependent love, and "Januarye" notifies us that the pastoral world of *The Shepheardes Calender* is fragmented. With the "Aprill" eclogue Spenser introduces the remedy for his fragmented world in the figure of Elisa/Elizabeth, bride and queen. The fruitful love she both stands for and offers would restore the world to itself again. That Colin's song, couched in a frame of private revelation, remains only an ideal, an ideal not even Colin can use, underlines Spenser's didactic purpose. Elizabeth and her harmony are not less "real" for Colin's silence and exile, but they are less actual. Colin, or any citizen, can break the triadic motion of true liberality by refusing to accept the harmony of Elizabeth and thereby not return again.

The "Aprill" eclogue portrays a world of apparent paradox and irreso-lution. Both the lay and the woodcut to "Aprill" describe particular ideals and praise Elizabeth in specific ways as both bride and prince from whose beauty, virtue, and rule proceeds the harmony of an ideal-ized pastoral world. Spenser thereby exploits the celebration of Eliza-beth as the glorious bride of the Song of Solomon and as an English Solomon who decked the bride, England, and turned a barren land into the fruitful garden. The "actual" world of both the "Aprill" eclogue and *The Shepheardes Calender* contains discord, misdirected love, self-interest, and death, all forces that threaten the Golden Age. Although the actual and metaphoric figure of Elizabeth is the remedy for this world of silent poetry, broken friendships, foolish lovers, and corrupt clergy, the remedy is only effective if the inhabitants of that world choose to use it. The lesson does more than glance at Englishmen, for Elizabeth herself must be alive to her value as a symbol of England's peace. By casting Elisa as the bride of the Canticle and using the epithalamium as the underlying structure for Colin's lay, Spenser im-plicitly addressed the series of concerns directly relevant to the queen and the country's image of itself and its sovereign that Churchyard, Sidney, and Stubbs also addressed. By using the eclogue to praise Elizabeth as a bride, Spenser offered his queen an image of herself as the chaste or celestial Venus, whose virgin state engendered peace and plenty. In so doing, he used his praise of his queen as the veil through which he advised her, suggesting that her plenty lacked nothing, that she needed neither husband nor child to assure her own immortality or her country's stability. In its image of nascent fruitfulness, the marriage song of "Aprill" contrasts sharply with the potential for anguish and sterility outlined in the amoeban dialogues of "March" and "August."

"March" and "August" dramatize the deadly effect Cupid and Venus can have on human affairs. In "March" Willye and Thomalin discuss love and springtime, with Thomalin confessing his own heavy spirits, "For sithens is but the third morowe, / That I chaunst to fall a sleepe with sorowe, / And waked againe with griefe" ("March," ll. 46–48). Thomalin testifies, not to an annual re-creation of spirit, but to leaden spirits, to problems with his flock, and, finally, to an unlucky encounter with the winged love God. Out hunting one holiday, Thomalin finds a creature in a bush, "a naked swayne, / With spotted winges like Peacocks trayne" ("March," l. 79–80). Thomalin pursues the creature, but it draws its own bow, "And hit me running in the heele" ("March," l. 97). Willye tells Thomalin the identity of his antagonist, Cupid, thereby providing Thomalin with a name for the disease that now affects him. The eclogue is fittingly placed early in the calendrical sequence, for it chronicles in mythic terms the passage from youth to adolescence, when as yet unspecified desire inevitably takes the form of sexual frustration, frustration that changes boyhood's easy days to the relatively care-filled days and nights of pubescent anguish.[58] As E. K. is at great pains to point out, "by wounding in the hele, is meant lustfull loue." Such wounds inspire thoughts of recreation, but, as "August" makes clear, the object of our desires inevitably determines their ends.

If "March" raises the question of desire, "August" provides its target—beauty. The eclogue opens with a dialogue between Perigot and Willye concerning Perigot's unhappy state. Perigot describes himself in language that recalls Colin's "Januarye" complaint: "Love hath misled both my younglings, and mee: / I pyne for payne, and they my payne to see." ("August," ll. 17–18; cf. "January," l. 48). As a remedy, Willye suggests a singing match, as prescribed a feature of the classical pastoral as the drinking bowl he offers as his half of the pledges. The description of the scene carved on his mazer is at once conventional and unusual, for, like the entire *Calender*, this miniature pastoral relief evokes a number of classical and contemporary scenes while copying none:[59]

---

58. Leo Spitzer (1950) suggested that "March" chronicles a sexual awakening.

59. Hughes (1923) discusses the motif of the glyptic ornament as it was used by poets of the Pléiade. See also Tuve (1937).

Then loe *Perigot* the Pledge, which I plight:
A mazer ywrought of the Maple warre:
Wherein is enchased many a fayre sight
Of Beres and Tygres, that maken fiers warre:
And ouer them spred a goodly wild vine,
Entrailed with a wanton Yuie twine.

Thereby is a Lambe in the Wolues iawes:
But see, how fast renneth the shepheard swayne,
To saue the innocent from the beastes pawes:
And here with his shepehooke hath him slayne.
Tell me, such a cup hast thou euer sene?
Well mought it beseme any haruest Queene.
                              ("August," ll. 25–36)

The scene is a sort of microcosm within a microcosm, a pastoral insert wherein we see line drawings of scenes fleshed out in the *Calender*. Like the world of *The Shepheardes Calender*, the world the mazer depicts is like the natural, and inevitably fallen, world. The bears and tigers and the lamb in the wolf's jaws mark it as postlapsarian, as does the commingling of the natural wild vine "entrailed" with a *wanton* "Yuie twine." The lines suggest the realities of life in the Iron Age. Not only do obvious dangers abound, but the entrailed vines—one natural and wild, one wanton and presumably unnatural or fallen—depict the peculiar mixture of good and evil that the world presents to man. The very adjectives "natural" and "wanton" imply the difficulties in identifying, let alone disentangling, good and evil. The scene depicted on the mazer is, however, less pessimistic or even realistic than hopeful, for our sense of it changes with the catalytic "but." The conjunction arrests what might easily become a catalogue of decay, turning our attention to the shepherd, whose vigilance and care saves the innocent lamb. Willye's final comment about the mazer, that it might "beseme" any "haruest Queen," evokes the "maiden Queene," whom Colin decks with gifts of nature and grace in his "Aprill" lay. The mazer, fit as England itself for a harvest queen, serves to remind us of that balance between pastoral ease and pastoral responsibility that the *Calender* is designed to demonstrate. Like the world of the *Calender*, for which it is a kind of mirror, the scene on the mazer implies that pastoral peace can be maintained only by pastoral vigilance.

The roundelay between Willye and Perigot, which comprises the eclogue's third element, seems hardly worth either the mazer or the spotted lamb Perigot offers as his pledge. Led by the suffering Perigot, it recounts a vision that, with remarkable fidelity to its original, is an inverted reflection of the picture Colin paints of Elisa in "Aprill." In fact, the roundelay makes doggerel of the lay. Instead of the complicated stanzas of "Aprill," Perigot uses a singsong rhythm and simple rhymes to describe the object of his frustration, a lass in pastoral dress, crowned with a chaplet of violets, a lass whose eyes shine into his heart with the force of Phoebus, a thunderclap, or Cynthia's rays. Her glance is Cupid's arrow, moving through his eyes to his heart. Like all heirs of Amant in the *Romance of the Rose*, Perigot cannot remove the arrow's head from his heart, where it now festers, "Ne can I find salue for my sore" ("August," l. 103).[60] Willye's undersong, in echoing Perigot's lines, has the effect of undercutting our appraisal of Perigot's wounds, for lines like "hey ho gracelesse griefe" are hardly designed to make us take grief seriously.

Finally, Cuddie, who "judges" the match and whom Willye suspiciously compares to that other infamous arbitrator, Paris, ends the eclogue by singing Colin's mournful sestina, the poetic echo of Colin's unrequited love for Rosalind. The sestina not only echoes Colin's grief but calls upon nature to echo the plight captured by the song:

> Thou pleasaunt spring hast luld me oft a sleepe,
> Whose streames my tricklinge teares did ofte augment.
> Resort of people doth my greefs augment,
> The walled townes do worke my greater woe;
> The forest wide is fitter to resound
> The hollow Echo of my carefull cryes. . . .
> ("August," ll. 155–60)

Like a true Narcissus, Colin exists in a vast echo chamber, where nature and art reflect his own futile love. In fact, the sestina is a distorted echo of his lay to Elisa. That lay, tuned to the "Waters fall" ("Aprill," l. 36), celebrates a potentially fruitful love, describing her outward beauty as a reflection of inward virtue and her virtue as a reflection of heavenly verities. The figure he bids rise ("Ryse vp Elisa, decked as thou art,"

---

60. Thus Amant describes the first of Love's five arrows, "But the point that pierced me drew no blood . . . the barbed point called Beauty was so fixed inside my heart that it could not be withdrawn. It remains within; I still feel it, and yet no blood has ever come from there" (1715–20).

["Aprill," l. 145]) is a symbol for true beauty, while the poem Colin sings is an echo or reflection of truly regenerative life. When echoing Elisa, herself a kind of echo, Colin's song is genuinely recreative; when echoing himself, his song fittingly doubles back on itself, augmenting the sterile world of his own grief and frustration.

Taken together, the three Recreative eclogues are at once recreative and re-creative, suggesting the potential gains and losses that accompany desire. Theologians and philosophers agreed: Love is born of lack. Plato described love as the child of poverty, while Bishop Jewell remarked that "no man loveth a thing before he felt himself stand in need of it."[61] The three Recreative eclogues explore the nature of love: "March" chronicles the stirrings of that sense of lack; "Aprill" and "August" provide us with two opposing images of its operation. "Aprill" describes the celestial Venus, whose power manifests itself in pastoral harmony and well-being, while "August" describes the earthly Venus—any lass, a bonnibell or a Rosalind—whose power drives through the eye to the heart, fracturing all peace. Colin's plight suggests that he chooses to erect one image rather than the other in his heart, thereby turning himself into the shrine of his own frustration. The two eclogues are even more closely tied, for each depicts a fallen pastoral world, one where friendships and loves are broken, a realm sorely in need of the care and vigilance hinted at in the scene on the mazer.

"Aprill" promises fruit, but we must look to Colin's other major poem in the *Calender*, his elegy for Dido in "Nouember," for the fulfillment of "Aprill's" hints of re-creation. Not only must this elegy be seen in relation to Colin's complaint in "December," but "Nouember" should also be seen in relation to "Aprill" as directed to Queen and country, to the myth of Elizabeth and England. Despite the fact that the Dido of the elegy cannot be absolutely identified with Elizabeth, it seems likely that Spenser intended the name to evoke, at the very least, the *idea* of the Queen. E. K. implies such an association in the Argument for the eclogue, "In this xi. AEglogue he bewayleth the death of some mayden of great bloud, whom he calleth Dido. The personage is secrete, and to me altogether vnknowne, albe of him selfe I often required the same. This AEglogue is made in imitation of Marot his song, which he made vpon the death of Loys the frenche Queene." The phrase "mayden of great bloud" and the allusion to Marot's elegy

---

61. Jewell II:1018. Jewell's sermon was on Matthew 9:37–38. He first discussed Plato, then went on to discuss Saint Augustine, who was contemptuous of scripture before he felt his own lack.

obviously associate Dido with royalty.[62] Moreover, by placing the elegy in November, the month of Accession Day festivities, Spenser more closely links the poem to his country's virgin queen. If Spenser meant his very use of the name Dido to evoke Carthage's queen, the reference could not have been more pointed.[63] Dido is, as Virgil describes her, the symbol, the keystone, of civic prosperity and peace and the symbol of civic decay. In relation to the *Aeneid*, already alluded to in the emblem for "Aprill," Dido's dalliance with Aeneas is reprehensible because she begins to ignore her responsibilities to her people, her very role as queen. The private woman comes to overshadow the public figure as the queen's two bodies lose their single focus. Spenser's real intent, however, in naming the object of the "Nouember" elegy after the queen of Carthage is probably forever and intentionally hidden. No Elizabethan judge could charge him with Stubbs's crime of ingratitude or treason, for, as usual, E. K. has the last word, "out of dout I am, that it is not Rosalind" ("Nouember," glosse, l. 38).·

While it may seem odd to eulogize Elizabeth in 1579, when she was only forty-six, the subject of the elegy is less her death than her immortality, the "fruit" of her virtuous earthly existence. Where "Aprill" describes Elisa as a bride, "Nouember" describes Dido as having engendered not literal children, but figurative, and more lasting, offspring. Here Spenser seems to reflect and exploit the issues of the day, for the two subjects most closely linked to the subject of the Queen's marriage were her future children and her death. Both issues were intimately associated with the succession question: The possibility of Elizabeth dying in childbirth was as seriously considered as the consequences of her living to a ripe old age, still a virgin queen. As Sidney's letter, Stubbs's *Gaping Gulf*, and records of high-level discussions on Elizabeth's marriage articles reveal, the consequences of bearing children were not left to chance; sex, religion, and education were crucial factors for children in line for the thrones of England and France. Spenser's elegy for Dido, taken together with the lay to Elisa, implicitly suggests a solution for these complexly interrelated problems, anticipating for Dido (and inevitably for England) the same sort of futurity he would later foresee for himself and his own bride in the final complete stanza of "The Epithalamion." As the stanza suggests, marriage is one means of cheating time since it is an institution that enables man to transcend

62. For a discussion of Spenser's exploitation of Marot in this eclogue, see Patterson, *Pastoral and Ideology*, 117–21.
63. See also McLane, chapter 4.

his own mortality. The most obvious means is children, one of the "ends" of marriage. The two other means of evading time are also proclaimed by Spenser in his role as Orphic bridegroom—the very poetry that confers brief immortality upon his bride further celebrates the reality of a new realm, a greater nature, of life in another form. Colin's elegy for Dido similarly proclaims her continued existence. First, the elegy begins by "unmaking" the "Aprill" lay, by reversing the process of decking Elisa with triumphal symbols.[64] The mythic creatures of "Aprill" exchange their symbols of life for those of death; the landscape becomes forbidding; and the shepherds no longer sing or care for their sheep now that Dido, whom Colin describes as a gift-giver, as the source of light, beauty, praise, and prosperity, is dead. However, the very fact that death exists in nature, that death has claimed Dido, leads Colin to consider those aspects of Dido that are deathless. Finally, Colin is able to proclaim Dido as living on and reigning in another realm, a pastoral world where "Fayre fieldes and pleasaunt layes there bene, / The fieldes ay fresh, the grasse ay greene" ("Nouember," ll. 188–89). The twice repeated "ay" and the stresses of the line suggest that the pastoral world Colin and his fellows inhabit is but an inverse reflection of a more perfect world. As he does in the "Aprill" lay, where he affirms his own special vision by using verbs and nouns denoting sight, Colin in the "Nouember" elegy bears witness to regenerative principles by exclaiming:

> I see thee blessed soule, I see,
> Walke in Elisian fieldes so free.
>   O happy herse,
> Might I once come to thee (O that I might)
>   O ioyfull verse.
>   ("Nouember," ll. 178–82)

Colin here sees far indeed, his gaze, like that of the bridegroom in "The Epithalamion," piercing beyond the veil of flesh thrown over human efforts. For shepheards and poets, Dido can lead the way to reclaimed worlds, can help us traverse the old way station, a Carthage destroyed by abrogated responsibility, and lead us on to a new kingdom whose plenty is our lack.

---

64. Hoffman 42–53.

Dido is gone afore (whose turne shall be the next?)
There liues shee with the blessed Gods in blisse,
There drincks she *Nectar* with *Ambrosia* mixt,
And ioyes enioyes, that mortall men doe misse.
The honor now of highest gods she is,
    That whilome was poore shepheards pryde,
    While here on earth she did abyde.
      O happy herse,
Cease now my song, my woe now wasted is.
      O ioyfull verse.
                ("Nouember," ll. 193–202)

Like poetry, Dido's hearse has assumed its proper function; both now serve as vehicles—as means of transport—between sublunary and celestial worlds.

Conclusion: Sundry Loves

All three Recreative eclogues concern the "matter of Venus." Each thus deals with the human desire for unity, pleasure, and futurity, which is love, born out of our discord, dissatisfaction, and mortality, that is, born out of our lack. As the poems imply, the quality and nature of love's object determines the characters of lovers. In the Recreative eclogues, Spenser depicts the two faces of Venus, one the bountiful manifestation of the celestial goddess, the subject of Botticelli's *Primovera*, the source of earth's chain of harmonies. As befits the celestial Venus, Colin's verse in "Aprill" is dignified, metrically refined, and syntactically elaborate. When she covers her immortal limbs with flesh, however, she is too often the source of earth's dissonance, grief, frustration, alienation, and war. Spenser's portrait of this Venus suits her manners since, in his efforts to adapt the themes and forms of what he conceived as Greek pastoral verse, he conveys the fundamental absurdity of Venus's game, a game that in *The Shepheardes Calender* as in Theocritus, Virgil, and Ovid, has little place for human dignity. Comic as that game may appear, it can entail serious penalties, as Colin's song in "August" and his entire legend suggest. What Colin forfeits to himself, to his own fixation, is his talent, or himself.

If love can produce discord in individuals—can wound a Thomalin in the heel, a Perigot in the eye, and a Colin in the heart, causing their friendships and flocks to suffer and their poetry to turn to doggerel or silence—what are the consequences for a country when Venus intervenes? This is a problem, of course, that Virgil brilliantly explored through his account of Dido in the *Aeneid*, the same problem that informed his *Bucolics*. What Brooks Otis calls *amor indignus*, "love which is essentially destructive and irrational and is implicitly inconsistent with (if not hostile to) a strong Roman-patriotic orientation,"[65] is the manifestation or sign of Venus's fire brand, of her intervention in human affairs. It may be one thing for a Mopsas or a Gallus, a Perigot or even a Colin to pursue limited goods. It is quite another for an Aeneas, a Dido, or an Elizabeth since sovereigns do not have the luxury of indulging only the mortal body but must also maintain the health of the body politic. Spenser's Recreative eclogues suggest just such an interpretation, but his lesson is cloaked in praise. The poems, especially when juxtaposed with "Nouember," proclaim that Elizabeth lacks nothing. In fact, by losing her status as a virgin queen, she stands to lose more than she can ever gain through marriage. What marriage might give her, she has already, in addition to the devotion and trust of a thankful people, goods she might see slip away if she abandons her role as the bride of God and England to become the wife of France. The "fruit" of "March" can be found in "August," of "Aprill" in "Nouember." Elizabeth herself can choose.

Rather than preach to his queen, however, Spenser praised, providing his age with a language that dominated English poetry for at least the following twenty years. In the hands of lesser poets and less astute observers, such effects either devolved into royal pageantry—of which numerous examples abound—or degenerated into the sort of literary flattery that is less interesting than it is distasteful. Unlike such works, the Recreative eclogues have an astringent effect; they amuse, tease, advise, and praise, all in an effort to explore what constitutes harmonious societies. Spenser thus created a picture of Elizabeth and England that reflects both the actual and the ideal queen and her country. His images—particularly of Elizabeth—are squarely based on contemporary attempts to find a language, or perhaps a myth, capable of communicating England's sense of its own identity, an identity very much bound up with its vision of its queen. From the distance of four hundred years, Spenser's decision to praise Elizabeth as Elisa rather than Judith

---

65. Otis, *Virgil, a Study in Civilized Poetry*, 130.

or Deborah or Athena seems inspired; for Elizabeth might find her youth, her vitality, and her virtue while the country might discover an image of itself as a special nation preserved in the mirror of *The Shepheardes Calender*. That the mirror also hints at the disparities between such images and reality, offering disturbing glimpses of the results of self-indulgence, is a tribute to its maker, who at once acknowledged the fallen state of human society and envisioned a new heaven and a new earth. For all the pain, conflict, and chaos hinted at in *The Shepheardes Calender*, the poem finally affirms the possibilities of human institutions if man turns his eyes from Venus's earthly to her heavenly face.

5

Conclusion: "These Alcion Daies"

t first glance, Spenser's decision to write a shepherd's calendar seems as deliberately and needlessly anachronistic as the Chaucerian English he employs throughout the work. In a decade that debated the theories of Copernicus, the meaning of recent astronomical discoveries and events, and the benefits of correcting the inaccuracies of the Julian calendar, Spenser's *Calender* seems to harken back to the more comfortable world of the *Kalender of Shepherdes*, where simple moral lessons and astrological lore suggested the fundamental harmony between humanity and nature. Spenser, however, offered more than a simple measure of time in his *Calender*; he used the calendar frame to capture the emerging conflicts between the stable truths of the past and a future at once threatening and alluring. While its form seems coherent and familiar, on closer scrutiny the *Calender* depicts humanity as out of harmony with the rhythms of the natural year. The very conventions Spenser evoked in the title, physical appearance, and general homeliness of his poem ultimately combine to suggest how disjointed the time of the *Calender* is. Spenser also used his *Calender* to thrust himself and England into the future, for he embeds within a medieval calendar a modern, Elizabethan one, a calendar of revolutionary time, that motion whereby bodies return to their original and pure identities.

As Spenser was no doubt well aware, the word "calendar" had four meanings. First a calendar was a system that fixed the beginning and length of the year, as well as its division into parts. Second, a calendar

was a table showing the divisions of a given year. Third, a calendar was
a guide or a directory, an example or a model. Finally, a calendar was
a list or register of any kind, sometimes a list arranged chronologically.[1]
Each of these meanings describes an effort to impose order or meaning
on seasons, events, and things by arranging them according to a particu-
lar external principle. In the final poem to the *Calender*, Spenser inti-
mates just how well he understood the uses of calendars:

> Loe I have made a Calender for euery yeare,
> That steele in strength, and time in durance shall outweare:
> And if I marked well the starres reuolution,
>   It shall continewe till the worlds dissolution.
> To teach the ruder shepheard how to feede his sheepe,
> And from the falsers fraud his folded flocke to keepe.

Claiming for his poem the combined functions of kalander/almanac,
perpetual calendar, and literary calendar, Spenser says that he has cre-
ated a system of dividing the parts of the year that is stronger than steel
and more durable than the time it measures. He then describes the
poem as a table marking the motions of the heavens, saying that it shall
continue until time itself ends. He ends by describing the work as a
moral guide for the "ruder shepheard."

Significantly, each of these types of calendar was associated with the
idea of reform. For medieval or Catholic England, the kalendar—
found in prayer books and listing holy days and saints' days—and the
almanac—a series of yearly tables listing such things as the signs of the
zodiac, phases of the moon, equinoxes, and perhaps the tides—were
distinct from one another. Not until 1540 were the two issued together
for popular use.[2] The Henrician reforms, which inevitably affected the
calendar, necessitated a cheap and handy book that provided useful
information about the year. The Prognostication—a table predicting
the weather or important natural events—frequently formed a separate
section of this English hybrid, the kalander/almanac. Thus an early
English almanac page might list important liturgical, astronomical, civil,
and perhaps agricultural information. Later in the century, almanacs
became more elaborate, providing information about court terms, the

---

1. *OED*, v. *calendar*.
2. Bosanquet. See also Capp. My remarks in this chapter are based upon an examination
of English kalendars and almanacs from Elizabeth's accession to the throne until 1580.

locations and dates of fairs, ecclesiastical holidays, and planetary con-
junctions and phases of the moon. Such an almanac testified to En-
gland's new status and newly perceived needs, for, in however mundane
a fashion, these Elizabethan calendars proclaimed themselves signs of
the spiritual and material needs of a new age. The calendars in Elizabe-
than prayer books likewise reflected this awakening sense of national
and religious identity. Prayer books, primers, and devotionals, whether
composed in Latin or English, sought to offer their readers a new way
of ordering time. Thus the *Preces Privatae* included a prayer for each of
the four seasons followed by a passage instructing the reader about the
overall significance of the calendar and a calendar for the new English
Church. It ended with a series of verses on the significance of each
month. The relationship between such Protestant devotionals and the
medieval Catholic book of hours is, or course, obvious; for Elizabethan
England sought less to destroy its past than to transform or reform it,
to replace a corrupt form with a primordial one.

Spenser may or may not have realized the links between the kalendar
or almanac and reform, but he was surely aware of the reformist associa-
tions of the literary calendar. From its earliest appearance in England,
the *Kalender of Shepherdes* had been tagged with charges of Lollardy.
The *Zodiac of Life* was concerned with reform in a more theoretical way,
focusing upon the individual's efforts to apprehend God, or light, and
thus to recognize and shrug off the corruptions of the world. Whereas
the *Kalender of Shepherdes* and the *Zodiac of Life* were, for the most part,
intended to prompt personal spiritual reform, Ovid's *Fasti* praised
Rome for its enactment of actual reforms. Ovid took as his pretext the
Julian reforms of the old Roman calendar. He used that new form, the
Julian calendar, as an occasion to celebrate the idea of Rome by includ-
ing tales and legends from the various nations and tribes united under
Roman rule, recounting the history of Roman institutions and record-
ing agricultural and religious information. As an effort to translate a
Greek literary form into one magnifying the ethnic, civil, and religious
achievement of the new Roman age, the *Fasti*, like the *Kalender of
Shepherdes* or the *Zodiac of Life*, offered a highly specific perspective
upon time.[3]

The Shepheardes Calender displays the key features of a well-wrought

3. See Otis, *Ovid as an Epic Poet*, 9, 22. For a discussion of the medieval and renaissance
understanding of the *Fasti*, see Alton (1926); Binns. The commentaries in early printed
editions of the *Fasti* describe the work as a calendar; sometimes astrological tables are included.
Iser (1980), 7, links calendars and almanacs with prophecy and thus with the idea of reform.

calendar or almanac. Like literary calendars, *The Shepheardes Calender*
provides moral and spiritual advice, suggests links between the human
life cycle and the macrocosm, and underlines the ways in which mutabil-
ity is the law of both the greater and the lesser worlds. The issue of
fruitfulness, central to the language of the *Calender*, is likewise an
informing principle of works like the *Kalender of Shepherdes*, which
admonishes its reader to live each day with an eye to judgment or
harvest. The more vulgar almanac underlined the need for literal fruit-
fulness with its agricultural information and, more implicitly, in the
word commonly employed for autumn, *harvest-time*, meaning the
months of September, October, and November. Furthermore, the var-
iegated texture and tone of Spenser's *Calender* suggest its antecedents
since it was not unusual for an Elizabethan almanac to contain spiritual
advice mingled with more practical information, a curious blend of
the lofty and the worldly that Spenser sustained throughout. Finally,
Spenser's claim that he has made a calendar for every year suggests
that his calendar, like many published throughout the century, was
perpetual, a table that enabled people to "find Easter forever" or foretell
the tides for years into the future.

The *Calender* seems designed to jog our literary memories and present
us with pictures or situations that recall earlier and more conventional
treatments of time, treatments that Spenser himself echoes in the pag-
eant of the months in the *Mutabilitie Cantos*. Only in its superficial
details, however, is the *Calender* faithful to its model.[4] Traditionally,
each month was assigned a labor linking human activity to the rhythms
of the natural year.[5] These labors, with some minor variations, remained
constant throughout late classical and medieval Europe. Thus January
was usually depicted as a scene of New Year's feasting and gift-giving,
February as an old man sitting by a fire, March as a man readying a
vineyard, and so on. However, there are problems in attempting to
link the eclogues of the *Calender* with the conventional Labors of

4. For remarks about Spenser's familiarity with medieval treatments of the year, see Cullen,
chapter 2; Durr; Hamilton (1956); Hawkins; Heninger (1962); Luborsky (1980, 1981);
Parmenter (1930). For a discussion of medieval ways of considering time, see Johnson, *The
Voice of the Gawain-Poet*, 40–69. For remarks about Spenser's interest in time, see Hieatt;
Fowler, *Spenser and the Numbers of Time*. For a discussion of the importance of scientific
poetry to the intellectual life of renaissance England, see Schuller (1985). See also Harbison
185ff.; Quinones, Introduction.

5. For discussions of the convention of the Labors of the Months, see Male 64–75; Tuve,
Seasons and Months.

the Months. First, the two series do not quite correlate. In fact, the similarities between the poem and the conventional Labors point up the differences between the two. If Thenot in "Februarie" recalls the traditional *senex*, a fitting emblem for the last month before the vernal equinox, then what do we do with "Nouember," where we do not find a man feeding pigs or preparing for winter, but an elegy that gives the lie to mutability, death, and winter? If "Aprill" and "Maye" evoke traditional associations between spiritual and sexual renewal, then how does "Januarye" relate to the conventional labor for January or "September" to scenes of vintage and harvest? For every eclogue that captures the sense of a traditional scene or emblem, another forces us to admit that Spenser, and not an external scheme, is the master of his poem.[6]

A consideration of Colin Clout in relation to these conventions is equally unsatisfactory. He seems an antitype of the *Kalender of Shepherdes'* Master Shepherd, the spokesman for the work's moral wisdom who points out the ways in which humanity should bring itself into harmony with the cycles of the natural year. In contrast, Colin is a figure of zodiacal disproportion; by ignoring time's power and disavowing the relationship between humanity and nature, Colin becomes a prisoner of time.[7] What Colin laments in "Januarye"—his sense of waste, of the disjunction between past and present, of pastoral irresponsibility and conflict, of the effects of unrequited love—provides the *Calender* with its underlying tone of discontent. Similarly, Colin's description of the world as a mirror of the self and of himself as a tree whose buds are already blasted supplies the *Calender* with images that Spenser uses, as a composer would a *leitmotif*, throughout the succeeding eclogues. As the "Januarye" eclogue suggests, the rejuvenation through love that Colin seeks—both for himself and his poetry—is illusory, for unlike the world of nature, humanity too often seeks only the carefree pleasures of a literal and not a metaphoric spring. In so doing, people ignore the duties and demands of all four seasons. That humanity, exiled from Eden, searches for a means of passage back to the lost garden, Spenser and his contemporaries did not doubt; rather, they were at pains to scrutinize the ways humanity attempted to regain this timeless paradise.

6. I have found no model that does fit exactly; attempts to correlate Spenser's months with a scheme involving the proper planetary houses for each sign of the zodiac, with the plan of the *Kalender of Shepheardes*, or with the calendar in the English prayer book all yield the same frustrating result.

7. On the convention of the zodiacal man, see Boker.

Too often, as the *Calender* suggests, people choose to claim an actual—and therefore illusory—flower that, like themselves, is bound by the laws of mutability.

Spenser used Colin to explore humanity's confrontation with the strictures of a finite and thus mutable world. Colin appears in six of the eclogues and casts his shadow over the others. Cuddie's exuberant sexuality in "Februarie" and the love wound featured in "March" foreshadow Colin's account in "December" of his movement from the objectless idyll of youth to the frustrations and pain of love, when desire is focused by a single objective. Palinode's words in "Maye" echo Colin's lay in "Aprill," for he translates Colin's platonic celebration of Elisa into his own cruder and literal pantheism. Morrell's disclaimer of the past, like Colin's, is a refusal to admit responsibility for the abuses of the present. In "September," Hobbinoll reminds the wasted and confused Diggon Davie that he left home for the world nine months ago, "Thrise three Moones bene fully spent and past" ("September," l. 20). His words suggest a kinship between Diggon Davie and Colin, whose lament (nine eclogues previously) introduced a pastoral world characterized by exile, regret, conflict, and waste. Finally, the problems of poetic vocation considered in "October" ultimately concern Colin, who has ignored the inspiration of the heavenly Venus in favor of his desire for Rosalind, thus exiling himself from his own art ("October," ll. 89–94). These eclogues flesh out the portrait sketched in "Januarye," "June," and "December," in which Colin describes his increasing alienation from his pastoral world. "December" summarizes Colin's year, or the year of the natural man. It is a year of frustration and blighted harvest because its focus is the self. Colin's desire for Rosalind, Thenot's and Palinode's desires for a vanished youth, Morrell's desire for high station, and Cuddie's desire for comfort cannot finally be satisfied. Colin and his fellows can only dramatize the inability of natural man to find satisfaction, to erect harmonious societies, or to live in time since the members of this pastoral world are turned inward upon a narrowly conceived world. Spenser prepares us for such a world in "Januarye," where Colin introduces one of the poem's most important images, the mirror, an image long associated with the themes of nature, history, art, and time, in addition, of course, to the legend of Narcissus.[8]

Colin begins his lament in "Januarye" by comparing his own spiritual state with nature's physical privation, using the conceit as a means of

8. See Bradley.

justifying his own barrenness. Thus in the second stanza of his lament, he addresses nature as "thou barrein ground," like himself a prisoner of time past. The landscape once enjoyed milder seasons but "now is come thy wynters stormy state, / Thy mantle mard, wherein thou maskedst late" ("Januarye," ll. 23–24). He here intimates that winter constitutes a blot on nature by describing it as infertile rather than fallow. He goes on to link himself to his own interpretation of this landscape, saying "Such rage as winters, reigneth in my heart, / My life bloud friesing with vnkindly cold" ("Januarye," ll. 25–26). He characterizes himself as old and wintry in spirit, if not in years. In the following stanza, he describes the trees in relation to their past glory:

> You naked trees, whose shady leaues are lost,
> Wherein the byrds were wont to build their bowre:
> And now are clothd with mosse and hoary frost,
> Instede of bloosmes, wherwith your buds did flowre:
> I see your teares, that from your boughes doe raine,
> Whose drops in drery ysicles remaine.
>
> ("Januarye," ll. 31–36)

Rather than blossoms, these trees now bear icicles, which Colin describes as tears. The fifth stanza echoes or mirrors the fourth, for Colin describes himself in terms of his own account of the wintry trees, as a tree whose buds are blown away with wailing, whose blossoms are borne away with sighes, whose branches drip tears "As on your boughes the ysicles depend" ("Januarye," l. 42).

These stanzas are a good deal more complicated than they appear. Indeed, when reading them we need to recall the distinction between the poet and the poem he has made, a distinction suggested by the emphasis on poetic craftsmanship in the front matter of the *Calender*. These four stanzas evince more than Spenser's artful deployment of a conventional *topos*, for behind Colin is Spenser, poet and ironist. Spenser does not compare Colin to a winter landscape; Colin compares himself to a landscape that he glosses even as he describes it. After depicting nature as "mard" by winter, the trees as naked, and icicles as tears, Colin then uses his own metaphors to describe, and implicitly to justify, his present apathy, misgovernment, and waste. Immerito, in fact, transforms the mirror of Narcissus into verse; Colin finds a human face in nature, then compares nature's face to his own. His use of nature has even more serious implications, for where the motif of the seasons was traditionally used as a means of urging responsibility and self-awareness upon man, Colin uses the *speculum naturae* to point up his regret. He therefore uses nature as an emblem of a vanished past, as suggested by the line "naked trees, whose shady leaves are lost." "Naked" and "lost" imply that a tree's natural season is spring or summer, when for half the year a tree is naturally bare. I am not quarreling with Colin's preference here, but with his underlying assumption that winter is an unnatural season. His refusal to see the year as a unit renders him incapable of living comfortably in the present because he sees only the most tenuous connection between it and the past. He thus identifies his "sight" of Rosalind ("such sight hath bred my bane" l. 53) as the point when the weather changed for the worse, but disavows any responsibility for the change or any possibility of reclaiming a lost golden age. Since he ignores his own culpability, he rules out the opportunity for genuinely creative remorse. That is, he rules out the possibility of using or resurrecting the past and thus of rectifying the present.[9]

Colin is not alone in projecting himself upon the external world, for the pastoral world of the *Calender* is populated by figures who use the mirrors afforded by literature, history, and nature to reflect the self rather than to seek to know either the self or the celestial realm. For example, Thenot, like Colin, glosses nature as in a protracted state of decay:

> Must not the world wend in his commun course
> From good to badd, and from badde to worse,
> From worse vnto that is worst of all,
> And then returne to his former fall?
> ("Februarie," ll. 11–14)

Thenot here echoes the common enough medieval and renaissance assumption that the world declines steadily toward its eventual destruction; however, his description also reflects his appraisal of human life as a decline from youthful vigor to crabbed old age. He depicts winter

---

9. The most resonant of the renaissance treatments of time is that of Lancelot Andrewes in the Ash Wednesday sermon he preached before the Queen at Whitehall in 1602. See Andrewes, 202ff. For an official Elizabethan discussion of the individual's relation to time, see the important "Homily of Repentance, and of True Reconciliation to God," in Corrie, 525ff. Throughout the *Calender* Spenser seems to evoke the language of this homily.

as he sees himself, "breme winter with chamfred browes, / Full of wrinckles and frostie furrowes" ("Februarie," ll. 43–44). When he looks out upon winter, Thenot finds the outlines of his own aging face. As his subsequent remarks to Cuddie and the fable of the Oak and the Briar suggest, Thenot sees little hope in age, only the prospect of increasing powerlessness and decay, followed by betrayal and destruction. Since Thenot finds little to smile at in his own state, he fails to mention to Cuddie that spring succeeds winter, that those "wrinckles and frostie furrowes" are the seedbed of a new year.

Palinode uses nature as a mirror for frustrated sexuality. He thus describes May as a month reserved for the young, despite the reawakened vigor and sexual longing the month inspires in both old and young:

> Is not thilke the mery moneth of May,
> When loue lads masken in fresh aray?
> How falles it then, we no merrier bene,
> Ylike as others, girt in gawdy greene?
> Our bloncket liueryes bene all to sadde,
> For thilke same season, when all is ycladd
> With pleasaunce: the grownd with grasse, the Wods
> With greene leaues, the bushes with bloosming Buds.
>
> ("Maye," ll. 1–8)

His words sketch a tableau of riotous array. Youths and nature are masked or clad in fresh clothing and clear colors; only the priest, dressed in sober and prescribed clothing, stands apart from the season's revels. Palinode describes May in elegiac language, as a fleeting masque his priestly vestments prevent him from joining; he can only envy the young and unfettered and recall the dissatisfactions of the present. Throughout the eclogue his remarks suggest just how dangerously inadequate his view of time is, for his notion of rejuvenation is literal or physical rather than spiritual. In sharp contrast to Colin's lay for Elisa in the "Aprill" eclogue, which celebrates Elisa as a principle of life, creativity, and stability, Palinode celebrates spring for its beauty and brevity. Moreover, Palinode uses many of the same flowers with which Colin decks Elisa ("Hawthorne buds, and swete Eglantine, / And girlonds of roses and Sopps in wine," ["Maye," ll. 13–14]) as tokens of a landscape he interprets in terms of his own frustrated sexual desire.

Morrell's use of history in "Julye" is equally solipsistic; here the past is a means of justifying to Thomalin his own elevation above his fellows. Although their debate sounds like a conventional enough schoolmen's quarrel about clerical living, with one authority matched against another, their argument actually concerns the proper use of the past, of history. Whereas Thomalin uses the *speculum historiae* as a means of understanding the workings of providence and thus of seeking guidance for the present, Morrell uses the mirror to justify the *status quo*. Morrell's vision of history is thus highly selective. In justifying his elevated status, he mentions only hills sanctioned by myth and legend. Not only do his seven examples suggest the seven hills of Rome, symbol of ecclesiastical elevation and abuse, but he seems much more comfortable discussing profane history. He leaves sacred history to Thomalin, discounting Thomalin's more elaborate and pedagogical view of it. Morrell thereby signals his genuine disinterest in the past except insofar as it supports his own inclinations to comfortable living.

The majority of the speakers on the *Calender*'s pastoral stage reject the idea of enlightenment that informed the medieval and renaissance use of the trope of the *speculum*, or mirror. Though figures like Piers and Thomalin rhetorically employ the metaphoric mirror of history, while Piers in "October" refers to beauty as an immortal mirror, their listeners follow the Kidde in "Maye" in preferring a mirror that only reflects an image of the person holding it. Spenser's shepherds resist the lessons of works like the *Kalender of Shepherdes* and the more humble almanac, which suggest that man pattern himself upon nature and translate nature's literal cycle of fruit and harvest into a metaphoric cycle. Aligned with its medieval *figura*, Spenser's *Calender* seems a table chronicling time's violence on an inert landscape. The eclogues describe a world dominated by commerce and cupidity similar to the one that Ovid describes in his account of the Age of Iron. In Spenser's portrayal, man is out of tune with his world, his fellows, and himself.

The time the *Calender* tells therefore has little relevance to astronomical time, and is as inadequate a measure of motion as those models by which sixteenth-century Englishmen expressed their relation to the universe. Spenser's decision to write a shepherds calendar in 1579 seems especially curious since the very subject of the calendar was so provocative.[10] For centuries scientists had been aware that the Julian calendar was becoming increasingly inaccurate, that, as Roger Bacon

10. See Coyne, et al., particularly the essays by Gingerich; Hoskin; North; Ziggelaar. For a study of the world of chronological research in the century before 1582, see Grafton (1985).

said, it was "intolerabilis omni sapienti, et horribilis omni astronomo, et derisibilis ab omni computista."[11] In the early 1570s, Pope Gregory XIII heeded a long-standing call for calendrical reform and appointed a commission to study ways of bringing the Julian calendar into line with the natural year. The commission produced a number of recommendations, the most well-known of which was the suggestion that ten days be dropped from the calendar, thereby aligning the actual vernal equinox with its intended Julian date. From 1578, when the Pope issued these recommendations in the form of a compendium, which he sent to all Catholic princes, until 1582, when, with the bull *Inter gravissimas*, he introduced the Gregorian calendar, the Julian calendar was the subject of a good deal of debate throughout Europe. Since the date of Easter is determined in relation to the vernal equinox, and calendar reform would inevitably affect other holy days as well, the matter was referred to ecclesiastical as well as scientific authorities for discussion. In England, Elizabeth and her cabinet supported the new calendar, passing it to John Dee for his opinion. As one of England's most important scientists, Dee was naturally aware of the inadequacies of the Julian calendar. Though he quibbled with some parts of the Gregorian reform and wrote a treatise on the subject of the calendar for Queen Elizabeth, in the end Dee advised her to support what he called a "reformation of tyme." His verdict was then referred to a committee composed of Thomas Digges, Henry Savile, and a Mr. Chambers, who endorsed Dee's findings. Though Queen, council, and learned advisors favored reform, England's ecclesiastical authorities resisted the change. Despite acknowledging the inadequacies of the existing calendar, England's churchmen were loath to join a reform instigated by Rome. Some even went so far as to say that since the world would not last much longer, there was no need to worry about the future problems England might face with its absurdly inaccurate calendar. Their resistance was sufficient to maintain England in its own time until 1752, when, despite continued opposition, England dropped

---

11. Quoted in North (1983), 75. In *The Castle of Knowledge*, Robert Recorde noted,
. . . about the incarnation of Christ, the equinoctiall point or instaunte happened aboute the 25 daye of Marche, and now it is aboute the tenth of the same moneth.
. . . For althoughe the Sonne do at the yeares eande retourne to the same poynte in the starrye skye where hee was at the beginninge of the same yeare yet is he not exactly so nighe vnto the Equinoctiall pointe as he was before, but doth ouerrunne it euery yeare, and thereby in continuance of tyme it cometh to passe, that men may sensibly perceaue that the stars are runne eastward from that equinoctiall point. (277)

the eleven days from September 2 to September 14 and adopted the calendar that knowledgeable Elizabethans had supported nearly two hundred years before.

In 1572 the scientific and religious communities had also been shaken by the sudden appearance of a new star in the constellation of Cassiopeia. Tycho Brahe, the important Danish astronomer, took a number of careful observations, enabling him to identify it as belonging to the region of the fixed stars.[12] The star and Tycho's remarks about it were unsettling in two ways. First, any event like a comet (of which there were two that decade) or an eclipse was thought to conceal a meaning: "The signes of the tymes who can them comprise? the tokens of troubles what man could deuise? And yet in that boke who rightly can reade, to all secrete knowledge it will him straighte leade." In the Preface to the Reader of his popular astronomical handbook *The Castle of Knowledge*, Robert Recorde thus compared the heavens to a book of unknown semiotics. The new star caused some to speculate about the end of the world; Theodore Beza linked it to the Second Coming, when the King of France and other tyrants would reap the justice they so richly deserved for their persecution of Protestants. In fact, with its political tensions and stellar disturbances, the decade spawned a certain amount of apocalyptic speculation, and several, among them Melanchthon, looked to the end of the world in the early part of the 1580s.[13] Even more potentially upsetting about Tycho's observations was the thought that the universe was subject to change, that a new star could appear in what was considered a changeless part of the sky. Colin's perception in "Nouember" of the new realm Dido inhabits has a similar effect in the *Calender*. His electric "I see thee blessed soule, I see" ("Nouember," l. 178) is his reaction to an observation or sighting, not a testimony to belief grounded in faith. What Colin sees changes his feelings about death because it substantially alters his conception of the boundaries and the structure of the universe.

During the 1570s, a new universe must have seemed fearfully eminent to learned Elizabethans, who were probably aware that Copernicus in his *De revolutionibus Orbium Coelestium* (1542–43) had proposed a "reformed" model of the universe. Copernicus described a heliocentric universe in which each of the planets, including the earth, revolved around the sun in its own time and at its own distance. Only the moon

12. On Tycho Brahe and the new star, see Berry, 135–36.
13. See Camden, 190; Sheltoo a Geveren.

revolved around earth. Copernicus's model was conservative in that it retained the basic structure of the Ptolemaic model, substituting the sun for the earth at the center of what was still a mathematically ordered and thus limited universe. Copernicus's contemporary supporters saw him as a revivalist, as one who had resurrected a worldview first propounded by the early Pythagoreans.[14] Among Protestant countries, England accorded Copernican thought a relatively mild reception. Both Robert Recorde, the learned mathematician and scientific writer, and John Dee were knowledgeable about, if not sympathetic to, the theories of Copernicus. Dee's library, which attracted many visitors, contained two copies of *De revolutionibus*.[15] But the most important English Copernican was Thomas Digges, a friend of both Edward Dyer and Gabriel Harvey.[16] In 1576 Digges reissued his father's *Prognostication euerlasting*—one of the best and most popular perpetual almanacs of the time—with an appendix containing a free translation of parts of *De revolutionibus*. Copernicus had a vigorous and intelligent English supporter in Digges, whose volume went through seven editions between 1576 and 1605.[17]

The revised *Prognostication euerlasting* embodies the paradoxes of the third quarter of the sixteenth century. The first and longest section of the book, Leonard Digges's original work, epitomizes the concerns and stances of an earlier age. It contains information about the influence of celestial bodies on the weather, the four quarters of the year, the auspicious signs for such activities as bloodletting and bathing, and the means of determining certain important church holidays in any natural year. In addition, it provides tables for the months, tides, and shadows for every grade of the sun's height. However, when juxtaposed with his son's essay, Leonard's work, though more than respectable and thoroughly scientific, seems old-fashioned. The second section, written by Thomas, can be described as a proclamation for a new era, an era

14. Heninger, *The Cosmographical Glass*, 48. See also Berry 106ff.; Johnson, *Astronomical Thought in Renaissance England*, chapter 5; Kocher, chapter 9; Kuhn 129ff.; Russell (1973). Giordano Bruno was also a Copernican. See *The Ash Wednesday Supper*, 28, 44–45, 207ff.

15. See Berry, 127; Russell (1973), 191–92.

16. For discussions of Digges, see Johnson, *Astronomical Thought in Renaissance England*, 169ff.; Johnson and Larkey (1934). Johnson also outlines the university debate between Aristotelians and Copernicans, or between Aristotelians and Ramists. Harvey was both a Copernican and a Ramist, and his passionate championship of Ramus formed the core of his lectures at Cambridge during this period. Johnson, in effect, suggests that the name "Ramus" was sometimes a synonym for "Copernicus."

17. Russell (1973), 194.

that sought to distinguish itself as the guardian of ancient and often obscured truths. Thus Thomas Digges, proclaiming man's newly redis-covered powers of reason and observation, heralded a universe that reflects indisputable truths about human nature and divine wisdom. He argued eloquently for a new order, as shown in a Letter to the Reader where he compares the new and the old:

> Among other things I haue founde a description or Modill of the world, & situation of Spheres Coelestiall and elementary according to the doctrine of Ptolomie, whereunto all vniuersities (led thereunto chiefly by the authoritie of *Aristotle*) sithens have consented. But in this our age, one rare wit . . . hath by long study, painefull practise, and rare inuention deliuered a new Theorick or Modill of the world, shewing that the Earth resteth not in the Center of the whole worlde, but not onely in the Center of this our mortall world or Globe of Elements, which enuironed and enclosed in the Moones orbe, and together with the whole Globe of mortalitie is caried yearely round aboute the Sunne, which like a king in the middest of all raigneth and giueth lawes of motion to the rest, sphaerically dispersing his glorious beames of light through all this sacred Coelestiall Temple. And the Earth it selfe to bee one of the Planets, hauing his peculiar and strange courses turning euery 24. houres round vpon his owne Centre: whereby the Sunne and great Globe of fixed starres seeme to sway about and turne, albeit indeed they remayne fixed. So many waies is the sense of mortall men abused.

This Letter is important in several ways. It provides both a new model for the universe and a language—the Neoplatonic language that Copernicus himself adopted—with which to describe that universe. Just as Palingenius had used a poetic language underpinned by the metaphysics of light to organize his *Zodiac of Life* around the sun, so Digges drew upon a language already sanctioned by philosophers and theologians.[18] He therefore intimated the logic of heliocentricity by comparing the sun to a king, suggesting that we adduce the nature of the universe by observing the laws and hierarchies that operate in the human sphere. Second, he suggested that our understanding of the nature of motion demands that we first recognize and understand

18. Suchodolski; Yates, *Giordano Bruno and the Hermetic Tradition*, 152, 153.

perspective. Because we move, we think the sun moves: Our senses are "abused" by our own motion. Finally, he consented to preserve—to publish anew—his father's earlier account of the older model for the universe "to the end such noble English mindes . . . might not be altogether defrauded of so noble a part of Philosophie." As is apparent from the body of the essay, however, Digges, or Copernicus, offered a new perspective upon motion in offering a new cosmos, and consequently suggested a new philosophy to replace the old. Even more important about Digges's essay is his underlying assumption that Copernicus's theories of heliocentricity and his own belief in the infinity of the universe constitute a reformation of natural law. He argued for the dominance of the intellect over the senses; man's "abused" senses have convinced him of what is false, that he stands still while the heavens move. Digges rebutted this notion with reason, matching Aristotle and Ptolemy with Plato, Martianus Capella, and Copernicus, darkness and error with light and truth, scientific supposition with scientific observation. In a manner familiar to any observer of the Elizabethan religious and political scene, Digges therefore defends the new as "ancient doctrine reuiued" (sig. N2^r).

Digges's essay, "A Perfit Description of the Coelestiall Orbes, according to the most ancient doctrine of the Pythagoreans: lately reuiued by Copernicus, and by Geometricall Demonstrations approued," made Copernicus's mathematical calculations and astronomical observations accessible to those without specialized mathematical or scientific knowledge. After first summarizing earlier theories of universal motion, Digges summarized Copernicus's theory of heliocentricity, going on to describe briefly the length of the orbits of each of the planets, including earth, about the sun. He then devoted a good deal of space to a discussion of the nature of motion, beginning with Aristotle. Aristotle described two types: simple or right motion (up or down movement) and circular motion (movement around a center). Circular motion is only proper to heavenly bodies. Ptolemy felt that the earth could not have circular motion because, in its violence, this movement would disturb the right motion of earthly elements and eventually dissolve and scatter earth. To this characterization of motion as inevitably violent, Digges counterposed a theory of natural motion:

> But hee that will maintaine the Earths Mobilitie, may say that this motion is not violent but naturall. And these thinges which are naturally mooued haue effects contrarie to such as are vio-

lently carried. For such motions wherein force and violence is used, must needes bee dissolued, and cannot bee of long continuance: but those which by nature are caused, remaine still in their perfite estate, and are conserued and kept in their most excellent constitution. (sig. N3^r)

Digges used the verbs "move" and "carry" to distinguish between natural or inherent motion and external or forced motion. Since earth is limited, and motion is only a property of finite bodies, "why doe we yet stagger to confesse motion in the Earth, being most agreeable to his forme and nature, whose bounds also and circumference wee knowe, rather then to imagine that the whole worlde should sway and turne, whose ende wee knowe not, ne possiblie can of any mortall man be knowne" (sig. N3^v). Stressing earth's natural circular motion, he then turned to the issue of simple or right motion. If earth moves in an orbit about a central point, earth's elements likewise seek their "right state or perfection naturall" (sig. N4^v). He ended his rebuttal of Aristotle by redefining gravity as a species of natural motion: "For grauitie is nothing else but a certaine procliuity or naturall coueting of parts to be coupled with the whole: which by diuine prouidence of the Creator of all, is giuen and impressed into the parts, that they should restore themselues into their unitie and integritie, concurring in Sphericall forme" (sig. O^r). Like earth itself, earth's elements move, seeking their original integrity and order.

The essay ultimately suggested the logic of heliocentricity by demonstrating the varieties of motion peculiar to earth and its elements. Following Copernicus, Digges echoed hermeticists in calling the sun a "visible god": "Thus doth the Sun like a King sitting in his throne, governe his Courtes of inferiour powers" (sig. N^r). Digges praised the symmetry of a universe governed by stability and light: "Hereto wee may adioyne, that the condition of immobilitie is more noble and diuine then that of chaunge, alteration, or instabilitie: and therefore more agreeable to Heauen then to this Earth, where all things are subiect to continuall mutabilitie" (sigs. N4^v–O^r). For Digges, who called Earth the Orb of Decay, it made little sense to assume an unstable center for the universe; instead, marrying common sense to scientific observation, he urged a new universe whose center provides light, life, and order for all bodies within its radiant sphere.

Though in Digges Copernicus had a fine and shrewd apologist, his ideas seemed nonetheless waiting to be translated into poetry. In the

two Elizabethan eclogues of *The Shepheardes Calender*, we can detect
hints of a model for the universe whose proportions and stability can,
like Copernicus's model, be described as "ancient doctrine reuiued."
The "Aprill" eclogue blazons a sun-centered universe. In his lay, after
comparing Elisa to Phoebe, goddess of chastity, or to the moon, Colin
compares Elisa to Phoebe's brother, Phoebus, or to the sun:

> I sawe Phoebus thrust out his golden hedde,
> > vpon her to gaze:
> But when he sawe, how broade her beames did spredde,
> > it did him amaze.
> He blusht to see another Sunne belowe,
> Ne durst againe his fyrye face out showe:
> > Let him, if he dare,
> His brightnesse compare
> With hers, to haue the ouerthrowe.
>
> > > ("Aprill," ll. 73–81)

Colin describes an unusual phenomenon: Rising and encountering
another body, like himself described as a radiant sphere, the sun sets.
However, the sun's eclipse has no darkening effect on the world, for
Elisa's "broade beames" illuminate it. The woodcut for "Aprill" even
more strongly suggests that Elisa functions as a sun for her world. The
artist displaces the actual sun, situating it in the right-hand corner of
the woodcut, and places a regal Elisa, the metaphoric sun, in the center
of the composition, providing the symmetrical grouping of shepherds
and Muses with a central focal point.

In "Aprill" Spenser described his sovereign as a sun, a figure who
places all other bodies in proportional distribution. In the remaining
stanzas of the lay, Colin praises Elisa as a principle of pastoral order:
The music of Calliope and the Muses, the dances of the Graces, the
"beuie of Ladies bright, / raunged in a rowe," and the shepherds'
daughters, hair bound and waists girded, function as a series of tropes
magnifying the idea of order embodied by and emanating from Elisa.
The final catalogue of flowers is similarly informed by the idea of order:

> Bring hether the Pincke and purple Cullambine,
> > With Gelliflowres:
> Bring Coronations, and Sops in wine,
> > worne of Paramoures.
> Strowe me the ground with Daffadowndillies,

And Cowslips, and Kingcups, and loued Lillies:
The pretie Pawnce,
And the Cheuisaunce,
Shall match with the fayre flowre Delice.
("Aprill," ll. 136–44)

Colin's measured language and careful choice of flowers suitable for
England's paramour, bride, and queen bely any suggestion of riot or
randomness that such an array might otherwise suggest. As the blazon
dressing Elisa in the robes of splendor and symmetry ends, leaving
Thenot and Hobbinoll grimly aware that Colin no longer sings songs
to his "visible god," the sun sets, leaving the pastoral world lighted only
by the lesser stars. The eclogue ends with two Virgilian emblems:

Thenots Embleme.
O quam te memorem virgo?
Hobbinols Embleme.
O dea certe.

It is a fitting close to the eclogue, for in echoing Aeneas's exclamation
of recognition and loss when he encounters his divine mother, Venus,
just outside the precincts of Carthage (*Aeneid* I, ll. 327–28), Spenser
echoes the effect of Colin's lay upon the pastoral world that the entire
eclogue depicts.[19] Even as we perceive Elisa as the only stable center
for the *Calender*'s world, vision recedes, leaving us aware of earth's
instabilities and our own insufficiencies.

If in "Aprill" Spenser celebrated his sovereign as a manifestation of
universal symmetry, thus adumbrating a *metaphoric* heliocentricity, in
"Nouember" he explored the change natural to all earthly bodies. Co-
lin's elegy for Dido describes death as motion, demonstrating that what
he first thought violent or unnatural motion is, in fact, natural and
providential. He therefore first describes death as powerful, violent,
and disruptive (see lines 119, 122, 123), depicting earth as holding, or
encompassing, Dido's buried body. However, the downward motion
whereby Dido is carried into the earth is shown to be the natural
gravitational motion of the body, the part seeking the whole, to adopt
Digges's vocabulary. Moreover, Colin demonstrates that Dido herself

---

19. I am indebted to T. M. Krier's paper, "Prying into Mysteries," delivered at the 1986
meeting of Spenser at Kalamazoo, for starting this train of thought.

is master of the situation because once "vnbodied of the burdenous corpse" ("Nouember," l. 166), her soul seeks its own *patria*, heaven. It is that downward gravitational pull that provides Dido with the lightness, the spring she needs for what Digges or Aristotle would call a type of right motion, levity and not gravity. The elegy strongly suggests what ten eclogues of the *Calender* imply: that earth is the wrong place to seek stability. The permanence we crave is located beyond what Digges, referring to all elements enclosed within the orb of the moon, described as the "globe of Mortality, because it is the peculiar Empire of death" (sig. M2ʳ). Dido's death, like the changing seasons or Colin's slow decay, should be seen as evidence for earth's mobility, its inherent and natural motion. But in the very eclogue that describes the motion appropriate to citizens of this orb of decay, Spenser offers a link between earth's impermanence and the stability figured in the sun of "Aprill." In his reply to Thenot, who wishes to hear a merry song, Colin says that merry songs are "meetest" for May:

> But nowe sadde Winter welked hath the day,
> And *Phoebus* weary of his yerely taske,
> Ystabled hath his steedes in lowlye laye,
> And taken vp his ynne in *Fishes* haske.
> ("Nouember," ll. 13–16)

These lines have teased Spenserians for years, especially since E. K.'s gloss only underlines the riddle:

> In fishes haske) the sonne, reigneth that is, in the signe Pisces all Nouember. a haske is a wicker pad, wherein they use to cary fish.

The line seems to refer to the constellation Pisces, which E. K., ignoring the woodcut for "Nouember" that depicts Sagittarius, incorrectly ascribes to November. Since any sixteenth-century child would catch that error and since Spenser carefully superintended the printing of his works, it seems likely that the mistake is deliberate. *Fishes* is possibly a singular possessive noun, referring to the Dauphin (Dolphin) of France; the line thus might describe Elizabeth, or the sun, as in danger of being caught by France.[20] Spenser may well have intended it to refer

---

20. Parmenter, 214; McLane, 54.

to Elizabeth's metaphoric death if she allowed herself to be trapped by Alençon's marriage proposals, but it would have been impossible to prove without first defining *haske*.

Here the *OED* is more helpful than E. K. Since Spenser coined the word, he obviously wanted it to sound like a more familiar word and thus to evoke a common meaning or meanings.[21] The most likely homonym here is *haspe*, an indigenous word used throughout the medieval and renaissance periods in England. As a noun, *haspe* referred to a fastening or clasp, a reelful of yarn, or a reel or hinge. As a verb it could also mean clasp, embrace, or confine. With its interrelated meanings, *haspe* is probably what Spenser wished to evoke with his employment of the nonce word, *haske*. Taken one way, the line might well refer to Elizabeth's marriage, to the likelihood of the Queen's being embraced or confined by the Fish, as the Dauphin was sometimes called. However, if we take the more common meaning of *haspe* as a clasp, fastening, or reel of yarn and apply it to the zodiacal constellation of Pisces, it would refer to the star Alpha Piscium, the star that Robert Recorde described in the *Castle of Knowledge*: "The Fyshes tyed by the tayles with a common Lyne. . . . and where those two lines are knitte togyther, there is one starre more, which is called the Knotte" (267).[22] *Alpha Piscium* was and is commonly known as the Knot of Pisces since the constellation is compared to two fish connected by a "ribbon."

The Knot of Pisces not only marks the point where the ribbon is tied, but the point when the sun departs from Pisces and enters Aries around the time of the vernal equinox.[23] Spenser thus used *haske* as a particularly complicated pun. As a homophone, it evoked *haspe*, meaning hinge or fastening or reelful of yarn. *Haspe* then recalls that knot joining the ribbons that connect the fishes in the constellation Pisces. If we take the *Fishes haske* to mean the *fish*'s embrace, then the sun has taken up its habitation or abode in the fish's embrace and is therefore caught. However, if we take the *Fishes haske* to mean the *fishes*' knot, the sun has taken as its *temporary* dwelling the Knot of Pisces, or is just

21. For a discussion of Spenser and word play, see Hamilton (1973). Regarding "haske," the word *hassocke* existed. In his *Alvearie*, John Baret defined it as "a baskette made of twigges, & rushes. Scirpiculum, li., n. g. colum. Vn petit panier faict de ionc."

22. The Latin word for knot, *nodus*, was likewise used to designate *Alpha Piscium* by Latin writers. See Cicero, *Arati Phaenomena*, 251 (17); Germanicus Iulius Caesar, *Aratea Epigrammata*, 370.

23. I am indebted to Anthony Aveni of the Department of Astronomy at Colgate University for providing me with this information. See also Fowler, *Spenser and the Numbers of Time*, 146. In Canto 1 of the *Purgatorio*, Dante associates Pisces with the vernal equinox and hence with the theme of resurrection.

leaving the constellation of Pisces. The one describes the end of action, the other announces a new age.

Though the line seems to presage only a consideration of mortality, like the elegy it introduces, it describes not a setting but a rising sun. What Spenser concealed in this line is a different way of organizing the year, a new calendar based on a metaphoric vernal equinox, the beginning of the sun's dominance. Spenser placed his celebration of the mortal Dido in November, the month from which England dated its reformation; in April, the month in which Rome celebrated its founder's day, Spenser placed his blazon of Elisa as an immortal figure of stability and magnificence whose rising ushers in a new era. Just as Elizabethans frequently dated the year from the beginning of Elizabeth's accession to the throne, in November of 1558, so Spenser offered his readers a new Elizabethan calendar. November and its apparent decline is designed to turn us away from the moving earth, from the mortal Dido, and towards the sun celebrated in "Aprill," for, as E. K. notes, November is that season "when the sonne draweth low in the South toward his Tropick or returne" ("Nouember," Glosse, 15).

An underlying concern with reform links *The Shepheardes Calender* to its time. On Good Friday of 1570, in response to the Papal Bull releasing Englishmen from any fealty to their sovereign, John Foxe preached "A Sermon of Christ Crucified."[24] He concluded that sermon by urging Londoners to "learne another ioyning," pleading with them to see themselves as *English*men and not as subjects of a foreign spiritual power. The prayer at the end of the sermon voiced the hopes and the concerns of the age: "it hath pleased thy grace to give us these Alcion daies . . . so many Enemies we haue, that enuie us this rest and tranquillity, and do what they can to disturb it." That concern is echoed throughout a decade that saw itself as poised in a moment of "rest and tranquillity" like the fourteen days of calm weather believed to occur about the winter solstice when the halcyon, or kingfisher, was brooding. Thus Englishmen questioned the fitness of their own institutions, cautioning lest envy, ingratitude, greed, or any other form of self-interest threaten the pastoral world that burgeoned under Elizabeth.[25] As Foxe

24. This sermon was reissued in 1575, 1577, 1585, and 1609.

25. See, for example, Edwin Sandys's Accession Day sermon (1577?) in *Sermons*. Sandys preached on Canticle 2, "Take us the little foxes which destroy the vines; for our vines hath flourished." Sandys noted that an incredible peace flourished in England, which "hath fructified and brought forth his natural fruit, which is plenty" (61), warning that if Englishmen were wicked, the vineyard "shall be laid waste." Sandys cautioned against living in complacency and security, instead urging vigilance.

ushered in the decade, foreseeing England's halcyon's respite, Spenser capped it, signaling his presentiment that the time of rest drew near its period. He therefore used his first poem to proclaim the need for reform. The word itself, frequently and allusively used, demands some attention; for *reform* could signify a process of renewal or restoration to an original form or state or of conversion into another and better form. Or *reform* was sometimes *re-form*, meaning to rebuild or to form a second time. English Reformers thus traced the English Protestant Church to Joseph of Arimathea and pre-Roman Britain; jurists and historians noted the excellencies of their medieval forebears; architects suggested with wood and plaster the outlines of Gothic style. All these affirmations of the continuity between past and present were ultimately, as the *Calender* suggests, efforts to forge a new identity for what was perceived as a new nation, at once a fulfillment and a transformation of the past.

In the *Calender* Spenser revealed his shrewd appraisal of his age. Each detail was designed to betray its links with the past. The form and appearance of the poem evoke earlier denizens of the literary market-place; the pastoral mode links the *Calender* to European and classical traditions. With his combined urbanity, garrulousness, and erudition, E. K. at once suggests such comic and indigenous figures as Chaucer's famous go-between, Pandarus, and the more Olympian go-betweens, authors of countless glosses upon classical texts. Similarly, the three kinds into which E. K. divides the eclogues of the *Calender* adumbrate a tradition whose roots can be traced both to classical philosophy and the study of wisdom and to sacred scripture and Solomon's poetry. The *Calender*, in fact, seems intended to deceive, for it harkens back to earlier conventions and configurations, apparently rooted in the fashions and modes of thought of earlier eras. However, when we compare its details and strategies to their medieval or classical analogues, it becomes clear that the poem is less an imitation than an attempt to recover the original clarity and purity of its models, transforming those older forms into linguistic structures suitable for the new age. Thus while each of the various *ranckes* of eclogues suggests earlier literary forms, Spenser built upon the achievements of his elders, fashioning Elizabethan Canterbury tales, myths, and idylls that do not so much pass on a tradition as create new forms and suggest new ways of thinking about and using one's literary heritage.

Spenser's formal and poetic interest in the strategies of reform is matched by his concern with the theme of reform. He thus focused each of the *ranckes* of eclogues upon a particular element of the body politic. In the Moral eclogues for the most part, he used the indigenous conventions of moral literature to explore those bonds holding together the social body. But the eclogues depict a body politic bound by corrupt economic policies whose outcome can only be bankruptcy and by a language that does not function as a common medium of exchange. In the Plaintive eclogues, Spenser fused the themes of the speculative tradition with the classical techniques of the mythographer. Using the legend of Narcissus as the analogue for his portrait of Colin Clout, he described a self at odds with its own talent, desire, and drives. Like Narcissus, whom Ovid described as choosing infertility and death, Colin chooses a figurative barrenness that renders him equally vulnerable to the wasting power of time. If the shepherds who assume center stage in the Moral eclogues seem to lack direction, Colin lacks the force necessary for creative change. In the Recreative eclogues, Spenser drew upon the conventions of the Greek idyll and the biblical epithalamium to depict the force of love. As these eclogues intimate, only by focusing our wills on an immortal principle of beauty, manifested through earthly creatures and institutions, may we join together in harmonious relationships, creative song, and fruitful union. In each of the *ranckes* Spenser depicted the realities of fragmentation, implicitly the likely outcome of ignoring our fundamental identities as stewards. The poem suggests that neither the humble shepherd, the successful bishop, the most talented poet, nor the sovereign can with impunity sever those ties binding the self laterally to its fellows and vertically to its maker.

Finally Spenser offered us a choice in the two calendars contained within a work ambiguously entitled *The Shepheardes Calender*. As *The Shepheardes' Calender*, a title that evokes the older *Kalender of Shepherdes*, the volume presents a calendar of retrogradation, a scheme of measuring time by which Colin and his fellows point up the grim realities of mutability and man's utter inadequacy in the face of harvest and judgment. But in *The Shephearde's Calender*, Spenser provided his readers new identities and with a calendar based upon a metaphoric vernal equinox, thus realigning them with the patterns and harmonies of the universe. The world hinted at in that second calendar is one where Colin and his fellows transcend their own limitations: elegies turn to epithalamia; grief turns to recognition; destructive love and silence turn into gracious song. The central focus of the *Calender* is thus on the "Aprill" eclogue where Colin praises not the mortal Elisa but the virtue manifested through her, arraying Elisa in the immortal robes of the sun. For the brief moment during which Hobbinoll sings Colin's lay, the individual dissatisfactions and discordant impulses of the *Calender*'s pastoral world are suspended and that world is rearranged in a harmonious distribution. The lay offers us a glimpse of what Foxe might call a "new ioyning," a world of motion arranged around a point of light. Significantly, Spenser located the first month of England's new age in the fourth of the *Calender*'s eclogues, in April, the month of the Roman founder's day. Spenser therefore offered England a vision of itself as a reformed Rome whose citizens, poets, and queen together achieve a gracious congruence, a harmony that magnifies the greater pattern of proportionate distribution, of motion, that lies just outside our own sphere of uncertainty and change.

Works Cited

Primary Works

"A Meditation wherein the godly English giveth thankes to God for the Queene's Majesties prosperous government hitherto, and prayeth for the continuance thereof to God's glory." From vol. IX of *Harleian Miscellany*. Ed. T. Park. London, 1812. 136–39.

Alanus de Insulis. *Expl. in Cantica Canticorum*. Vol. 210 of *Patrologiae cursus completus, Series Latina*. Ed. J. P. Migne.

Alciati, Andrea. *Emblemata cum commentariis*. Padua, 1621. New York: Garland, 1976.

Ambrose, Saint. *Comm. in Cantica Canticorum*. Vol. 15 of *Patrologiae cursus completus, Series Latina*. Ed. J. P. Migne.

———. *De Isaac et Anima*. Vol. 14 of *Patrologiae cursus completus, Series Latina*. Ed. J. P. Migne.

———. *Exposition Evang. Secundum Lucam*. Vol. 15 of *Patrologiae cursus completus, Series Latina*. Ed. J. P. Migne.

Andrewes, Lancelot. *XCVI Sermons*. London: 1632.

Arber, Edward, ed. *A Transcript of the Registers of the Company of Stationers of London; 1554–1640*. Birmingham, 1894.

Arcandam. London, 1568.

Bacon, Francis. *De Sapientia Veterum*. London, 1609. *The Wisedome of the Ancients*. Trans. Sir Arthur Gorges. London, 1619. New York: Garland, 1976.

Baldwin, William. *A Treatyce of Morall philosophy containing the sayinges of the wise*. London, 1557?

Bale, John. *The Image of Both Churches*. London, 1548? or 1550?

Baret, John. *Alvearie or Triple Dictionarie*. London: H. Denham, 1573.

Bateman, Stephen. *A Christall Glasse of Christian Reformation*. London, 1569.

Bat[e]man, Stephen. *The New Arival of the three Graces into Anglia*. London, 1580?

Bat[e]man vppon Bartholome, his Booke, De Proprietatibus Rerum. Trans. Stephen Bat[e]man. London, 1582.

Benson, Larry D., ed. *The Riverside Chaucer*. Boston: Houghton-Mifflin: 1987.

Bentley, Thomas. *The Monument of Matrones*. London, 1582.

Bernard, Saint. *Sermones in Cantica Canticorum*. Vol. 184 of *Patrologiae cursus completus, Series Latina*. Ed. J. P. Migne.

Beza, Theodore. *A Tragedie of Abrahams Sacrifice*. Trans. Arthur Golding. Ed. Malcolm W. Wallace. University of Toronto Library, 1906.

Bible, English. *A misticall devise of the love between Christ and the Church*. Trans. Jude Smith. London, 1575.

―――. Bishops' Bible. London, 1568.

―――. Coverdale Bible. Cologne? 1535.

―――. *Ecclesiastes. Otherwise Called the Preacher*. Trans. Henry Lok. London, 1597.

―――. *Here begynneth the Proverbs of Salomon*. London, 1540.

―――. *The Geneva Bible*. A facsimile of the 1560 edition. Intro. Lloyd E. Berry. Madison: University of Wisconsin Press, 1969.

―――. *The Gospels of the fower Euangelistes translated in the olde Saxons tyme*. London, 1571.

―――. *The Poem of Poems or Sions Muse Contayning the diuine Song of King Salomon, deuided into Eight Eclogues*. Trans. Gervase Markham. London, 1596?

Boaistuau, Peter. *Theatrum Mundi*. Trans. John Alday. London, 1581.

Bode, G. H., ed. *Scriptores Rerum Mythicarum, Latini tres* (1834). Hildesheim, 1968.

Brentius, John. *Newes from Niniue to Englande, brought by the Prophete Ionas*. Trans. Thomas Tymme. London, 1570.

Bruno, Giordano. *The Ash Wednesday Supper*. Ed. and trans. Edward A. Gosselin and Lawrence S. Lerner. Hamden, CT: Archon Books, 1977.

Brutus, Junius (pseud.). *A Defense of Liberty Against Tyrants*. London, 1579. Trans. 1689. Intro. Harold J. Laski. London, 1924.

Bryskett, Lodowick. "A Discourse of Civil Life." *Literary Works*. Ed. J. H. P. Paffold. Gregg International Publishers, 1972.

Bunny, Edmund. *Certeine prayers and other godly exercises, for the seventeenth of November*. London, 1585.

Callistratus. *Descriptions in Philostratus the Elder, Imagines*. Trans. Arthur Fairbanks. New York: G. P. Putnam's Sons, 1931.

Camden, William. Selected chapters of *The History of the Most Renowned and Victorious Princess Elizabeth*. Ed. Wallace T. MacCaffrey. Chicago: University of Chicago Press, 1970.

―――. *The History of the Most Renowned and Victorious Princess Elizabeth*. London, 1688.

Carnicelli, D. D., ed. *Lord Morley's Triumphes of Fraunces Petrarch*. Cambridge, MA: Harvard University Press, 1971.

Cartari, Vicenzo. *Le Imagini Degli Dei*. Venice, 1571. New York: Garland, 1976.

Cartwright, Thomas. *A Dilucidation, or Exposition of the Epistle of St. Paul the Apostle to the Colossians, diliuered in sundry sermons*. Ed. A. B. Grosart. Edinburgh, 1864.

Cartwright, Thomas. *In Librum Salomonis, qui inscribitur Ecclesiastes*. London, 1604.

―――. *In Proverbis Salomonis*. Amsterdam, 1638.

Caxton, William. *Mirrour of the World*. Ed. Oliver H. Prior. London, 1913.

―――. Trans. *The History of Reynard the Fox*. Ed. Donald B. Sands. Cambridge, MA: Harvard University Press, 1960.

Caxton's Aesop. Ed. R. T. Lenaghan. Cambridge, MA: Harvard University Press, 1967.

Charbonnier, F. *Pamphlets protestants contre Ronsard, 1560–1577*. Paris, 1923.

Cheke, Sir John. *The hurt of Sedition*. London, 1569.

Clay, W. K., ed. *Preces Privatae*. Vol. 37 of *Private Prayers, Put forth by authority during the Reign of Queen Elizabeth*. Cambridge: Parker Society, Cambridge University Press, 1851.

Collier, J. P. *Broadside Blackletter Ballads*. London, 1868.

———, ed. *The Egerton Papers*. Camden Society London: John Bowyer Nichols and Son, 1840.

Collins, Arthur, ed. *Letters and Memorials of State . . . written and collected by Sir Henry Sidney, Sir Philip Sidney, Robert, Earl of Leicester, and Viscount Lisle*. 2 vols. London, 1746.

Comes, Natalis. *Mythologiae*. Venice, 1567. New York: Garland, 1976.

Corrie, J. E., ed. *Certain Sermons, appointed by the Queen's Majesty, 1574*. Cambridge: John W. Parker, 1850.

Cunliffe, John W. ed. *The Complete Works of George Gascoigne*. 2 vols. Cambridge: Cambridge University Press, 1907.

Curteys, Richard, Bishop of Chichester. *The 14th. day of Marche, 1573*. London: Henry Bynneman, 1579.

De Boer, C., ed. *Ovide Moralisé*. Vol. 15 of *Verhandelingen der Koninklijke Akademie van Wetense happen te Amsterdam*. Amsterdam: J. Muller, 1915.

de la Primaudaye, Pierre. *The French Academy*. Trans. T. B. 3d edition. London, 1594.

de Lorris, Guillaume, and Jean de Meun. *The Romance of the Rose*. Trans. Charles Dahlberg. Princeton: Princeton University Press, 1971.

Dee, John. *The Mathematical Preface to the Elements of Geometrie of Euclid of Megara (1570)*. Intro. Allen G. Debus. New York: Science History Publications, 1975.

The Dialoges of Creatures Moralized. Antwerp, 1535.

Digges, Leonard. *A Prognostication euerlasting*. London, 1556. Revised by his son Thomas and reissued; London: Thomas Marsh, 1576.

Drant, Thomas. *Two Sermons Preached*. London, 1572.

Drayton, Michael. *Works*. Ed. J. William Hebel. 5 vols. Oxford: Basil Blackwell, 1961.

DuBartas, Guillaume De Salluste Sieur. *Works*. Ed. U. T. Holmes, John Coreden Lyons, and R. W. Linker. Chapel Hill: University of North Carolina Press, 1935.

DuBellay, Joachim. *Le Deffence et Illustration de La Langue Francoyse*. Ed. H. Chamard. Paris: Didier, 1948.

Dyson, H., collector. *All Such Proclamations as Were Published During the Reign of Elizabeth*. London, 1618.

Estienne, Charles. *Dictionarium Historicum, Geographicum, Poeticum*. Paris, 1596. New York: Garland, 1976.

Fering, W. *A newe yeres gift, entituled, A Christal glas*. London, 1569.

Fills, Robert, trans. *The Lawes and statues of Geneva, translated out of frenche into Englishe*. London, 1562.

Fortescue, Sir John. *A learned commendation of the politique lawes of England*. Trans. Robert Mulcaster. London: R. Tottel, 1573.

Foxe, John. "A Sermon of Christ Crucified." London, 1570.

———. *The Acts and Monuments*. 8 vols. New York: AMS, 1965.

———. "The Epistle to the Reader." *The Whole Works of W. Tyndall, John Frith, and Doct. Barnes*. London: John Daye, 1573.

Fraunce, Abraham. *The Third part of the Countesse of Pembroke's Yuychurch*. London, 1592. New York: Garland, 1976.

Ghisalberti, Fausto, ed. *Integumenta Ovidii*. Milan, 1933.

Gildas. *De excidio*. Ed. John Josseline (?). London: John Davis, 1568.

―――. *A Description of the State of Great Brittain*. London: John Hancock, 1652.

Glossa Ordinaria. Vol. 113 of *Patrologiae cursus completus, Series Latina*. Ed. J. P. Migne.

Golding, Arthur, trans. *The woorke of the excellent Philosopher Lucius Annaeus Seneca concerning Benefyting, that is too say the dooing recyuing, and requyting of good Turnes*. London, 1578.

Grafton, Richard. *A Chronicle . . . and History of the affayres of Englande.* . . . London, 1569.

Green, Henry, ed. *Whitney's "Choice of Emblemes," A Facsimile Reprint*. London: Lovell Reeve and Co., 1866.

Greville, Fulke. *Life of Sir Philip Sidney*. Oxford, 1907.

Grueber, H. A. *Medallic Illustrations of the History of Great Britain and Ireland to the Death of George II*. London: 1911.

Hake, Edward. "A Commemoration of the Most prosperous and peaceable Raigne of our gratious and deere Soveraigne Lady Elizabeth." London, 1575. In vol. 9 of *Harleian Miscellany*. Ed. T. Park. London, 1812. 123–38.

Harvey, Gabriel. *Ciceronianus*. Trans. C. A. Forbes. University of Nebraska Studies. Lincoln, 1945.

―――. *Marginalia*. Ed. G. C. Moore Smith. Stratford-upon-Avon, 1913.

Heffner, R., D. E. Mason, F. M. Padelford, comp. *Spenser Allusions in the Sixteenth and Seventeenth Centuries*. Chapel Hill: The University of North Carolina Press, 1972.

Holliwell, J. O., ed. *The Private Diary of Dr. John Dee and The Catalogue of His Library of Manuscripts*. Camden Society. London: John Bowyer Nichols and Son, 1842.

Hooker, Richard. *The Laws of Ecclesiastical Polity. Works*. Ed. John Keble. Oxford: The Clarendon Press, 1874.

Hugh of St. Victor. *In Salomonis Ecclesiasten*, Hom. XIX. In vol. 175 of *Patrologiae cursus completus, Series Latina*. Ed. J. P. Migne.

James, William. "A Sermon Preached Before the Queenes Maiestie at Hampton Court the 19. of February laste paste." London: 1578.

Jewel, John. Vol. 24 of *The Works of John Jewel*. Ed. John Ayre. Cambridge: Parker Society, Cambridge University Press, 1847.

The Kalender of Shepherdes. The Edition of Paris 1503 in Photographic Facsimile, A Faithful Reprint of R. Pynson's Edition of London, 1506. 3 vols. Ed. H. Oskar Sommer. London, 1892.

Knewstubb, John. "A Sermon preached at Paules Crosse the Fryday before Easter . . . in the yeere of our lorde, 1579." London, 1579.

Lamond, Elizabeth, ed. *A Discourse of the Common Weal of This Realm of England*. Cambridge: Cambridge University Press, 1893; rpt. 1954.

Langham, Robert. *A Letter*. Ed. R. J. P. Kuin. Vol. 2 of *Medieval and Renaissance Texts*. Leiden: E. J. Brill, 1983.

Lemon, Robert, ed. *Calender of State Papers*. Vol. 19 of the Domestic Series. London, 1856. Nendelm Liechtenstein: Kraus Reprint, 1967.

Lucan. *The Civil War*. Ed. and trans. J. D. Duff. New York: G. P. Putnam's Sons, 1928.

Luther, Martin. *Lectures on the Song of Solomon*. Vol. 15 of *Luthor's Works*. Ed. J. Pelikan. St. Louis: Concordia Press, 1972.

MacDonald, Robert H., ed. *The Library of Drummond of Hawthornden*. Edinburgh: Edinburgh University Press, 1971.

Marot, Clément. *Oeuvres Lyriques*. Ed. C. A. Mayer. London: The Athlone Press, 1964.

Mayor, J. E. B., ed. *The English Works of John Fisher*. London, 1887.

Memmo, Paul Eugene, Jr. *Giordano Bruno's the Heroice Frenzies, a Translation with Introduction and Notes*. Chapel Hill: University of North Carolina Press, 1964.

Murdin, William, comp. *A Collection of State Papers Relating to Affairs in the Reign of Queen Elizabeth, 1571–1596* (left by William Cecil). London: William Bowyer, 1759.

Mustard, W. P. *The Eclogues of Baptista Mantuanus*. Baltimore: The Johns Hopkins Press, 1911.

Nichols, John, ed. *The Progresses and Public Processions of Queen Elizabeth*. 3 vols. London, 1823. New York: AMS, 1960.

North, Thomas, trans. *The Morall Philosophy of Doni*. London: Henry Denham, 1569/70.

Opera Virgiliana. Lyons: J. Crespin, 1529.

Osborn, J. M., ed. *The Queenes Maiestes Passage through the Citie of London to Westminster the Day Before her Coronation*. New Haven: Yale University Press, 1960.

Ovid. *Metamorphoses* (incl. glosses of Pierre Bersuire). Lyon, 1518. New York: Garland, 1976.

Ovid's Metamorphoses, Englished, Mythologized, and Represented in Figures. Ed. Karl K. Hulley and Stanley F. Vandersoll. Foreword by Douglas Bush. Lincoln: University of Nebraska Press, 1970.

Palengenius, Marcellus. *The Zodiake of Life*. Trans. Barnabe Googe, with an introduction by Rosemond Tuve. Delmar, NY: Scholars' Facsimiles and Reprints, 1947.

Patten, William. *Calender of Scripture*. London, 1575.

Pausanius. *Description of Greece*. Trans. and ed. W. H. S. Jones. 6 vols. New York: G. P. Putnam's Sons, 1918.

Peacham, Henry. *Minerva Britanna* (1612). English Emblem Books No. 5. Ed. John Harden. Hamden, CT: Scholar Press, 1969.

Peter Lombard. Vol. 191 of *Patrologiae cursus completus, Series Latina*. Ed. J. P. Migne.

Petrarch, Francis. *Petrarch, Opera con li commenti sopra li Triumphi, Soneti, Canzoni*. Ed. Bernardo Lapini (Bernardo Illicino). Milan, 1512.

Philip of Harvengt. *Cantici Canticorum Explicatio*. In vol. 203 of *Patrologiae cursus completus, Series Latina*. Ed. J. P. Migne.

———. *Responsio de Damnatione Salomonis*. In vol. 203 of *Patrologiae cursus completus, Series Latina*. Ed. J. P. Migne.

Philostratus. *Les Images*. Trans. Blaise de Vigenere. Paris, 1614. New York: Garland, 1976.

Pit, I. "A Prayer and also a thanksgiving . . . to be sung the xvii day of November." London, 1577.

Plutarch's Lives of the Noble Grecians and Romans englished by Sir Thomas North (1579). Intro. George Wyndham. New York: AMS Press, 1967.

Pollard, A. W., and G. R. Redgrove, comp. *A Short Title Catalogue of Books Printed in England, Scotland, and Ireland, and of Books Printed Abroad, 1475–1640*. London, 1926.

Pollard, A. W., ed. *The Queen's Majesty's Entertainment at Woodstock, 1575*. Oxford, 1910.

Pontanus, Jacobus. *Symbolarum. Libri XVII Virgilieu.* Augsburg, 1599. New York: Garland, 1976.

Prime, John. "A Sermon Briefly Comparing the Estate of King Solomon and his Subiects togither with the condition of Queene Elizabeth and her people." Oxford, 1585.

Puttenham, George. "The Partheniades." In vol. 2 of *Ballads from Manuscript.* Ed. F. G. Furnivall and W. R. Morfill. Hertford: The Ballad Society, Stephen Austin and Sons, 1873. 72–91.

———. *The Arte of English Poesie. A Facsimile Reproduction.* Intro. Baxter Hathaway. Kent: Kent State University Press, 1970.

Radbertus, Paschasius. "Expositio in Ps. XLIV." In vol. 120 of *Patrologiae cursus completus, Series Latina.* Ed. J. P. Migne.

Recorde, Robert. *The Castle of Knowledge.* London, 1556.

Reynolds, Henry. *Mythomystes.* Vol. 1 of *Critical Essays of the Seventeenth Century.* Ed. J. E. Spingarn. Oxford, 1908.

———. *The Tale of Narcissus.* The Orinda Booklets, Extra Series, III. Hull: J. R. Tutin, 1906.

Richard of St. Victor. *Explicatio in Cantica Canticorum.* Vol. 196. *Patrologiae cursus completus, Series Latina.* Ed. J. P. Migne.

Rogers, Thomas. *A Golden Chaine. taken out of the rich Treasurehouse the Psalmes of King David: also, the pretious Pearles of King Salomon.* London: H. Denham, 1579.

Rupert. *In Librum Ecclesiastes.* In vol. 168 of *Patrologiae cursus completus, Series Latina.* Ed. J. P. Migne.

Sabinus, Georgius. *Metamorphosis Seu Fabulae Poeticae.* Frankfurt, 1589. New York: Garland, 1976.

Sandys, Edwin. Vol. 41 of *Sermons.* Ed. John Ayre. Cambridge: Parker Society, Cambridge University Press, 1841.

Scott, Edward G. L., ed. *Letter-Book of Gabriel Harvey.* Camden Society, N. s. 33. Westminster, Nicholas and Sons, 1884.

Shakespeare's Ovid, Being Arthur Goldings Translation of the Metamorphoses. Ed. W. H. D. Rouse. Carbondale: Southern Illinois University Press, 1961.

Sheltoo a Geveren. *Of the ende of this worlde.* Trans. T. Rogers. London, 1577.

Sidney, Sir Philip. *Poems.* Ed. William Ringler. Oxford: Clarendon Press, 1962.

———. *Works.* Ed. Albert Feuillerat. 4 vols. Cambridge: Cambridge University Press, 1922.

Sixe Idillia, That is, Sixe Small, or Petty Poems, or AEglogues, chosen out of the right famous Sicilian Poet Theocritus, and translated into English Verse. Oxford: Joseph Barnes, 1588.

Skeat, Walter W., ed. *Chaucerian and Other Pieces.* Oxford: Clarendon Press, 1897.

Skelton, John. *Merie Tales.* London: Thomas Colwell, 1567.

Spagnuoli, Baptista. *The Eglogs . . . turned into English verse.* Trans. George Turberville. London, 1572.

Spenser, Edmund. *The Shepheardes Calender. A Facsimile Reproduction.* Ed. S. K. Heninger, Jr. Delmar, NY: Scholars' Facsimiles and Reprints, 1979.

———. *The Yale Edition of the Shorter Poems of Edmund Spenser.* Ed. William A. Oram, et al. New Haven: Yale University Press, 1989.

———. *Works.* A Variorum Edition. 11 vols. Ed. Edwin Greenlaw, et al. Baltimore: The Johns Hopkins University Press, 1966.

Stockwood, John. "A Sermon Preached at Paules Crosse on Bartholomew Day, being the 24. of August, 1578." London, 1578.

Stow, John. *The Chronicles of England from Brute vnto this present yeare of Christ, 1580*. London, 1580.

Stubbs, John. *Gaping Gulf with Letters and Other Relevant Documents*. Ed. Lloyd E. Berry. Charlottesville: The University of Virginia Press, 1968.

Theodore de Beze. *Comm. in Iobus, Ecclesiastes*. London, 1589.

Thomas of Perseigne. *Comment. in Cantica Canticorum*. Vol. 206 of *Patrologiae cursus completus, Series Latina*. Ed. J. P. Migne.

Tusser, Thomas. *Five Hundred Pointes of Good Husbandrie, The Edition of 1580 collated with those of 1573 and 1577. Together with a Reprint from the Unique Copy in the British Museum, of "A Hundreth Good Pointes of Husbandrie," 1557*. Ed. W. Payne and Sidney J. Herrtage. London: Trübner, 1878.

Twyne, Thomas. *The Schoolmaster, or Teacher of Table Philosophie*. London: Richard Jones, 1576.

Valerius, Cornelius. *Casket of Iewels: contaynynge a playne description of Morall Philosophie*. Trans. I. C. London, 1571.

van der Noot, Jan. *A Theatre for Voluptuous Worldlings, A Facsimile Reproduction*. Intro. Louis S. Friedland. Delmar, New York: Scholars' Facsimiles and Reprints, 1977.

Virgil. *Bucolica Virgilij cum commento familiari*. London: Wynken de Worde, 1522.

———. *Bucolics*. Naples, 1510.

———. *Eclogues*. Comm., Michael Barth. Lipsiae, 1570.

———. *The Bucoliks of Publivs Virgilivs Maro . . . translated into English verse by A. F.* (Abraham Fleming). London, 1589.

———. *Opera*. Venice, 1507.

———. *Opera Virgiliana*. Lyons: John Crespin, 1529.

White, Beatrice, ed. *The Eclogues of Alexander Barclay*, from the original edition by John Cawood. London, 1928.

Willes, Richard. *De Re Poetica*. Trans. A. D. S. Fowler. Oxford: Published for the Luttrell Society by Basil Blackwell, 1958.

Wimbledon, R. "A Sermon No lesse fruitfull then famous. Made in the yeare . . . 1388. And founde out hyd in a wall." London, 1579.

Woolton, John. *A Newe Anatomie of Whole Man*. London, 1576.

Young, John. "A Sermon preached before the Queenes Maiestie, the second of March. 1575." London, 1576?

Youngs, Frederic A., Jr., ed. *The Proclamations of the Tudor Queens*. Cambridge: Cambridge University Press, 1976.

Secondary Works

Adams, Marjorie. "Ronsard and Spenser: The Commentary." *Renaissance Papers presented at The Renaissance Meeting in the Southeastern States*. Duke University, April 23–24, 1954. Durham: Southeastern Renaissance Conference. 25–29.

Adams, Robert P. "Opposed Tudor Myths of Power: Machiavellian Tyrants and Christian Kings." *Studies in the Continental Background of Renaissance English Literature, Essays Presented to John L. Leevsay*. Ed. Dale B. J. Randall and George Walton Williams. Durham: Duke University Press, 1977.

Alpers, Paul. "The Eclogue Tradition and the Nature of Pastoral." *CE* 34 (1972): 352–71.

————. *The Singer of the Eclogues: A Study of Virgilian Pastoral*. Berkeley: University of California Press, 1979.

————. "Pastoral and the Domain of Lyric in Spenser's *Shepheardes Calender*." *Representing the Renaissance*. Ed. Stephen Greenblatt. Berkeley: University of California Press, 1988.

————. "What is Pastoral?" *CI* 8 (1982): 437–60.

Alton, E. H. "The Mediaeval Commentators on Ovid's *Fasti*." *Hermathena* 44 (1926): 119–51.

Anderson, Judith. *The Growth of a Personal Voice: Piers Plowman and The Faerie Queene*. New Haven: Yale University Press, 1976.

Baroway, I. "The Imagery of Spenser and the Song of Solomon." *JEGP* 33 (1934): 23–45.

Beilin, Elaine V. *Redeeming Eve*. Princeton: Princeton University Press, 1987.

Bell, James. *Queen Elizabeth and a Swedish Princess*. London, 1926.

Berger, Harry, Jr. "The Aging Boy: Paradise and Parricide in Spenser's *Shepheardes Calender*." *Poetic Traditions of the English Renaissance*. Ed. Maynard Mack and George deForest Lord. New Haven: Yale University Press, 1982.

————. "A Secret Discipline: *The Faerie Queene*, Book VI." *Form and Convention in the Poetry of Edmund Spenser*. Ed. William Nelson. New York: Columbia University Press, 1961. 35–75.

————. "Orpheus, Pan, and the Poetics of Misogyny: Spenser's Critique of Pastoral Love and Art." *ELH* 50 (1983): 61–81.

————. "The Mirror Stage of Colin Clout: A New Reading of Spenser's *Januarye* Eclogue." *Helios* 10 (1983): 139–60.

————. "Mode and Diction in *The Shepheardes Calender*." *MP* 67 (1969): 140–49.

Bergeron, David M. *English Civic Pageantry, 1558–1642*. Columbia: University of South Carolina Press, 1971.

Bergman, Martin S. "The Legend of Narcissus." *AI* 41 (1984): 389–411.

Berry, Arthur. *A Short History of Astronomy From Earliest Times Through the Nineteenth Century*. New York: Dover Publications, rpt. 1961.

Bevington, David. *Tudor Drama and Politics*. Cambridge: Harvard University Press, 1968.

Billington, James H. *Fire in the Minds of Men*. New York: Basic Books, 1980.

Binns, J. W., ed. *Ovid*. London: Routledge and Kegan Paul, 1973.

Boker, H. "The Zodiacal Miniature of the 'Tres Riches Heures' of the Duke of Berry—Its Sources and Meaning." *JWCI* 11 (1948): 1–34.

Bond, Ronald B. "Supplantation in the Elizabethan Court: The Theme of Spenser's February Eclogue." *Spenser Studies* 2 (1981): 55–66.

Bosanquet, Eustace F. *English Printed Almanacks and Prognostications, A Bibliographical History to the Year 1600*. London: Chiswick Press, 1917.

Braden, Gordon. *The Classics and English Renaissance Poetry*. New Haven: Yale University Press, 1978.

Bradley, Sister Ritamary. "Backgrounds of the Title *Speculum* in Mediaeval Literature." *Speculum* 29 (1954): 100–115.

Buck, P. M., Jr. "Spenser's Lost Poems." *PMLA* 23 (1908): 80–99.

Bush, Douglas. *Mythology and the Renaissance Tradition in English Poetry*. Minneapolis: University of Minnesota Press, 1932.

Butterworth, Charles C. *The English Primers (1529–1545)*. Philadelphia: University of Pennsylvania Press, 1953.

Byrom, H. G. "Edmund Spenser's First Printer, Hugh Singleton." *The Library*, Fourth Series, 14 (1933): 121–56.

Cain, Thomas. "Spenser and the Renaissance Orpheus." *UTQ* 41 (1971): 24–47.

———. *Praise in The Faerie Queene*. Lincoln: The University of Nebraska Press, 1978.

Campbell, Lily B. "The Use of Historical Patterns in the Reign of Elizabeth." *Huntington Library Quarterly* 1 (1937–38): 135–67.

———. *Divine Poetry and Drama in Sixteenth-Century England*. Berkeley: University of California Press, 1959.

Capp, Bernard. *English Almanacs 1500–1800*. Ithaca: Cornell University Press, 1979.

Castor, Grahame. *Pléiade Poetics*. Cambridge: Cambridge University Press, 1964.

Cheney, Donald. "The Circular Argument of *The Shepheardes Calender*." *Unfolded Tales: Essays on Renaissance Romance*. Ed. George M. Logan and Gordon Teskey. Ithaca: Cornell University Press, 1989. 137–61.

Colie, Rosalie. *The Resources of Kind: Genre Theory in the Renaissance*. Ed. B. K. Lewalski. Berkeley: University of California Press, 1973.

Colvin, Sidney. *Early Engraving and Engravers in England (1545–1695)*. London, 1905.

Constable, Giles. "The Popularity of Twelfth-Century Spiritual Writers in the Late Middle Ages." *Renaissance Studies in Honor of Hans Baron*. Ed. A. Maeho and J. A. Tiedeschi. Florence, 1971.

Cooper, Helen. *Pastoral: Mediaeval into Renaissance*. Totowa: Rowman and Littlefield, 1977.

Courcelle, P. *Recherches sur les Confessions de Saint Augustine*. Paris, 1950.

Coyne, G. V., S. J., M. A. Hoskin, and O. Pedersen, eds. *Gregorian Reform of the Calendar, Proceedings of the Vatican Conference to Commemorate Its 400th Anniversary, 1582–1982*. Vatican: Pontifical Academy of Sciences, 1983.

Craig, D. H. "A Hybrid Growth: Sidney's Theory of Poetry in *An Apology for Poetry*." *ELR* 10 (1980): 183–201.

Cullen, Patrick. *Spenser, Marvell, and Renaissance Pastoral*. Cambridge, MA: Harvard University Press, 1970.

Davies, Horton. *Worship and Theology in England, 1534–1603*. Princeton: Princeton University Press, 1970.

DeNeef, A. Leigh. "Of Dialogues and Historicisms." *SAQ* 86 (1987): 497–517.

———. *Spenser and the Motives of Metaphor*. Durham: Duke University Press, 1982.

Dick, Hugh G. "Thomas Blundeville's *The fine order and methode of wryting and reading Hystories* (1574)." *Huntington Library Quarterly* 3 (1939–40): 149–70.

Dickens, Arthur G. *The English Reformation*. London: Batsford, 1964.

Donaldson, E. Talbot. "Chaucer the Pilgrim." *PMLA* 69 (1954): 928–36.

Droz, E., ed. *Aspects de la Propagande Religieuse*. Vol. 28 of *Travaux D'Humanisme et Renaissance*. Geneva, 1957.

Dufour, Alain. *Histoire Politique et Psychologie Historique: Le Mythe de Genève aux temps de Calvin*. Geneva, 1966.

Durr, Robert Allen. "Spenser's Calendar of Christian Time." *ELH* 24 (1957): 269–95.

Eisenstein, Elizabeth L. *The Printing Press as an Agent of Change*. New York: Cambridge University Press, 1979.

Ferguson, Margaret W. " 'The Afflatus of Ruin,' Meditations on Rome by DuBellay, Spenser, and Stevens." *Roman Images,* Selected Papers from the English Institute. N.s. 8. Ed. Annabel Patterson. Baltimore: Johns Hopkins University Press, 1984. 23–50.

Fowler, Alastair. *Spenser and the Numbers of Time*. New York, 1964.

————. *Kinds of Literature: An Introduction to the Theory of Genres and Modes.* Cambridge, MA: Harvard University Press, 1982.

Garrett, C. H. *The Marian Exiles.* Cambridge: Cambridge University Press, 1938.

Gingerich, O. "The Civil Reception of the Gregorian Calendar." *Gregorian Reform of the Calendar, Proceedings of the Vatican Conference to Commemorate Its 400th Anniversary, 1582–1982.* Ed. G. V. Coyne, S. J., M. A. Hoskin, and O. Pedersen. Vatican: Pontifical Academy of Sciences, 1983. 265–80.

Goldberg, Jonathan. "Colin to Hobbinol: Spenser's Familiar Letters." *SAQ* 88 (1989): 107–26.

————. *Voice Terminal Echo.* New York: Methuen, 1986.

Goldin, Frederick. *The Mirror of Narcissus in the Courtly Love Lyric.* Ithaca: Cornell University Press, 1967.

Golding, Louis Thorn. *An Elizabethan Puritan: Arthur Golding.* New York: 1937.

Gombrich, E. H. *Symbolic Images: Studies in the Art of the Renaissance.* London: Phaidon, 1972.

Goyau, Georges. *Une Ville-Eglise: Genève, 1535–1907.* Paris, 1919.

Grafton, Anthony. "From *Die Natali* to *De Emendatione Temporum:* The Origins and Setting of Scaliger's Chronology." *JWCI* 48 (1985): 100–143.

Grant, William Leonard. *Neo-Latin Literature and the Pastoral.* Chapel Hill: University of North Carolina Press, 1965.

Greene, Thomas M. *The Light in Troy: Imitation and Discovery in Renaissance Poetry.* New Haven: Yale University Press, 1982.

Greg, W. W. *Pastoral Poetry and Pastoral Drama.* New York: Russell and Russell, 1959.

Haller, William. *Foxe's Book of Martyrs and the Elect Nation* London: 1963.

Hamilton, A. C. "Our New Poet: Spenser, 'Well of English Undefild.' " *A Theatre for Spenserians.* Ed. J. M. Kennedy and J. A. Reither. Toronto: University of Toronto Press, 1973. 101–23.

————. "The Argument of Spenser's *Shepheardes Calender.*" *ELH* 23 (1956): 171–82.

————. *Sir Philip Sidney: A Study of His Life and Work.* Cambridge: Cambridge University Press, 1977.

Hanning, Robert W. *The Vision of History in Early Britain.* New York: Columbia University Press, 1966.

Harbison, Craig. *The Last Judgment in Sixteenth-Century Northern Europe: A Study of the Relation Between Art and the Reformation.* New York: Garland Press, 1976.

Harley, Marta Powell. "Narcissus, Hermaphroditus, and Attis: Ovidian Lovers at the Fontaine d'Amors in Guillaume de Lorris' *Roman de la Rose.*" *PMLA* 101 (1986): 324–37.

Hawkins, Sherman. "Mutabilitie and the Cycle of the Months." *Form and Convention in the Poetry of Edmund Spenser,* selected Papers from the English Institute. Ed. William Nelson. New York: Columbia University Press, 1961; rpt. 1967. 76–102.

Helgerson, Richard. *Self-Crowned Laureates.* Berkeley: University of California Press, 1983.

Heninger, S. K. *The Cosmographical Glass, Renaissance Diagrams of the Universe.* San Marino: The Huntington Library, 1977.

————. *Touches of Sweet Harmony.* San Marino: The Huntington Library, 1974.

————. "The Implications of Form for *The Shepheardes Calender.*" *Studies in the Renaissance* 9 (1962): 309–21.

Hieatt, A. Kent. *Short Times Endless Monument: The Symbolism of Numbers in*

Edmund Spenser's "Epithalamion." Port Washington, NY: Kennikat Press, 1960.

Hoffman, Nancy Jo. *Spenser's Pastorals.* Baltimore: Johns Hopkins University Press, 1977.

Hollander, John. *The Figure of Echo: A Mode of Allusion in Milton and After.* Berkeley: University of California Press, 1981.

Hoskin, M. A. "The Reception of the Calendar by Other Churches." *Gregorian Reform of the Calendar, Proceedings of the Vatican Conference to Commemorate Its 400th Anniversary, 1582–1982.* Ed. G. V. Coyne, S. J., M. A. Hoskin, and O. Pedersen. Vatican: Pontifical Academy of Sciences, 1983. 255–64.

Howard, Jean E. "The New Historicism in Renaissance Studies." *ELR* 16 (1986): 13–43.

Hughes, Merritt Y. "Spenser and the Greek Pastoral Triad." *SP* 20 (1923): 184–215.

Hume, Anthea. *Edmund Spenser: Protestant Poet.* Cambridge: Cambridge University Press, 1984.

———. "Spenser, Puritanism, and the 'Maye' Eclogue." *RES* 20 (1969): 155–67.

Iser, Wolfgang. "Spenser's Arcadia: The Interpretation of Fiction and History." *Protocol of the Colloquy of the Center for Hermeneutical Studies in Hellenistic and Modern Culture* 38 (1980): 1–19.

Jahn, Robert. "Letters and Booklists of Thomas Chard (or Chare) of London, 1583–4." *Library,* 4th ser., 4 (1923): 219–37.

Jameson, Fredric. *The Political Unconscious.* Ithaca: Cornell University Press, 1981.

Jardine, L. "Humanism and Dialectic in Sixteenth Century Cambridge: A Preliminary Investigation." *Classical Influences on European Culture. A.D. 1500–1700.* Ed. R. R. Bolgar. Cambridge: Cambridge University Press, 1976.

Jayne, Sears. *John Colet and Marsilio Ficino.* New York, 1963.

———. *Library Catalogues of the English Renaissance.* Berkeley: University of California Press, 1956.

Jenkins, Raymond. "Who is E. K.?" *Shakespeare Association Bulletin* 19 (1944): 147–60.

Johnson, F. R., and S. V. Larkey. "Thomas Digges, the Copernican System and the Idea of the Infinity of the Universe, in 1576." *Huntington Library Bulletin* 5–6 (1934): 69–117.

———. *Astronomical Thought in Renaissance England.* Baltimore, 1937. Reprint. Octagon Books, 1968.

Johnson, Lynn Staley. "Chauntecleer, Son of Troy." *Chaucer Review* 19 (1985): 225–44.

———. "Elizabeth, Bride and Queen: A Study of Spenser's April Eclogue and the Metaphors of English Protestantism." *Spenser Studies* 2 (1981): 75–91.

———. "Old Wine in New Bottles: Thomas Blenerhasset's Elizabethan Shepherd's Pageant." *Journal of the Rocky Mountain Medieval and Renaissance Association* 5 (1984): 107–18.

———. *The Voice of the "Gawain"-Poet.* Madison: University of Wisconsin Press, 1984.

Jones, R. F. *Triumph of the English Language.* Stanford: Stanford University Press, 1953.

Judson, Alexander C. *The Life of Edmund Spenser.* Vol. 11 of *The Works of Edmund Spenser, a Variorum Edition.* Ed. Edwin Greenlaw, et al. Baltimore: The Johns Hopkins University Press, 1966.

Kerling, Johan. *Chaucer in Early English Dictionaries.* Leiden: Leiden University Press, 1979.

King, John N. *English Reformation Literature: The Tudor Origins of the Protestant Tradition*. Princeton: Princeton University Press, 1982.

———. "Spenser's *Shepheardes Calender* and Protestant Pastoral Satire." *Renaissance Genres: Essays on Theory, History, and Interpretation*. Ed. Barbara Kiefer Lewalski. Harvard English Studies 14. Cambridge, MA: Harvard University Press, 1986. 369–98.

———. "The Godly Woman in Elizabethan Iconography." *Renaissance Quarterly* 38 (1985): 41–84.

———. "Was Spenser a Puritan?" *Spenser Studies* 6 (1985): 1–31.

———. Rev. of *Spenser's "Faerie Queene" and the Cult of Elizabeth,* by Robin H. Wells. *Huntington Library Quarterly* 47 (1984): 139–40.

Kingdon, Robert M. *Geneva and the Coming of the Wars of Religion in France, 1555–1563*. Geneva, 1956.

Kinney, Arthur F. *John Skelton: Priest as Poet. Seasons of Discovery*. Chapel Hill: University of North Carolina Press, 1987.

Kipling, Gordon. *The Triumph of Honor: Burgundian Origins of the Elizabethan Renaissance*. Leiden: Leiden University Press, 1977.

Kocher, Paul H. *Science and Religion in Elizabethan England*. San Marino: Huntington Library, 1953. Rpt.; New York: Octagon Books, 1969.

Kolve, V. A. "*Everyman* and the Parable of the Talents." *Medieval English Drama*. Ed. Jerome Taylor and Alan H. Nelson. Chicago: The University of Chicago Press, 1972.

Kuhn, Thomas S. *The Copernican Revolution*. Cambridge, MA: Harvard University Press, 1979.

LaCapra, Dominick. *Rethinking Intellectual History: Texts, Contexts, Language*. Ithaca: Cornell University Press, 1983.

Leach, Eleanor W. *Virgil's Eclogues. Landscapes of Experience*. Ithaca: Cornell University Press, 1974.

Lee, Sidney. *The French Renaissance in England*. Oxford, 1910.

Lemmi, Charles. *The Classic Deities in Bacon*. Baltimore: The Johns Hopkins University Press, 1933.

Lewalski, Barbara Keifer. *Protestant Poetics and the Seventeenth-Century Religious Lyric*. Princeton: Princeton University Press, 1979.

Luborsky, Ruth Samson. "The Allusive Presentation of *The Shepheardes Calender*." *Spenser Studies* 1 (1980): 29–67.

———. "The Illustrations to *The Shepheardes Calender*." *Spenser Studies* 2 (1981): 3–53.

MacCaffrey, Isabel G. "Allegory and Pastoral in *The Shepheardes Calender*." *ELH* 36 (1969): 88–109.

MacCaffrey, Wallace T. "Place and Patronage in Elizabethan Politics." *Elizabethan Government and Society, Essays Presented to Sir John Neale*. Ed. S. T. Bindoff, et al. London: University of London, 1961. 95–126.

———. *Queen Elizabeth and the Making of Policy*. Princeton: Princeton University Press, 1981.

———. "The Anjou Match and the Making of Elizabethan Foreign Policy." *The English Commonwealth 1547–1640*. Ed. Peter Clark, Alan G. P. Smith, Nicholas Tyache. New York: Barnes and Noble, 1979. 59–75.

Mâle, Emile. *The Gothic Image*. Trans. Dora Nussey. New York: Harper and Row, 1958.

Mallette, Richard. "Spenser's Portrait of the Artist in *The Shepheardes Calender* and *Colin Clouts Come Home Again*." *SEL* 19 (1979): 19–41.

Martin, Charles. *Les Protestant Anglais réfugiés à Genève au temps de Calvin*. Geneva, 1915.

Martines, Lauro. *Society and History in English Renaissance Verse*. Oxford: Basil Blackwell, 1985.

McCanles, Michael. "*The Shepheardes Calender* as Document and Monument." *SEL* 22 (1982): 5–19.

McFarlane, Ian. *A Literary History of France: Renaissance France, 1470–1589*. London: Benn, 1974.

McLane, Paul E. *Spenser's Shepheardes Calender: A Study in Elizabethan Allegory*. Notre Dame, Indiana: University of Notre Dame Press, 1961; rpt. 1970.

Meyer, Russell J. " 'Fixt in heauens hight': Spenser, Astronomy, and the Date of the *Cantos of Mutabilitie*." *Spenser Studies* 4 (1983): 115–29.

Miedema, Hessel. "The Term *Emblema* in Alciati." *JWCI* 31 (1968): 234–50.

Miller, David. "Abandoning the Quest." *ELH* 46 (1979): 173–92.

———. "Authorship, Anonymity, and *The Shepheardes Calender*." *MLQ* 40 (1979): 219–36.

Miskimin, Alice. *The Renaissance Chaucer*. New Haven: Yale University Press, 1975.

Montrose, Louis Adrian. " 'Eliza, Queen of Shepheardes,' and the Pastoral of Power." *ELR* 10 (1980): 153–82.

———. "Interpreting Spenser's February Eclogue: Some Contexts and Implications." *Spenser Studies* 2 (1981): 67–74.

———. " 'The perfecte paterne of a Poete': The Poetics of Courtship in *The Shepheardes Calender*." *Texas Studies in Literature and Language* 21 (1979): 34–67.

———. "Of Gentlemen and Shepherds: The Politics of Elizabethan Pastoral Form." *ELH* 50 (1983): 415–59.

———. "Renaissance Literary Studies and the Subject of History." *ELR* 16 (1986): 5–12.

Moore, John W., Jr. "Colin Breaks His Pipe: A Reading of the 'January' Eclogue." *ELR* 5 (1975): 3–24.

Murrin, Michael. *The Veil of Allegory*. Chicago: The University of Chicago Press, 1966.

Neale, J. E. *Elizabeth I and Her Parliaments, 1559–1581*. New York: St. Martin's Press, 1958.

———. *Queen Elizabeth I*. New York: Doubleday, 1957.

Nohrnberg, James. *The Analogy of the Faerie Queene*. Princeton: Princeton University Press, 1976.

Norbrook, David. *Poetry and Politics in the English Renaissance*. Boston: Routledge and Kegan Paul, 1984.

North, J. D. "The Western Calendar—'Intolerabilis, Horribilis, et Derisibilis.' " *Gregorian Reform of the Calendar, Proceedings of the Vatican Conference to Commemorate Its 400th Anniversary, 1582–1982*. Ed. G. V. Coyne, S. J., M. A. Hoskin, and O. Pedersen. Vatican: Pontifical Academy of Sciences, 1983. 75–116.

Olson, Paul A. "The Reeve's Tale: Chaucer's Measure for Measure." *SP* 59 (1962): 1–17.

Orgel, Stephen K. "Sidney's Experiment in Pastoral: 'The Lady of May.' " *JWCI* 26 (1963): 198–203.

Otis, Brooks. *Virgil: A Study in Civilized Poetry*. Oxford: Clarendon Press, 1963.

———. *Ovid as an Epic Poet*. Cambridge: Cambridge University Press, 1966.

Palliser, D. M. *The Age of Elizabeth*. New York: Longman, 1983.

Panofsky, Erwin. *Problems in Titian, Mostly Iconographic*. New York, 1969.

———. *Renaissance and Renascences in Western Art*. New York, 1972.

Parmenter, Mary. "Spenser [sic] *Twelve Aeglogues Proportionable to the Twelve Monethes*." *ELH* 3 (1936): 190–217.

Partner, Nancy F. *Serious Entertainments: The Writing of History in Twelfth-Century England*. Chicago: The University of Chicago Press, 1977.

Patterson, Annabel M. *Pastoral and Ideology: Virgil to Valéry*. Berkeley: University of California Press, 1988.

———. "Re-Opening the Green Cabinet: Clément Marot and Edmund Spenser." *ELR* 16 (1986): 44–70.

———. *Censorship and Interpretation*. Madison: University of Wisconsin Press, 1984.

Pearsall, Derek. *John Lydgate*. London: Routledge and Kegan Paul, 1970.

Phillips, James E. "Daniel Rogers: A Neo-Latin Link Between the Pléiade and Sidney's 'Areopagus.'" *Neo-Latin Poetry of the Sixteenth and Seventeenth Centuries*. Los Angeles: William Andrews Clark Memorial Library, 1965. 5–28.

———. "Spenser's Syncretic Religious Imagery." *ELH* 36 (1969): 110–30.

———. *Images of a Queen: Mary Stuart in Sixteenth Century Literature*. Berkeley: University of California Press, 1964.

Pineaux, Jacques. *La Polemique protestant contre Ronsard*. 2 vols. Paris: Didier, 1973.

Poggioli, Renato. *The Oaten Flute*. Cambridge, MA: Harvard University Press, 1975.

Prescott, Anne Lake. *French Poets and the English Renaissance*. New Haven: Yale University Press, 1978.

———. "Licia's Temple: Giles Fletcher the Elder and Number Symbolism." *Renaissance and Reformation* 2 (1978): 170–81.

Pulman, Michael Barraclough. *The Elizabethan Privy Council in the Fifteen-Seventies*. Berkeley: University of California Press, 1971.

Putnam, Michael. *Virgil's Pastoral Art*. Princeton: Princeton University Press, 1970.

Quilligan, Maureen. *Milton's Spenser*. Ithaca: Cornell University Press, 1983.

Quinones, Richard J. *The Renaissance Discovery of Time*. Cambridge, MA: Harvard University Press, 1972.

Quint, David. *Origin and Originality in Renaissance Literature*. New Haven: Yale University Press, 1983.

Rasmussen, Carl " 'Quietnesse of Minde': *A Theatre for Worldlings* as a Protestant Poetics." *Spenser Studies* 1 (1980): 3–27.

Richmond, Hugh M. *Puritans and Libertines: Anglo-French Literary Relations in the Reformation*. Berkeley: University of California Press, 1981.

Ringler, William, A. "A Book Worth Reading." *Huntington Spectator* (1983), Winter.

Robertson, D. W., Jr. *A Preface to Chaucer*. Princeton: Princeton University Press, 1962.

Robinson, Forest. *The Shape of Things Known*. Cambridge, MA: Harvard University Press, 1972.

Roche, Thomas P., Jr. "The Calendrical Structure of Petrarch's *Canzoniere*." *SP* 71 (1974): 152–72.

Rosenberg, Eleanor. *Leicester, Patron of Letters*. New York: Columbia University Press, 1955.

Rosenzweig, Sidney. "Ascham's Scholemaster and Spenser's February Eclogue." *SAB* 15 (1940): 103–9.

Røstvig, Maren-Sofie. "*The Shepheardes Calender*—A Structural Analysis." *Renaissance and Modern Studies* 13 (1969): 49–79.

Russell, Daniel. "DuBellay's Emblematic Vision of Rome." *Yale French Studies* 47 (1972): 98–109.

Russell, John L. "The Copernican System in Great Britain." *The Reception of Copernicus' Heliocentric Theory*. Ed. Jerzy Dobrzycki. Boston: D. Reidel, 1973. 189–240.

Sacks, Peter. *The English Elegy*. Baltimore: The Johns Hopkins University Press, 1985.

Sandison, H. E. "Spenser's 'Lost' Works and Their Probable Relation to His *Faerie Queene*." *PMLA* 25 (1910): 134–51.

Schuller, Robert M. "Theory and Criticism of the Scientific Poem in Elizabethan England." *ELR* 15 (1985): 3–41.

Seznec, Jean. *The Survival of the Pagan Gods*. Trans. B. F. Sessions. New York, 1953.

Shepherd, Simon. *Spenser*. Atlantic Highlands, NJ: Humanities Press International, 1989.

Shore, David R. *Spenser and the Poetics of Pastoral*. Montreal: McGill-Queen's University Press, 1985.

Smith, G. Gregory. *Elizabethan Critical Essays*. 2 vols. Oxford: Clarendon Press, 1904.

Smith, M. C. "Ronsard and Queen Elizabeth I." *Bibliothèque d'Humanisme et Renaissance* 29 (1969): 93–119.

Spearing, A. C. *Medieval to Renaissance in English Poetry*. London: Cambridge University Press, 1985.

Spitzer, Leo. "Spenser, Shepheardes Calender, March." *SP* 47 (1950): 494–505.

Stahl, William Harris, and Richard Johnson, with E. L. Burge. *Martianus Capella and the Seven Liberal Arts*. 2 vols. New York: Columbia University Press, 1971.

Starnes, D. T. "Spenser and E. K." *SP* 41 (1944): 181–200.

Stephenson, Edward A. "Some Stylistic Links Between Spenser and E. K." *Renaissance Papers, 1956*. Columbia: University of South Carolina Press, 1956. 66–71.

Stern, Virginia F. *Gabriel Harvey: His Life, Marginalia, and Library*. Oxford: Clarendon Press, 1979.

———. "The *Bibliotheca* of Gabriel Harvey." *Renaissance Quarterly* 25 (1972):1–62.

Stirling, Brents. "Spenser and Thomas Watson, Bishop of Lincoln." *PQ* 10 (1931): 321–28.

Stone, Lawrence. *The Crisis of the Aristocracy, 1558–1641*. Oxford: The Clarendon Press, 1965.

Strong, Roy. *The Cult of Elizabeth*. London: Thames and Hudson, 1977.

Strype, John. *Annals of the Reformation*. Oxford, 1824.

Suchodolski, Bogdan. "The Impact of Copernicus on the Development of the Natural and the Human Sciences." *The Scientific World of Copernicus*. Ed. Barbara Bienkowska. Boston: D. Reidel, 1973. 95–106.

Surtz, Edward. *The Praise of Pleasure*. Cambridge, MA: Harvard University Press, 1957.

Thompson, J. W., ed. *The Frankfurt Book Fair: The Francofordiense Emporium of Henri Estienne*. Chicago: The Caxton Club, 1921.

Tuve, Rosemond. *Seasons and Months: Studies in a Tradition of Middle English Poetry.*
　　Totowa: Rowman and Littlefield, 1974.
――――. "Spenser and Medieval Mazars; with a Note on Jason in Ivory." *SP* 34
　　(1937): 138–47.
――――. "Spenser and the *Zodiake of Life.*" *Essays by Rosemond Tuve.* Ed. Thomas P.
　　Roche. Princeton: Princeton University Press, 1970.
Upham, Alfred. *The French Influence in English Literature.* New York: 1908.
Van Dorsten, J. A. "Literary Patronage in Elizabethan England, the Early Phase."
　　Patronage in the Renaissance. Ed. Guy F. Lytle and Stephen Orgel. Princeton:
　　Princeton University Press, 1981. 91–206.
――――. *Poets, Patrons, and Professors.* London: Oxford University Press, 1962.
――――. *The Radical Arts.* London: Oxford University Press, 1970.
Walker, D. P. "Orpheus the Theologian and Renaissance Platonists." *JWCI* 16
　　(1953): 100–120.
――――. "The *Prisca Theologica* in France." *JWCI* 17 (1954): 204–59.
Weiner, Andrew. *Sir Philip Sidney and the Poetics of Protestantism: A Study of Contexts.*
　　Minneapolis: University of Minnesota Press, 1978.
Wetherbee, Winthrop. *Chaucer and the Poets.* Ithaca: Cornell University Press,
　　1984.
White, Helen C. *Social Criticism in Popular Religious Literature of the Sixteenth
　　Century.* New York: The Macmillan Company, 1944.
Williams, Arnold, *The Common Expositor.* Chapel Hill: The University of North
　　Carolina Press, 1948.
Wilson, E. C. *England's Eliza.* Harvard Studies in English Vol. xx. London: Frank
　　Cass, 1966.
Wilson, E. Faye. "Pastoral and Epithalamium in Later Latin Literature." *Speculum*
　　23 (1948): 35–57.
Wind, Edgar. *Pagan Mysteries in the Renaissance.* New York: Norton, 1968.
Winternitz, Emanuel. *Musical Instruments and Their Symbolism in Western Art.*
　　London: Faber and Faber, 1967.
Wittkower, Rudolf. *Architectural Principles in the Age of Humanism.* London: Alec
　　Teranti, 1952.
Woods, Susanne. *Natural Emphasis: English Versification from Chaucer to Dryden.*
　　San Marino: Huntington Library, 1985.
Wrightson, Keith. *English Society, 1550–1680.* London: Hutchinson, 1982.
Yates, Frances A. *A Theatre of the World.* London: Routledge and Kegan Paul,
　　1969.
――――. *Astraea: The Imperial Theme in the Sixteenth Century.* London: Routledge
　　and Kegan Paul, 1975.
――――. *Giordano Bruno and the Hermetic Tradition.* New York: Vintage Books,
　　1964.
――――. *The Art of Memory.* Chicago: The University of Chicago Press, 1966.
――――. *The French Academies of the Sixteenth Century.* London: The Warburg
　　Institute, 1947.
Yeager, R. F. "British Library Additional MS. 5141: an unnoticed Chaucer *vita.*"
　　The Journal of Medieval and Renaissance Studies 14 (1984): 261–81.
Ziggelaar, A. "The Papal Bull of 1582 Promulgating a Reform of the Calendar."
　　*Gregorian Reform of the Calendar, Proceedings of the Vatican Conference to
　　Commemorate Its 400th Anniversary, 1582–1982.* Ed. G. V. Coyne, S. J., M.
　　A. Hoskin, and O. Pedersen. Vatican: Pontifical Academy of Sciences, 1983.
　　201–42.

Index

DATE DUE